The EMERGENCY PLAYBOOK

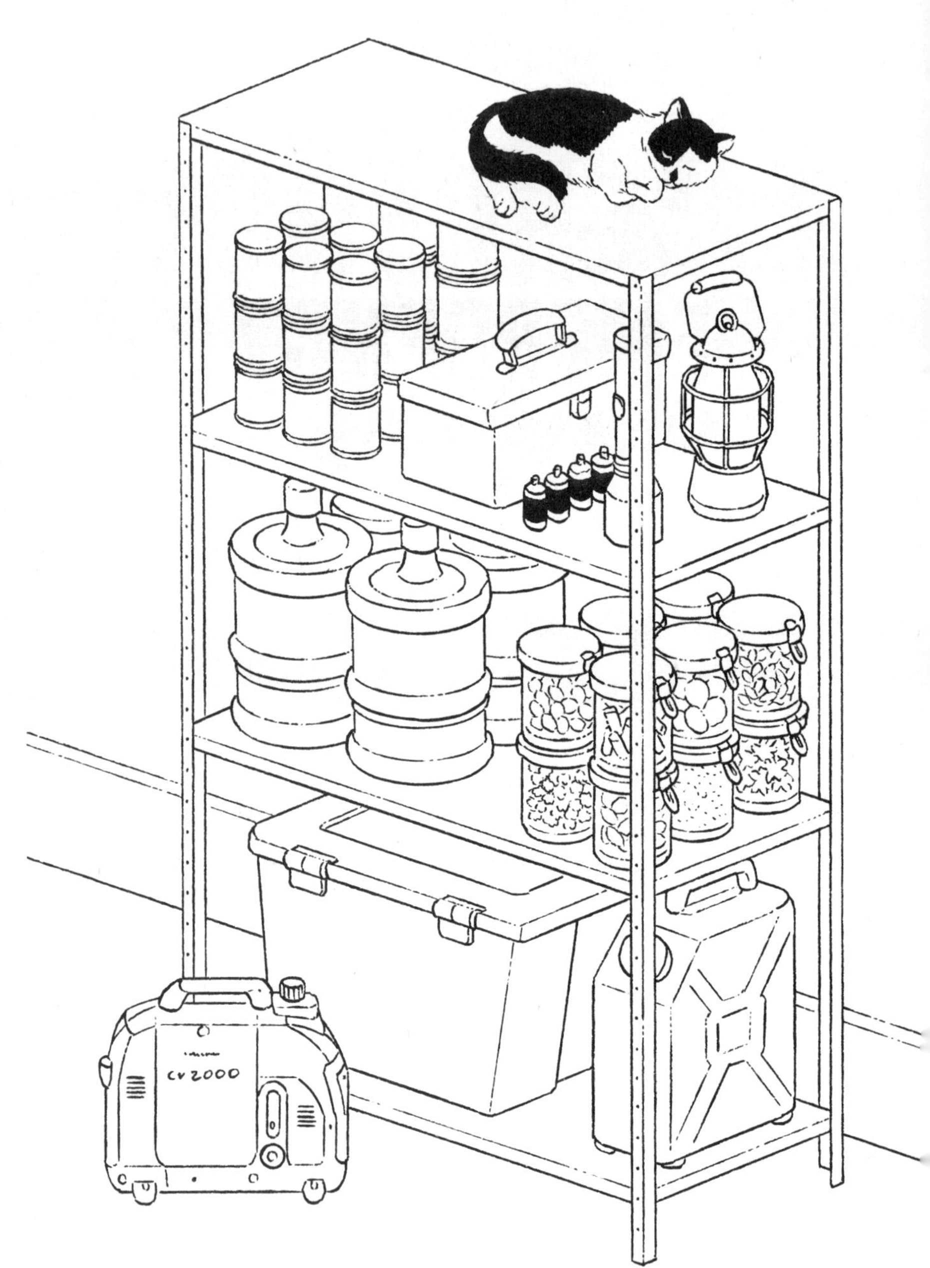
cv2000

The EMERGENCY PLAYBOOK

A BUNKER-FREE GUIDE TO DISASTER* PREPARATION

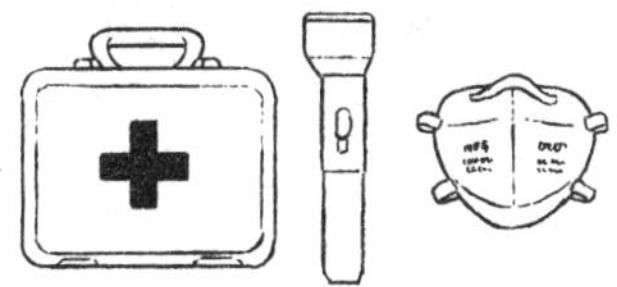

*FLOODS, EARTHQUAKES, WILDFIRES, BLACKOUTS, PANDEMICS, CIVIL UNREST, AND MORE

AMY EDELMAN & CHRIS BEGLEY

TEN SPEED PRESS
California | New York

CONTENTS

Part Three
How to Handle Worst-Case Scenarios

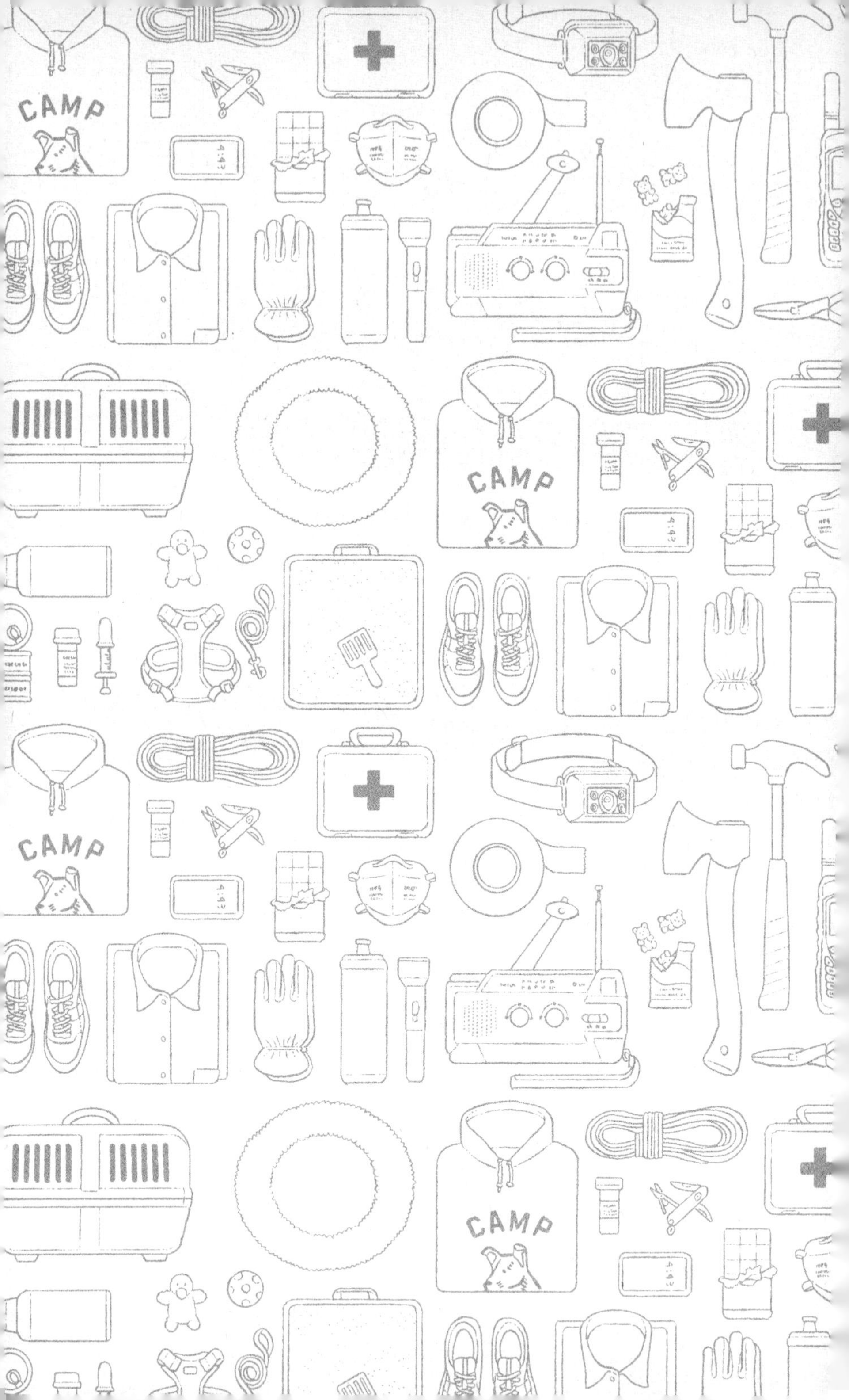
CAMP

INTRODUCTION

The Prepping Lifestyle

What goes up must come down.

—ISAAC NEWTON

Hi. Allow us to introduce ourselves: From where we live (Lexington, Kentucky, versus Northern New Jersey) to how we look (a six-foot man versus a barely five-foot woman), we are very different people. Chris is an archaeologist, a National Geographic Explorer, and a Fulbright scholar who also teaches wilderness survival skills. Amy spent most of her career in a different kind of "wilderness," specifically New York City in the mid-1980s, working in public relations and marketing and specializing in fashion, lifestyle, and consumer goods. In her spare time, she wrote several books, including a history of the little black dress. Chris doesn't mind getting his hands dirty, while Amy couldn't imagine life without her twice-monthly pedicure.

Chris's grandfather was an Appalachian folk hero, while Amy's immigrated from Austria and was the first Jewish man to attend Villanova University on a sports scholarship. Chris was named one of *Men's Journal*'s "50 Most Adventurous Men." After her husband died in 2001, Amy's greatest adventure became raising two young kids on her own while writing a fictional memoir about searching for a new husband. Chris filmed a BBC documentary in the jungle with actor Ewan McGregor.

Amy prefers *not* to explore jungles (but would make an exception for Ewan). Differences aside, we share many similarities: We are both married with children, we have developed insight into our collective future based on our knowledge and reading of science and history, and we are both planning accordingly for an increasingly tumultuous future.

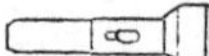

Amy's first brush with not being prepared came a couple of decades ago at her cousin's wedding. She was wearing a new pair of heels and an hour into the festivities had developed a blister the size of the bridal bouquet. After querying half the guests about the possible whereabouts of a Band-Aid, she was told that Uncle George always carried them. As he reached into the pocket of his tux and pulled out the OG boo-boo fix, Amy felt a huge sense of relief. From that day forward she swore she would always be prepared like Uncle George. How hard could it be to make room for a Band-Aid?

It was fifteen years later, after reading two climate change–related articles—David Wallace-Wells's *New York* magazine July 2017 cover story, "The Doomed Earth Catalog," and an academic paper, "How to Adapt to the End of the World," written by former professor of sustainability leadership at the University of Cumbria Jem Bendell and quoted by Bloomberg in September 2018—when Amy recognized that, collectively, we were going to need more than a Band-Aid to prepare for our uncertain future. And while both articles were well researched, ran in respected and recognized publications, and prompted some lively dinner party conversation, the subject was a dark one and most people preferred not to dwell on it. Amy, however, was not one of those people.

Chris's interest in preparedness is less surprising given his academic and career background and is spurred by a larger tragedy. As an archaeologist, he has lived and worked in some of the most remote areas of Central America, where much of the knowledge we think of as "survival" skills is employed in everyday activities. But when a member of his community died while looking for help after his car got stuck in the snowy mountains, Chris began teaching fundamental survival skills such as navigation, fire starting, and shelter building.

When Amy read Chris's book *The Next Apocalypse: The Art and Science of Survival* (2021), she felt she had found someone with the hardcore survival expertise she lacked and a similar outlook on the future. *The Next Apocalypse* focuses on community and uses historical examples to separate wild imagination from likely scenarios. Chris also knows from personal experience that having a plan can make an enormous difference in how individuals and communities come out on the other side of a disaster. Amy reached out to Chris about writing a practical guidebook that followed a community-focused, level-headed approach. Chris also recognized the need, so we got to work.

We wrote *The Emergency Playbook* because we think it's needed, desperately and immediately. While we'd like to say that our opinion is shared, we've noticed that most of our family, friends, and colleagues—folks who are otherwise educated, engaged, and involved—are not even remotely prepared for emergencies, even the presently unfolding ones, which is weird, because the billionaire class clearly knows something is up.

If you don't believe us, just Google "billionaire bunkers" and you'll find stories everywhere from *The Guardian* and *The Hollywood Reporter* to *Vice* and CNN about fully equipped and heavily armed custom-built luxury safe houses, crammed to their reinforced rafters with indoor pools, hydroponic gardens, gourmet kitchens, and private golf courses. The new question asked in these circles isn't how much money you make but rather how long you can survive when everything collapses. Mark Zuckerberg and other Silicon Valley tech bros keep their planes fully gassed and ready to fly to bunkers in New Zealand, stocked with everything they'll presumably need till the end of time. Maybe the preparedness gene has something to do with their success, but, hey, the ability to gather supplies and make a plan is available to the rest of us too. Why not take up their quest to survive what's coming? Is there something they know that we don't?

In the years since Amy read those articles about the potential damage we might see from climate change, the worst outcomes have proven to be true and have often occurred several years before predicted. In addition to having already breached the global warming threshold of 1.5 degrees Celsius beyond preindustrial levels set by the Paris Agreement, 2024 ranked second highest for the number of billion-dollar disasters in a calendar year. The subsequent list of such disasters from that year reads like "The Twelve Days of Christmas": seventeen severe storms, five tropical cyclones, two winter storms, one flooding event, one drought/heat wave, and one wildfire event. And what of the "partridge in a pear tree"? Many partridge populations are declining because of habitat loss, pesticide use, and overhunting, and the Italian grey partridge is now considered extinct in the wild. Fruit trees in general are struggling because severe droughts and flooding are making them more susceptible to poor growing seasons, pests, and fungal diseases.

Sounds bad, yes? And if climate disasters aren't enough to send you screaming into the abyss, we are also seeing a rise in civil strife and financial instability along with deadly viruses and pandemics (measles, tuberculosis, bird flu). You're probably thinking right about now that you should put down this book and slowly back away. But unlike the hard-core prepper manuals written by "doomers" that focus on being heavily armed and raise the question of whether you will or won't have to eat your neighbor, our book does not intend to overwhelm you with nightmares and hopelessness. Group identity is stronger than ever, and we understand that many people aren't interested in learning skills from folks who seem to be borderline conspiracy theorists or center their advice on guns and the defense of a stash of freeze-dried possum parts. Weapons and walls are unlikely to work in the long run, and who wants to live like that anyway?

The Emergency Playbook, on the other hand, is about knowing there is a light at the end of the tunnel and making sure you have a flashlight and enough gas in your car to get you there. It's about seeing the glass as half full and knowing how much water you need (and where to find it) so you can top off your stylish stainless steel flask and stay safe until the emergency is over. It's about believing you can survive as long as you have the fortitude, appropriate clothing, and two different ways of getting to your family's safe meeting destination.

In these pages you'll find well-organized information on how to plan for the specific disruption(s) you are most likely to face. After all, who has the time to sort through the particulars on how to escape a wildfire when you *really* need info on preparing for a hurricane? What you *won't* find are zombies and cannibals and bunkers. This is *not* prepping for doomsday. And even though the road ahead may look a little dark and unfamiliar, we don't lead with fear.

Why Is Being Prepared So Important?

It's hard to quantify the benefits of planning ahead until you have a coughing fit at the theater and no cough drop, plan a romantic evening and forget to bring condoms, or finish a long, hard day at work only to realize you're out of your favorite scotch. For many of us, that helpless feeling of not having *the one thing* that makes the difference between everything being okay or not didn't hit until early 2020, when we collectively realized we didn't have enough toilet paper to last until it was safe to leave our houses again.

Have you ever wondered why being organized—whether it's crossing the last item off your to-do list or asking Siri to remind you to call your mother—can be calming? It's not your imagination. There are thousands of studies showing that simply being prepared makes people less likely to freak out. It turns out we tend to fixate on loose ends. Called the *Zeigarnik effect* and named for the Russian psychologist who identified the phenomenon in the late 1920s, it describes a tendency to remember interrupted tasks more easily than those that have been completed. Naturally, preparing helps with those loose ends. And even though we still can't predict the future with a great degree of accuracy, planning helps even if we don't follow through.

Feeling helpless over something as overwhelming as a pandemic or natural disaster is admittedly a bigger deal than remembering to call your mom, but the impact on your mental and physical health can be lessened with a little forethought. Completing a task enables you to focus on more important and pressing issues, like rationing the toilet paper. Prepared, we can survive and thrive together. And while it does take some cash to compile all the goodies you need to be sufficiently prepared, there are lots of things you can do that cost little to nothing.

Involve Your Kids in Your Planning

Humans, even those of the younger and smaller variety, are resilient. Approaching a topic, even a potentially scary one, with a spirit of optimism and adventure tends to alleviate some of the fear. In most cases, being kept in the dark (both rhetorically and actually) is scarier than knowing the truth. And if you're a parent, you know that it's not only adults who feel better when they have some sense of control: Turns out this works for children too.

Many articles have been written in the past couple of years about how to talk to kids to alleviate their fears and anxiety, whether these are related to another pandemic or hurricanes or wildfires. What's interesting is that none of the stories we came across mentioned how having a plan can help. That could be because studies show that nearly half (49 percent) of parents *themselves* don't feel very prepared to protect their kids from disaster and only three-fifths (60 percent) report having some kind of emergency plan. That number becomes even more alarming when you consider that, according to Save the Children, each workday, sixty-nine million children are in school or childcare and thus are separated from their family should a disaster occur.

So, to calm both your stress and your children's, think about making an emergency plan as a family activity. Frame it as an adventure. Solicit and consider your kids' opinions. And most importantly, make sure they know that you're all in this together.

The Emergency Playbook is organized into three parts: "Planning," "The Essentials," and "Scenarios." In part one, we explain how and why to plan for the unknown. This involves debunking some survival myths and giving examples of methods that have worked in the past. In part two, we talk about necessary gear and supplies, and, equally as important, the skills and knowledge you should try to gain now, *before* an emergency occurs. In part three, we talk about strategies for facing specific scenarios—from extreme weather and financial uncertainty to a rise in authoritarianism, some of which we are already facing on the daily. We hope you'll read *The Emergency Playbook* from cover to cover, but we've also organized it for those times when you need information fast. It functions as a planning handbook as well as a quick-reference guide to toss in your go bag.

We wrote *The Emergency Playbook* because we knew there had to be a better way to approach the possibility of facing the end of the world (and lesser catastrophes) than the options we were seeing. But after several years of our *annus horribilis* (which by its very definition should be only twelve months long), we still haven't read a story on rising anxiety levels that offers as a solution the simple suggestion of being better prepared. We are optimistic that some of the challenges we face today, especially those that are systemic and long-term, will bring out the best in our community. Preparing for the rougher spots, expecting them, and even embracing them can change our future for the better. And while we don't expect anyone to welcome earthquakes or fascism, changes to our increasingly destructive buy-now-pay-later consumer lifestyles might be worth accepting in the long run.

So Why the Optimism?

Perhaps our rosy view comes from growing up watching too many Disney movies (*Bambi* aside). Or maybe it's more of an innate trait like eye color or aptitude at the piano. Whatever the reason, we want to imagine—even in the worst of circumstances—a story that ends happily, or at the very least hopefully. And after all, is thinking positively, a staple of self-help manuals for decades, so far from wrong?

Up until recently, admitting to being an optimist wasn't considered a controversial confession. But these days, when the prospect of doom and gloom hangs in the air like wildfire smoke drifting east from California, it seems downright foolish to admit it, especially considering the worst-case scenarios and end-of-the-world fantasies popping up everywhere. It's as if consuming disaster porn—spoon-fed to us by news outlets and social media—has left no room for less headline-grabbing, practical solutions.

You might think our optimism is misguided, a way of sticking our heads in the quickly eroding beach sand. Or perhaps it is merely hedonic adaptation, a way to describe the human tendency to return to a baseline level of happiness despite a change in fortune, even if that change includes the possibility of the end of the world as we know it. Yet while positive thinking might not change your reality at the moment, it sure can affect the future, and, historically, humanity has made it out of some tough spots before. The key takeaway from the relatively brief history of humankind is to face problems as a community and try to stay upbeat. Without a positive mental attitude, cortisol, the hormone generated by stress, wears down our bodies and brains faster than the time it takes to melt Greenland (which is pretty quick; between 2002 and 2021, the world's largest island shed approximately 280 gigatons of ice per year, 20 percent worse than previous estimates for that period and faster than any time in the past twelve thousand years). Prolonged cortisol exposure can also promote depression. And as your mental state deteriorates, so does your will to live, which, let's face it, in a life-or-death situation isn't all that optimal. This may be why most Boy Scout manuals claim that in an emergency a positive outcome depends on 80 percent attitude, 10 percent equipment, and 10 percent skill. Feeling good about a situation expands global thinking capacities in the brain, allowing for more innovation and creativity, while also relieving stress.

Another reason for optimism is that it is a myth that when disasters strike people become desperate and crazy (although if they're unprepared they may be more inclined to panic). The reality is much more hopeful. As author Rebecca Solnit noted in her book *A Paradise Built in Hell,* "In the wake of an earthquake, a bombing, or a major storm, most people are altruistic, urgently engaged in caring for themselves and those around them, strangers and neighbors as well as friends and loved ones." History supports this. After disasters, even apocalyptic ones, people regroup into communities and work together to get through.

For example, just days after the Los Angeles fires in early 2025, hundreds of people streamed into a parking lot near the Rose Bowl in Pasadena, California, to donate clothing, bottled water, and diapers. After Hurricane Helene almost wiped out Asheville, North Carolina, in 2024, residents emptied their fridges and freezers and pooled their food to feed themselves *and* their neighbors. Sixty thousand people jumped in to help rescue survivors after Hurricane Katrina crippled parts of New Orleans in 2005, and more than thirty thousand people volunteered after 9/11 (including Amy's stepson, a carpenter, who dug through the rubble for almost a week).

"

As an archaeologist, I've done projects all over the globe. And in almost every one, something goes wrong. Equipment malfunctions or breaks, permits are rescinded, the weather does not cooperate, or people get sick. Rarely,

however, do these things make or break a project; the key is how we handle the problems. Changing tactics, pivoting the focus a bit, adapting to the new realities, salvaging what we can, and focusing on what we can do will result in a successful project. Getting overly stressed, lamenting the changes, or focusing on what is no longer possible ensures failure.

—Chris

”

After more than thirty years of research, sociologists have found that the desire to do something constructive following a disaster is *universal:* Disasters stir empathy and inflame a feeling of powerlessness that can be alleviated only by stepping in to help. That is why, even with our current levels of division and animosity, we believe that when the crap hits the solar panels, people will find that what they need most is *not* a gun but enough food and water to keep their families going until help arrives.

We may be facing big challenges, but we won't overcome them by being heavily armed, hoarding supplies, and focusing on protecting our stash. We'll get through whatever life brings by relying on one another's strengths to fill in for our particular weaknesses and knowing we're more powerful as a group than we are on our own. And while we may have to face a harsher reality due to political, technological, or climate-related issues (or quite possibly all three at once), fear and dread—especially fear of *one another*—will not make things easier. We should instead consider what we're heading for, seemingly at warp speed, as a chance for a new beginning as opposed to a bad end.

Our optimism is not just reactive; it's our road map for getting through challenges. Our hope is to create a different kind of scenario where planning and preparing for an uncertain future with practical knowledge and a sense of adventure and openheartedness are the purview of *everyone* concerned for the future.

So rather than looking at the need to prepare from a negative place—the "All hell's breaking loose!" mentality—we choose to see it with a different attitude. Change is happening . . . period. Good or bad, we must deal with it. Wishing for things to stay the same or lamenting change will do you no good. The Girl Scouts (whose motto since 1907 has been "Be Prepared") aren't all doom and gloom when they're out selling Thin Mints. And poets, wilderness survivalists, and proponents of back-to-earth living like Henry David Thoreau, John Muir, and Bradford Angier weren't gun-toting nihilists—they just wanted to share the exaltation of being prepared for a new experience with little more than a sufficiently stocked backpack.

So allow us to share with you The Optimist's Five Commandments. Although there are a thousand details to remember during an emergency, if you can remember these few basic tenets, you'll be starting from a good place.

The Optimist's Five Commandments

1. Recognize that you are better off being prepared than not.
2. Keep your head during an emergency and try not to panic.
3. You may be afraid, but don't ever whine.
4. To the best of your ability, help and be kind to others.
5. Stay positive.

Let's be clear, though. Things are going to get grim much quicker than most of us imagine. Climate change will be behind much of it, but catastrophes could manifest in innumerable ways, from extreme weather to political repression. We might have prevented some of this, but we didn't. And becoming paralyzed by the truly unpleasant things facing us now will not help; it may even make things worse. When you start putting this book's advice into practice, you'll find that being prepared for whatever life throws at you is downright freeing.

So, welcome to *The Emergency Playbook,* where wearing black is both sensible *and* stylish, making room in your home for extra supplies works for both a short-term emergency *and* your interior design scheme, and being prepared is more of a mainstream activity, kind of like Dry January, Taco Tuesdays, and pickleball.

See you on the other side.

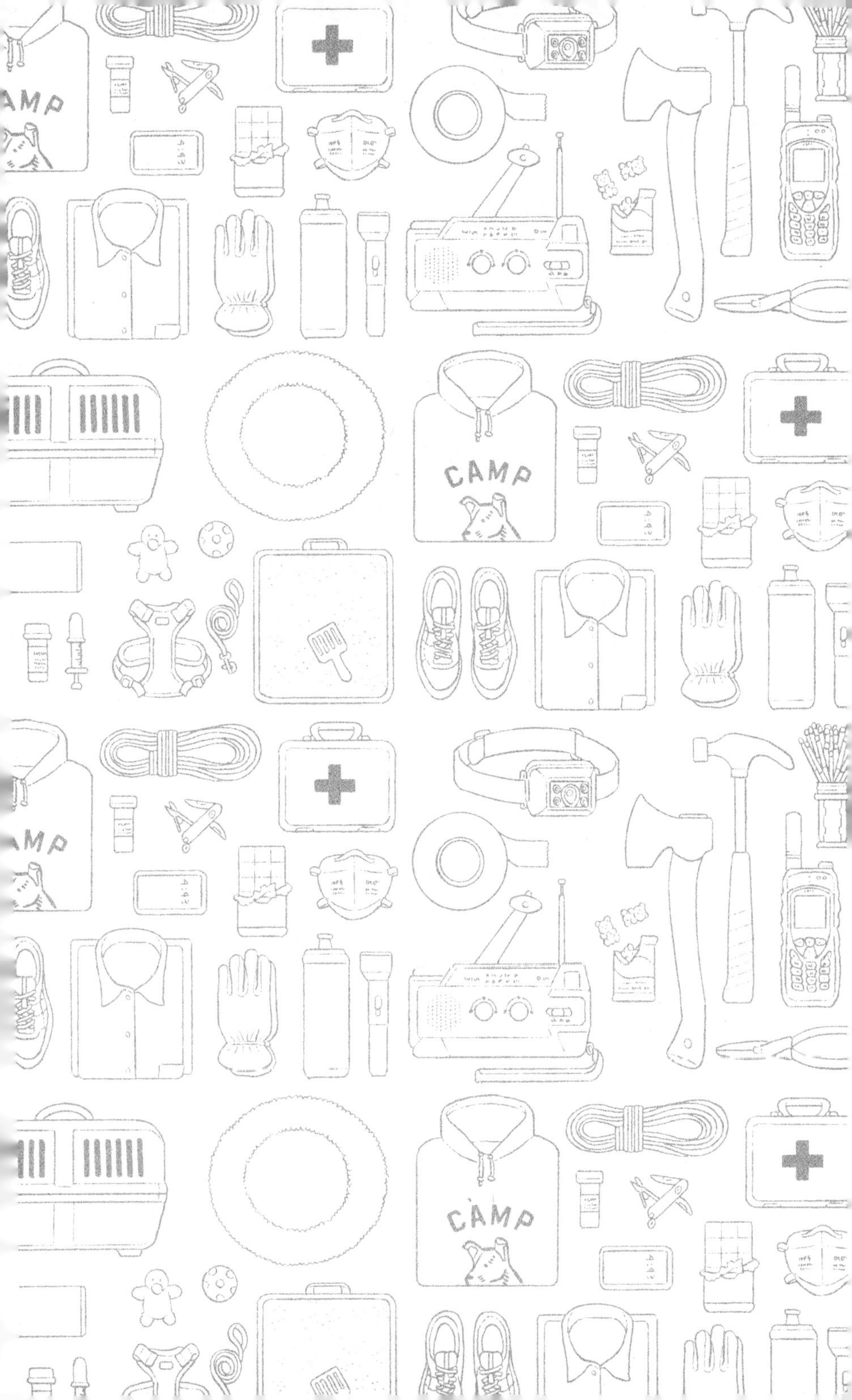
CAMP

PART ONE

Planning

By failing to prepare, you are preparing to fail.

—ATTRIBUTED TO BENJAMIN FRANKLIN

It is said that hindsight is 20/20, so what can we learn from the disasters of the past to help us plan for the emergencies we're likely to face today? This section examines the value of mining history for lessons that can inform how we approach our own catastrophes. And while you'll never know exactly what situation you're going to face, planning ahead for the most common ones is always a smart move.

1. What the Past Can Teach Us About the Future

You cannot stop things.
You can only be prepared for them to happen.

—ERIN MORGENSTERN, *THE NIGHT CIRCUS*

Chances are you haven't given much thought to the possibility that people have had to prepare for upheaval before. Focusing on the past to see into the future can be challenging. We don't always know what details to pay attention to or how to recognize which actions caused one set of circumstances to be different from another. But looking back, there are some common themes in the history of civilizations and people from which we can learn.

People are usually delusional. By this we mean that we all suffer from something called "normalcy bias," which encourages us to underestimate threats to a mind-boggling degree. From the thousands who refused to evacuate in advance of Hurricane Katrina (despite the obvious perils of staying) to the Jews who refused to leave Germany in the 1940s (despite the obvious perils of staying), the ability to recognize and counter normalcy bias is crucial for effective preparedness and response to potential crises.

With a few exceptions, crises build up over time. Environmental degradation can take decades to notice. Societies do not collapse suddenly. Like houses made of cards, both in terms of how long they take to construct and their fragility, all disasters—be they economic, ecological, or social—build for a long time before toppling. If we look at the fall of Rome in the fifth century A.D. or the decline of the Classic Maya in the ninth, we can see centuries of problems before a civilization's collapse. If you are not paying attention until the end, the failure may seem sudden, but unless a meteor or a supervolcano takes us out, it's not. Even looking back at the COVID-19 pandemic, we can see that the roots of the problems we faced—politicians stirring up mistrust in vaccines and science, a healthcare system that had issues with communication, supply lines that depended on a few megaports where container ships could unload their cargo—extend back a long time. None of these things started with COVID, but that's arguably what made those of us not suffering from normalcy bias take notice.

Knowing whom to listen to—and whom to ignore—could save your life. Not everyone with a public platform is trustworthy. Figuring out who is providing information you can trust can take some work, especially these days, when about five or six companies—owned by Bezos, Bloomberg, the Murdochs, and the Ellisons—control *90 percent* of American media. But there are fact checkers that can help identify politically biased sources. And by doing a bit of digging, especially in the neighborhood outside your "bubble," you will find certain providers of information (e.g., bona fide scientists, verified news sources) that are widely respected by more than one type of person. Getting information from various sources can help you assess credibility as well. If you know where to look and who to listen to, you may be able to read the signs a little sooner, giving yourself more time to prepare.

There is no single cause of the catastrophes we might face. Unless we're talking about an earthquake or meteor strike, the starting point for most crises isn't a single event. There may be a specific event that starts or exacerbates a situation, but all bets are off when the complex systems on which we depend are disrupted—for instance, when a particularly severe drought affects the agricultural system; a hurricane crashes the home insurance market; the folks in charge gut the budgets of the National Oceanic and Atmospheric Administration (NOAA) and the Federal Emergency Management Agency (FEMA), resulting in an inability to compile and forecast accurate weather data and subsequent emergency responses; or a lack of infrastructure investment results in a failed power grid. It's like cascading dominoes: A foundering in one system affects the others too. When we think about things falling apart and how to put them back together, we need to think in terms of giant and intricate *systems,* not small parts of those systems. Unfortunately, the scenarios are endless, but by seeing how things are interconnected we can better recognize what we will need to rebuild or reestablish after a disaster —and do it in a smarter and *fairer* way.

Even in the most apocalyptic scenario, there will probably be many survivors. In the case of some global, catastrophic event—and we have seen plenty in just the last few years—there will be millions or billions of people who need food, water, shelter, community, and all the other things that make life worth living. Here we are talking about all kinds of disasters; some (like weather) are relatively local, but even a global catastrophe like a pandemic will not look like it does in most movies. Imagine a horrific situation that results in the loss of 75 percent of the global population. That would still leave around two billion people on earth. Those apocalyptic stories with no other survivors in sight? An unlikely scenario. For better and for worse, no one gets through a collapse event alone, and it's always a community that comes out the other side. So, nurture your family, friends, and neighbors, even those who may have different views, and understand that you can't make it alone.

Heroes will not save us. Unlike in the movies, one person (or even a group of people) with superhuman powers and quick, dramatic action will not save the day. No billionaire with an ingenious invention (Hello, bioengineering!) or even a blond Hemsworth with a giant hammer can reverse the damage we've inflicted on our planet, the cruelty we've imposed on our fellow humans, or the resulting repercussions.

Surviving must be followed by rebuilding. After you have survived the initial disruption, gotten over the shock, and grabbed a beer or gummy from your stash, it's time to think about the long and hard task of rebuilding. What systems do we rely on, including agriculture, healthcare, and education? How do we build those back in ways that are fairer and more sustainable than what came before? Look around right now at your community leaders, organizers, and activists. See how hard their work seems, and how long it takes to make a difference? Now imagine that a thousand times over.

Be prepared for rebuilding to be very difficult—whether it's your neighborhood, your town, or the whole state—because it's not just *you* making decisions, it will be an *entire community.* The process will require patience, compromise, goodwill, and generosity—and, depending on what you've been through up to this point, you might not be feeling any of those things. So start with your family and close friends. Surely there's someone with a different point of view who makes attending holiday get-togethers difficult. But every year at Thanksgiving you realize that a different viewpoint is just *one* aspect of a person whom you otherwise love. Humans are complicated. No one is perfect. But few people, one on one, are as hateful as their comments on social media will have you believe.

Introduce yourself to your neighbors and make it a practice to interact with people who think or live differently than you do. Learn how to communicate outside of your bubble and to see the strengths and value of other ways of doing things. Working together at something, *anything*, will be better than a stalemate due to an inability to work together as a group. The more experience you have working with diverse groups of people and talking out solutions—even compromising sometimes—the better able you will be to work with others to move forward. In the end you'll realize that diversity isn't a negative feature, it's what makes families and communities resilient and strong.

The communities that have best endured tough times share some basic tenets.

- **Fairness:** Leadership often means compromise, and it's possible that nobody will be particularly happy with the outcome. But if an end result is relatively equitable and there is some history to show previous fair treatment, people can mostly accept the disappointment that accompanies a compromise. If a part of the population feels like they are not being treated fairly, things can go south quickly. We've seen this in the American Revolution, in the denouement of every authoritarian regime, and most recently in our own elections. Libya, Syria, and the disintegration of Yugoslavia are all complex situations where the resentment that built up within the population because of decades of abuse had a part in the way subsequent events played out.
- **Empathy and generosity:** Often considered feminine traits—and often for good reason—empathy and generosity are mostly missing from our current discourse. If we are to move forward as a community, the path must be different from the one that came before. This is not a screed about the horrors of toxic masculinity, but there's a good probability that if you're reading this book, (1) our world is in big trouble or (2) you expect our world to be in big trouble soon. In other words, what we're currently doing is not working and we clearly need to switch up our act. And while empathy and generosity aren't

often invoked in the final analysis of the success or failure of a community at a nation-state level, we certainly see them to a micro degree in our own lives. There are many reasons why things go wrong, but never giving anybody the benefit of the doubt (or anything else) creates communities that don't recognize one another, families who don't talk to one another, and work situations in which colleagues never communicate, much less collaborate.

- **Equitable distribution of voice, wealth, and power:** History shows—from the Classical Lowland Maya to the Western Roman Empire—that increasing wealth inequality consistently precedes collapse. So make sure that everyone in your community has a voice in decisions that will affect them and, if possible, an equal share of resources. In many societies, parts of the population are clearly poorer, have less influence, and possibly cannot meet their basic needs, like adequate food, decent housing, education, healthcare, and enough of any or all of the above to be happy and satisfied. If you look around and see this (in an emergency or elsewhere), figure out how to be part of the solution, even if you seem to benefit from the inequality. Eventually, this unfairness leads to problems that negatively affect everybody. From crime to ignorance to an unhealthy population, there are real-world consequences to leaving some people out.

Not all changes are bad, even dramatic ones. When we think of something collapsing or falling apart, it's usually not a good thing. But then again, a good deal of our modern lifestyle is neither fair nor sustainable. For instance, gone are the days when only white folks could eat at a lunch counter, and that's a good thing. Wouldn't it be nice if women could again regain control of their own reproductive systems? Yes, it would. And would it be all bad if we had to rely mostly on public transport or bicycles? What if more foods were produced locally, even if variety was reduced? In his book *Goliath's Curse,* Dr. Luke Kemp from the Centre for the Study of Existential Risk at the University of Cambridge notes that "for the citizens of early rapacious regimes, collapse often improved their lives because they were freed from domination and taxation and returned to farming. After the fall of Rome, people actually got taller and healthier." To evolve is a fact of life. Embrace change. Some of it will inevitably be for the better.

People are affected differently by change. Right now, in the United States, systems like healthcare and education aren't accessible and available to everyone equally. Subsequently, when those systems fall apart, they will not be mourned by everyone in the same way. Lowering meat consumption might benefit our health and the planet, but individuals, communities, and businesses that depend on raising livestock will have a hard time. Big box stores might be able to negotiate with vendors for lower prices but might in the process ruin small businesses, turning small-town Main Streets into ghost towns. Climate change might damage crops in one area of the country but not in another. Dramatic changes in the ninth century resulted in a collapse in the southern Maya area (the rainforests of Guatemala, for instance), while the northern part of the region (the Yucatán Peninsula in Mexico) saw unprecedented growth. In present circumstances, losing electricity for a week is very different if you live in a high-rise condo in the city than if you reside in a cabin in the woods. As we navigate through a tough time, it is important to understand who is negatively affected so that assistance can be deployed where it's most needed.

Not everyone experiences a catastrophe at the same time. Disaster hits some groups first, like residents near the coast in North Carolina and in wildfire regions of California, while others may not really be affected until much later. Those with money and power might be able to escape some of the worse effects of severe weather-related events that affect more vulnerable groups. Sure, circumstances may be all peaches and cream for you now, but others—potentially those you know and love—may already be suffering. And your suffering may begin while others are not yet affected.

Preparing can make all the difference. It might mean something as simple as stocking up on food and water or purchasing a solar-powered generator, but it goes way beyond that. Preparation also means knowing which experts and sources of information you can trust to create a course of action should you need one. Mark Twain taught us that history doesn't repeat itself but it often rhymes. We can't look to the past for specifics, but we can find some similarities to where we are at the moment. Identifying the rhymes, or patterns, can help us know how to prepare.

To that end, next up we talk about why it's so important to have a plan.

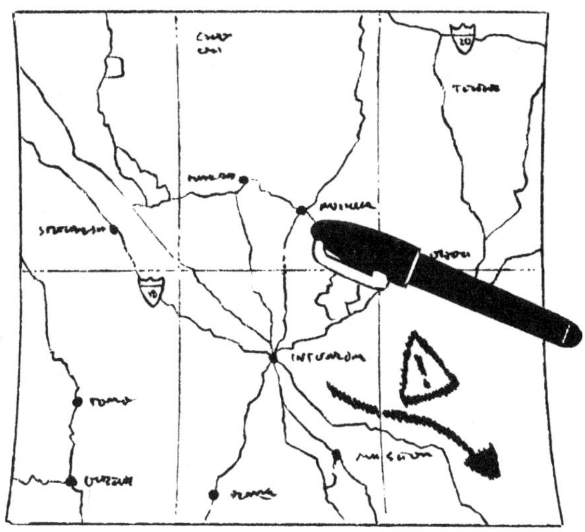

2. How to Make a Plan *Before* Things Go Tits Up

We should remember that good fortune often happens when opportunity meets with preparation.

—THOMAS A. EDISON

A recent national poll regarding personal preparedness found that those surveyed were (unsurprisingly) not ready for *any* type of crisis. Not even a little one. Only a few generations ago, our grandparents could handle almost any emergency using merely a penknife, a roll of duct tape, and a can of WD-40—and their skills were honed by more consequential issues than having to find an address without a GPS. They also probably spent more time socializing with friends, family, and neighbors than sitting on the couch with a bag of organic chips catching up on the latest shows.

Even though our ancestors had us beat in self-sufficiency, as a species we have a lousy history of preparing for the future. "We are inconsistent creatures who routinely court the catastrophes we most fear," said columnist Ezra Klein in a 2021 opinion piece in *The New York Times,* "because the future is an abstraction and the pleasures of this instant are a siren." Or as Bill Maher once noted on his show *Real Time,* regarding our inability to save ourselves from climate change, "As a world we made the decision to, like Thelma and Louise, hold hands and drive over the Grand Canyon."

Sure, sometimes we do plan for the short term, like what we're going to eat for dinner, what movie we're going to watch while we eat, or what we're going to wear on a hot date. Our preparedness efforts tend to be primarily focused on near-term events and are variations on the fight-or-flight reflex. This is how human brains are wired. While some of us have to-do lists on our phones, planning for an unknown future isn't the way we operate. It certainly doesn't help that technology and affluence have made some of us into habitual outsourcers. We can order in, but we can't cook. Our cars park themselves, but most of us don't know how to change a tire. We know we want to stop working at some point but avoid saving for our retirement. We know we will die someday but avoid writing a will. We know that eating a whole pizza is a bad idea, but sometimes we do it anyway.

The fact is that many of us prefer not to acknowledge that bad things can—and statistically *will*—happen. Some of us are even arrogant enough to think those bad things won't happen to us. But then again, ignorance is bliss right up until the time it bites you in the ass.

Recognizing that you're probably not quite ready—or even completely unprepared—for what's coming, from a blackout (Now, where'd I put the flashlight?) to a hurricane (Damn, I never repaired the storm shutters!), is the first step. Being realistic about your readiness tells you where to start; it's empowering! And it's not as if you need to go "full prepper" before the next full moon. Start with baby steps. Make your home more resilient by tightening the screws on your front door, buying a few flashlights, or getting to know your neighbors. Designate a backyard family camping night and break out all that gear you rarely use to be sure at least someone can figure out how to set up the tent. Create a map with at least two routes out of your neighborhood and make sure everyone in the household knows how to read it. Tell your kids it leads to buried treasure!

Be adventurous. Make it fun. Let go of the unnecessary anxiety and share your new pursuit. Like shopping for swimwear, getting prepared is a task that's better to do in the company of supportive and encouraging friends. After you've checked a few items off your list, sit back and enjoy the power that comes with knowing you are ready for whatever life throws at you.

Much like various kinds of milk (soy, oat, rice, sheep, cow), the types of catastrophes you should prepare for are practically endless (and listed at the end of this book). First up on most people's hit list are climate-related weather events, which now create chaos worldwide on the regular. Forget about those once-in-a-thousand-year storms. Some type of federal emergency declaration is now coming every three *days.* And why not? The year 2024 was the hottest on record, breaching the limit set by the Paris climate agreement. Heat waves shattered records (by *a lot*), as did tornadoes (the highest number ever recorded), and Beryl became the earliest observed Category 5 hurricane in the Atlantic. Helene was the second-deadliest U.S. hurricane since 2005. All these events caused more than $182 billion in damage. During just the first half of 2025 the trend continued, with $101 billion worth of climate and weather disasters.

If you think the need for planning doesn't affect you (or you need help convincing someone close to you that it does), let's try walking through our current reality with a variation on the Six Degrees of Kevin Bacon game, based on the idea that any actor can be linked to Kevin within six movie roles. Do you have a friend in California or a relative in North Carolina or a grandparent in Florida? Even if you didn't experience one of the more recent climate-related catastrophes firsthand, you probably know someone who did, possibly losing their insurance, their home, or even their community. But even without considering climate change and its related damage, we are still dealing with biodiversity loss; microplastics found in, well, everything; increased instances of disease outbreaks; unregulated AI and resource depletion; ongoing wars and domestic terrorism; and—just for shits and giggles—increasingly fraught political ideology and nukes. In fact, there's quite a formidable array of plights on the horizon. And all of these are multipliers, or a collection of crises, that could amplify one another and lead, sooner rather than later, to a polycrisis (see page 7).

So, yeah, you and everyone you love should have a plan. Actually you should have *two* plans: one for sheltering in place, and one for leaving, *fast* (but more on this later). While every situation is unique, they do have some elements in common, so in the interest of baby steps, here are a few things you can do right now (go ahead, we'll wait) to improve your readiness level:

DO: Stay alert, be it for extreme weather–related situations or rogue AI. (See page 120.)

DO: Familiarize yourself with the weather report lingo common to your area—a "watch" is different from an "advisory," which is different from a "warning." (See page 226.)

DO: Find some room in your home to store extra water, nonperishable food, flashlights, and toilet paper, even if you live in a small space. (See page 29.)

DO: Prepare a go bag so you don't have to run around looking for necessary (and possibly lifesaving!) items at the last minute. (See pages 42–48.)

DO: Create and print (yes, print!) at least two evacuation routes out of your neighborhood to your preplanned destination, because your electronic devices may not work when you need them. (See page 41.)

DO: Make (and regularly update) a home inventory. Sure, *you* pretty much know the contents of your home, but will you be able to reel off everything when your house is in shambles and you're under pressure by a harried insurance agent? Recovery is easier if you know what you've got. Document the contents of your home *before* a fire or flood occurs.

How to Make a Home Inventory

1. Video or photograph each room of your home, including inside drawers, closets, and your garage. Make note of important or expensive items like electronics, appliances, sports equipment, jewelry, and the like. This gives you "before" images to compare with the "after" in case of damage.
2. Describe your home's contents in your video or photographs. Note the price you paid and where and when you bought each item. Save the receipts for any major purchases and take pics of the bar codes and model stickers.
3. Keep your inventory, key documents, and receipts outside of your home or in a fireproof safe. You can keep video and photos in the cloud, but remember that you may not be able to access it, so have backup on a flash drive stored off-site or in a fireproof safe.

See how easy it is? You're still in part one and you've already taken some steps toward being prepared. Feels a little different from binge-watching all those episodes of *Doomsday Preppers,* doesn't it? That's because the mindset of *The Emergency Playbook* is different from that of a doomsday type. While the aim is mostly the same—to survive—the philosophy is less Mad Max and more the Power of Positive Prepping.

Once you have taken a couple of these small but important steps, you are hopefully feeling accomplished and ready to tackle more. Following is a checklist of considerations that you should start thinking about *now.* We'll address each of these in more depth later in the book (see the cross-references with each point if you want to turn immediately to that section), but this gives you an overview of what your complete emergency plan will look like.

Your Emergency Plan Overview

First think about where you live and how the location and type of home you live in might affect how you handle an emergency:

- **Are there particular disasters likely to affect your area that might require special planning?** For instance, floods and earthquakes may make travel impossible in their aftermath, whereas tornadoes might not. (See part three.)
- **Do you live in the city, where traffic may be an issue while trying to evacuate?** Or in the country, where you might have to drive farther to find a gas station or EV charger?
- **Are there details about your home that might affect your plans?** For instance, is your house located in a floodplain or perched on a hilltop? Is it built to modern standards to better resist disasters, or is it older? If you live in an apartment or condo: Does your building have a generator? And if so, is it powered via gasoline, diesel, propane, or solar? How long could it run in the event of a power failure without a resupply of fuel? And what could it power? Does your building have elevators and fire detection and suppression equipment?
- **How long could you live comfortably without power**—a few days? A week or longer? (See page 38.)

- **Do you have a space that stays cool,** like a basement, where you can go if temperatures rise but your power is out?
- **Do you have a heating source that does not depend on electricity,** such as a fireplace or wood stove? If so, make sure you have sufficient backup amounts of wood, coal, or some makeshift fuel. What constitutes "sufficient" depends on your situation and location, but you should know how much fuel you use per day and should plan for enough to keep you warm for at least a week or two.
- **What about the locks on your doors?** Are they old-fashioned mechanical locks or electronic locks that require electricity or a battery?
- **What tools, equipment, and supplies should you have in your home** if you, your family, and your pets have to shelter in place? (See page 112.)

Next think about how you will get information and communicate with friends, neighbors, and loved ones:

- **How will you know what's going on in an emergency?** How can you get news if the power is off or the phone systems are down? (See page 120.)
- **How will you communicate with others when a disaster occurs?** Do you have a primary emergency contact and a backup if the first is not available? What will you do when you can't contact everybody, or anybody? How long should you wait before you take action on your own? (See page 119.)
- **Have you identified everyone who needs to be aware of your plan** (or parts of it)? This should include your immediate family or housemates but could also comprise extended family or friends who live nearby, or even people in more distant areas, depending on what you are responding to. (See page 119.)
- **Define when the plan should be implemented.** There are various levels of emergency warnings, and sometimes evacuations

are suggested but not mandatory. What, or who, will cause your plan to go into effect? (See page 119.)

Next are the questions you should ask (and know the answers to) about the physical components of your plan—where you'll go, what you'll need to have on hand, and so on:

- **Is it safer to shelter in place or will you have to evacuate?** (See chapter 6.)
- **If you're sheltering in place,** what tools, equipment, and supplies do you need if you'll be holed up at home for a few days, a few weeks, or longer? Keep in mind that if you have a fireplace or wood-burning stove your supplies should include extra wood and tinder. (See page 112.)
- **If evacuating,** what tools, equipment, and supplies do you need to take with you? Do you have a go bag packed with all the essentials? Do you have one packed for each member of your family? What about for your pet(s)? Are the supplies it contains up to date? (See page 89.)
- **Do you have a preplanned destination,** a preplanned way to get there, and at least two backup routes? To paraphrase eighteenth-century Scottish poet Robert Burns, the best-laid plans of mice and men often go awry. Which is another way of saying that despite our most careful efforts, life's journey—especially the one out of town during an emergency—can be unpredictable.
- **And finally, you've survived the disaster. Now what?** Once you and your family have made it safely through, do you know the next steps? Will your insurance coverage and/or any government or community programs help you recover from property damage or loss? Do you have the documents you need, and do you know how to get them replaced if necessary? Do you have resources for helping with trauma or grief, or for medical

problems that might be associated with emergencies (such as inhaling toxic smoke during a fire)? (See page 267.)

While the chapters that follow will walk you through all the steps of formulating your emergency plan, there are some ways you can boost your knowledge and skills now that might end up being useful during a catastrophe. Let's take a look.

What You Can Do *Now* That Could Pay Off *Later*

Work out, bro. Most disaster scenarios (except for, perhaps, another pandemic) will probably involve more moving around than you're used to, unless your job or favorite pastime (say, jogging) requires regular physical activity. Staying active doesn't just give you rock-hard abs and bulging biceps, it's also great for mood and mental acuity. Whether from lifting weights, weekend Pilates classes, or working up a sweat doing daily chores, being in shape is definitely an asset in an emergency.

Get to know your neighbors. Introduce yourself. Say hello if you're in the elevator together or run into one another at the grocery store. Neighbors help one another out all the time—keeping watch when someone's out of town, watering plants, feeding pets, or collecting the mail. Once you establish a connection (often the hardest part), you can make a plan for semi-regular pizza-and-poker nights and check in on one another in case of an emergency.

Try your hand at foraging. Foraging is the practice of searching for and collecting food, such as plants, mushrooms, herbs, nuts, berries, and even edible insects, from your environment (but be careful to avoid poisonous or harmful plants and fungi). It's also a great way to connect with nature, discover new foods, and practice sustainable living. Also, breathing in the scent of soil has a physiological effect that stimulates the release of the hormone oxytocin, the same chemical that promotes social bonding and regulates stress. Coincidence? We think not.

You can learn about foraging via workshops and guided tours, local groups, community colleges, or agricultural programs at nature centers and botanical gardens, and through books and apps. Be aware, however, that learning to safely and effectively forage takes a lot of time, effort, and practice.

Take a first aid class. Being able to administer first aid (beyond kissing a boo-boo and applying a Band-Aid) can be crucial in an emergency. For example, knowing how to treat common minor injuries, stop bleeding, bandage a wound, save someone who is choking, splint a sprained or broken limb, deal with hypothermia or frostbite, and deploy a tourniquet properly can be lifesaving. Training in CPR or more advanced first aid or medical techniques is not just a good idea but also a great way to impress family and friends at a dinner party.

You can learn via courses offered by the Red Cross, the American Heart Association, and your local health centers, in addition to online resources including websites and apps.

Check out herbal medicine practices. Herbal medicine, which uses plants or plant extracts for medicinal purposes (via teas, tinctures, capsules, or oils), has been used for centuries to treat various health conditions. Plants contain compounds—often replicated for use in traditional medication such as aspirin and opium—that can help treat illnesses or improve health. Depending on your access to medical care during an emergency, herbal medicine could help you treat certain medical issues when more traditional medical care is no longer available or too expensive. Another plus: Herbal remedies often rely on materials that can be acquired or made locally.

You can learn about herbal medicine via local or online herbal medicine schools, university programs, or books, or from an herbalist. Check out *Forgotten Home Apothecary* by Nicole Apelian and *The Gift of Healing Herbs* and *Healing Magic* by Robin Rose Bennett.

Learn how to compost. Composting reduces waste and helps the environment by transforming organic waste into a nutrient-rich soil, lessening the need for chemical fertilizers and pesticides. It may also be important to know how to compost should you be in a situation where you need to dispose of human waste products (see page 141).

The principle is a simple one. Mix mostly brown (i.e., carbon-rich) plant material, such as dry, dead leaves and twigs, with a smaller amount of green (i.e., nitrogen-rich) material, including food scraps, grass clippings, and coffee grounds. Layer these materials, keep the pile moist like a damp sponge, and turn it regularly to aerate. Compost is ready when it's dark and crumbly and smells earthy.

You can learn more about composting by reading *Composting for a New Generation* by Michelle Balz, *Compost* by Charles Dowding, *Compost Stew* by Mary McKenna Siddals (for kids), or *Worms Eat My Garbage* by Mary Appelhof, or by watching how-to videos online.

Level up with wilderness survival training. This specialized training imparts the know-how needed to help you survive in the great outdoors. It includes most of what's covered in this book: knowing how to find and purify water, build a shelter, start a fire, navigate, and source food, among other essential skills.

You can learn via online courses, survival workshops and schools, outdoor adventure groups, wilderness survival communities, forums, and online communities. Some good ones include Justin McAffee's Substack newsletter *Collapse Curriculum* and Jamie Wheal's Substack newsletter *Homegrown Humans.*

Know how to fix your mode of transport. Basic car, motorcycle, and bicycle maintenance includes the tasks usually performed at your local auto repair shop, gas station, or bike shop that keep your ride in good working condition, extending its lifespan and ensuring your safety.

You can learn via online tutorials and videos, workshops and classes, books, and local car and bicycle maintenance clubs. Really, at the very least, you should know how to change a tire.

Train to keep yourself safe. Self-defense involves various techniques and strategies designed to protect yourself from physical harm in a threatening situation (shout-out to Sandra Bullock as undercover FBI agent Gracie Hart in *Miss Congeniality* for introducing us to the S.I.N.G.

acronym, which means to go for the Solar Plexus, Instep, Neck, and Groin). There are many different styles of self-defense, each with its own set of methods, philosophies, and techniques. Remember, a self-defense class or three won't transform you into a UFC fighter, but some knowledge is better than none, as long as you understand its limits.

Check out martial arts schools, self-defense workshops and classes, online tutorials and courses, personal safety seminars, and self-defense apps.

Hunt or catch your own food. Fishing and hunting are a more productive alternative to golf and pickleball. Like most skills, they're best learned by actually doing, and practice makes perfect. So, what are you waiting for?

Check out local hunting and fishing clubs and organizations, neighborhood fishing shops, tackle stores, or gun ranges. If you end up not needing this knowledge to survive, you'll still have plenty of fun.

The Rule of Three

There is a "rule of three" for everything from fashion and writing to photography and statistics. In survivalist circles it's a shorthand phrase to describe basic survival needs in order of urgency:

- You can survive three *minutes* without breathable air or in icy water.
- You can survive three *hours* in a harsh environment (extreme heat or cold).
- You can survive three *days* without drinkable water.
- You can survive three *weeks* without food.
- You can survive three *months* without hope, which is where the importance of optimism comes in.

While the above rules aren't *exactly* literal, they do get at the relative importance of each element. Each line assumes that the one(s) before it is met. For example, if you have a large quantity of food and water but are exposed to a hostile environment, then the harsh conditions rule applies.

But the real trick is not to have to sweat the rules because you're smart and you planned three *years* in advance. Being prepared will help you feel confident that you can handle whatever is coming your way. It can also prevent the rule that we didn't list here: You can survive only three *seconds* if you start to panic. We're not saying you'll expire after three seconds, but panicking sends you down a road from which you may not return. If you feel a bout of anxiety coming on, try some of the following practices to get back on track.

The Power of Positive Prepping (or How to Stay Calm and Control Your Stress)

- Think of something that makes you happy and then smile (even if you don't feel like it). Raising the upper corners of your mouth automatically releases tension.
- Breathe. In emergencies, the body naturally kicks into fight-or-flight mode. It's common to start breathing rapidly and shallowly as if you're running away from danger. And hell, given the subject of this book, you very well might be! You can override rapid breathing by taking long, deep breaths and focusing *only on your breath,* which is the basis for many forms of meditation. Breathe in, breathe out. And repeat. Tell your body you are calm, and your mind will follow. Easy peasy. And no money required.
- Take a broad view and try widening your field of vision. When your body's flight-or-fight response kicks in, it automatically narrows your field of vision, making it harder to find perspective.
- Immerse your face in cold water or place an ice pack against your cheeks and forehead. This can slow your heart rate and induce relaxation.

- Yawn. Prolonged exhaling lowers your heart rate and sends your body a signal to relax.
- Place your right hand above your heart and your left hand on your belly. Touch reduces your levels of cortisol, which is your body's main stress hormone.
- Focus on a goal. The magnitude of things going on during any given emergency—from wildfires to hurricanes—can be overwhelming. Practice tuning out everything *except the one thing you're doing.* If your house is on fire, focus on getting people out. If you are performing CPR, just do that one activity. If you're calling 911, focus on the conversation with the operator. It's easy to panic when you look up the road and see all the possible wreckage. Don't go there. One step in front of the other. One. Thing. At. A. Time. Even the Navy SEALs teach that. Solve one problem, then the next. Sooner or later, you will realize—for all our Gloria Gaynor fans out there—that you have survived.
- Get moving. Physical activity is a great (and proven) way to manage anxiety and pump up your endorphins.
- If it's safe, take a walk. Bonus points if you can do so among trees. Research shows that taking a walk *for as little as five minutes* in nature improves mood, self-esteem, and relaxation and yields noticeable changes in physiology: measurable decreases in cortisol (the stress hormone), respiration, blood pressure, and heart rate. Or at the very least step out your back door or onto your balcony or even stick your head out a window and breathe (again, if it's safe to do so).
- Play with your pet. It's time you won't spend worrying, and it may ground you for whatever you have to face next.
- Be bold. We—especially women!—are so attuned to following the rules that it can be difficult to break them

even when the situation calls for it. In emergencies it's perfectly okay to take measures like disturbing the peace, bossing around total strangers, ripping an item of expensive clothing, or taking charge of someone else's property to save lives. So go ahead. Become the superhero of your own story (yes, we did say earlier that superheroes won't save us, but there's no harm in a little role play). You may be surprised how much you enjoy it.

- Indulge when possible. Eat that ice cream you were avoiding even if it may wreak havoc on your cholesterol. Just because it may be the end of the world doesn't mean it has to *feel* like the end of the world.
- Laugh. It enhances oxygen intake; stimulates your heart, lungs, and muscles; increases the endorphins released by your brain; and activates and relieves stress. Or as comedy legend Mel Brooks put it, "Humor is just another defense against the universe."

It seems like we find ourselves facing situations that did not go as planned fairly often: The babysitter didn't show up. The bus was late. Our lunch date got canceled. And that's just the small stuff. When looked at this way, every day presents an opportunity to practice adapting to and embracing your stress. Experts say that people who practice adapting instead of resisting unplanned outcomes are calmer in general. The next time something small goes wrong in your day, view it as a chance to practice a critical survival skill.

Now that you're in a calm frame of mind, let's address the essentials you'll need to have on hand to be prepared.

FOOD
TOOLS

PART TWO

The Essentials

You always got to be prepared but you never know for what.

—BOB DYLAN, "SUGAR BABY"

Organization is to prepping what foreplay is to sex. Sure, you can do one without the other, but usually the results aren't as satisfying. So it goes for finding room for the "essentials," those items necessary for our *survival* (see the Rule of Three, page 24). And those seemingly frivolous items like lipstick or a delicious but unhealthy salty snack? There's always space for what makes us feel good. Yes, you could just make a pile and call it a day, but time counts during an emergency, and you really don't want to have to waste it digging around to find what you need. So best practices suggest that you:

- Keep items you'll need right away where you can easily find them.
- Keep related items together (there is no wrong way to do this—whatever makes sense to you and will easily be remembered is

best) and store smaller items in clear, marked plastic bags. You don't want to fumble in the dark if the lights go out.

- Continually rotate the items in your stash so nothing expires, but note that manufacturers' expiration dates are very conservative (more on this in the next few chapters).

Ask any city dweller about the downsides of living in a dense, urban environment and they'll probably mention something about having to shoehorn their belongings into smaller living spaces (even if that smaller living space is a "classic six" New York City apartment with Central Park views). There's hardly room for a second child, where do you expect them to store extra water? To make room in your home (regardless of its size) for essential emergency supplies:

- Declutter before you start adding more stuff.
- Use cabinets, cupboards, and shelves (go high and go low!) or under-sink areas to tuck away emergency items.
- If you have stairs, consider reconstructing the solid treads into hinged lids with storage compartments underneath. Hide supplies in plain sight in decorative baskets or cool-looking industrial storage units, in front of which you could hang a decorative canvas. Utilize storage bins you can keep out of sight under beds.
- Use multipurpose furniture that also features storage space (ottomans, benches, etc.).
- Camouflage storage bins with decorative curtains or hanging beads (so 1970s boho), or treat those backup soup cans like art (à la Andy Warhol) and design an interesting display.
- Hang your transportation (bike, scooter) to get it off the floor.
- Take advantage of separate storage spaces (garage, shed, communal storage area) that allow you to set aside emergency items.

If you don't have a lot of room, prioritize and arrange your essentials by their importance to your survival (e.g., water, food, a generator to prevent excess heat or cold should you suffer a power outage, and so on).

Now that we've taken a glimpse into the past and discussed why you should take action now and plan for the future, next up are the essentials. From what you'll need to keep warm when it's cold to how much food and water you should have on hand—we've got you covered.

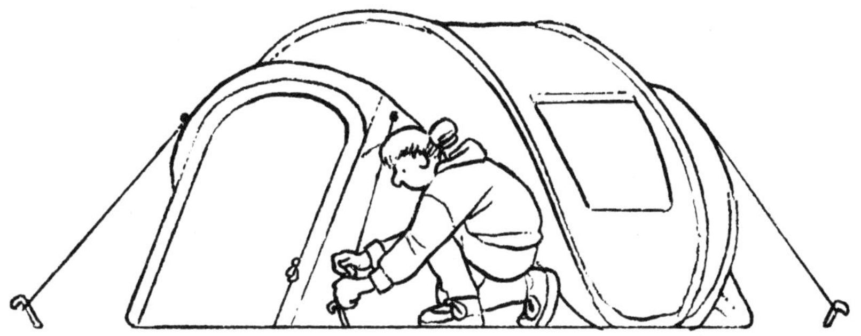

3. Protection from the Elements

A goal without a plan is just a wish.

—ANTOINE DE SAINT-EXUPÉRY, *THE LITTLE PRINCE*

According to the Rule of Three (see page 24), you can survive three *hours* in a harsh environment (and when we say "harsh," we're talking about the temperature, not the vibes). Depending on the type of emergency you are dealing with, you will be either hunkering down at home (or wherever you find yourself when disaster strikes) or evacuating. Ergo, this chapter is broken down into two sections. The first covers sheltering where you happen to be with no power (no heat! no cool air! no phone!), and the second addresses making friends with the elements should you need to evacuate.

Let's start with the preferred mode of action. Whether you live in the city, the suburbs, or a rural area, the default during an emergency that isn't directly threatening your home is to stay put. You (likely) have more resources where you live, you're familiar with the area, and you are (hopefully) part of a community that can help should you need it.

What You Need When You're Home and the Power Goes Out

If you live in a high-rise apartment building, even getting access to your home without electricity can be tricky, especially if you happen to live on the tenth or twentieth floor (it's all about the great views until you have to walk up a dozen flights of steps carrying canned goods and bottles of water). More than two million households lost power in New York and New Jersey after Hurricane (a.k.a. Superstorm) Sandy in 2012. Do you really want to risk not being prepared—even if that only means keeping a flashlight in your nightstand—should that happen again?

A power outage is when your "shelter in place" stash comes in handy. Find a decorative container (a vintage leather trunk, perhaps) that looks divine in your living room or something of similar dimensions to place at the foot of your bed (or both). At the very least the container should hold the items you'll need to find your way in the dark so you can get to your larger store of emergency supplies if it becomes necessary.

Here's what to store in your shelter-in-place emergency kit:

- **Enough drinking water and food that requires little preparation**—think energy bars and canned food (don't forget the manual can opener)—for everyone in your household (including pets and/or babies!) for a twenty-four- to forty-eight-hour period (in case you can't get to your larger store of supplies)
- **Extra batteries** for all devices
- **Light sources:** flashlights, headlamps, glow sticks (so festive!), and/or matches

- **N95 masks and air purifiers,** should you be in the vicinity of a wildfire
- **Power bank** for your phone
- **Weather radio:** battery powered or hand cranked

Most days, your home probably does a good job of protecting you from the elements. However, if you have lost power in a summer storm and it looks like a longer-term situation (more than a few hours), the outcomes could include your family overheating, the food in your fridge spoiling, and an inability to charge your devices (bigger picture: your sources of communication to the "outside").

If you lose power in a winter storm, you face similar possible outcomes: You (and possibly your pipes) could freeze, you'll be unable to charge your devices, and you won't even be able to watch that buzzy new show to take your mind off the crisis. You could potentially save some refrigerated items by tucking them into a snowbank outside, but if the storm is bad, you might not find them again until spring.

Dealing with a loss of power can be handled in a couple of ways. First, you can replace your electricity with a (solar-, gas-, or propane-powered) generator. Second, you can use the electricity you have stored in batteries; depending on the size, this could be enough to get you through until the lights go back on. Third, you can try a throwback activity, like swapping out streaming with the lights on for Scrabble by candlelight. Let's look at the first approach.

Pick Your Favorite Generator and Other Options

Some generators are already built and/or plugged into the gas line or propane tank of buildings and/or houses, and if you have access to that, you should know how to operate your own system. Others are portable and are available in various types, shapes, and sizes, each designed to serve different needs and environments. In the table on the next page you'll find the main types categorized by fuel source and intended use.

Choose Your Generator

Type of Generator	Pros	Cons
Gas-Powered Portable Generator (the regular kind, not the inverter generators discussed below)	Widely available fuel. Lower upfront cost compared to other types. Can power a wide variety of appliances.	Gasoline can be difficult to store for long periods. Shorter run time per tank of fuel. They can be noisy. Possible electrocution from improper use or via energizing other electrical systems.
Propane-Powered Portable Generator	Cleaner burning than gasoline, producing fewer emissions. Longer shelf life for fuel (propane tanks can be stored for long periods). Quieter operation compared to gasoline generators.	Propane can be harder to find depending on location. Generally higher upfront cost. May require an adapter to connect to propane tanks.
Diesel-Powered Portable Generator	More fuel-efficient than gasoline. Longer run time with larger fuel tanks. Powerful, making it ideal for heavy-duty equipment or job sites. Longer lifespan with proper maintenance.	Diesel fuel can be expensive and harder to find in some locations. Heavier and more expensive than gasoline-powered models. Typically noisier than propane or gas models.
Inverter Generator (mostly gasoline, but diesel, propane, and natural gas versions exist)	Clean, stable power output, ideal for sensitive devices like laptops, TVs, and smartphones. Quieter than conventional generators. More compact and lightweight, making it easy to transport. Energy-efficient with variable-speed engines that adjust to load requirements.	Generally, there is a lower power output compared to traditional generators. Higher initial cost. Can be less fuel-efficient at low loads.

Type of Generator	Pros	Cons
Dual-Fuel Portable Generator (either regular or inverter)	Offers the flexibility to run on either gasoline or propane, providing options in case one fuel is unavailable. Can operate for a longer time, as you can switch to a different fuel if one runs out. Cleaner-burning propane option when gasoline is not ideal.	Slightly more expensive than single-fuel generators. May be heavier than single-fuel models.
Solar-Powered Portable Generator	Environmentally friendly, as it uses renewable solar energy. Silent operation. Low maintenance and no fuel costs.	Limited power output, not suitable for high-power appliances or long-term use. Dependent on sunlight for recharging, so may not work well in cloudy conditions. Requires solar panels (some come bundled with panels, others require a separate purchase).

Another way to create the electricity you need is via solar panels, which will also require batteries for storage and sometimes electronic controls. Making your own solar power system without panels (or at least solar cells to make a panel) during or after an emergency is possible but not really feasible.

The most practical way to produce electricity without a generator or solar system is via a turbine, powered by wind or water. You can make one of these using a generator (like a car alternator) or an electric motor in reverse: You supply the turning power, and the motor will generate the electricity. This would work best for recharging batteries that would then be used to provide power. On a homemade, DIY generator, the voltage and current produced vary with many factors, so this could affect the utility. Like solar systems, if you don't have a solid understanding of how electricity works, it will be difficult to create a useful homemade turbine.

How to Get By Without Electricity

In many parts of the world, electricity is scarce or undependable, so people have to find ways of doing without. Let's flash back to one of the most important requirements in the Rule of Three: maintaining a livable environment, including temperature control (which means not getting too cold or, with the recent advent of heat domes, too hot), and having the ability to cook, communicate, shower, and see when it's dark.

Keeping Warm

In the United States, most modern houses need electricity for heat to function. If your heater is electric, your living space will get cold when the electricity goes out (Note: If your water heater runs on gas rather than electric you will still be able to take hot showers). Even houses warmed with gas usually require electricity to work, as the blower that sends the hot air through the building often runs on electric and the thermostat will not function for long if the power goes out.

If the usual heat source for your house or apartment is not functional, you can use a fireplace or wood-burning stove if you have one, assuming you laid in sufficient amounts of wood, coal, or some makeshift fuel for emergencies such as this. These features must be installed properly to avoid carbon monoxide poisoning, which will kill you. Make sure any wood-burning stove has proper ventilation. Also, be careful if you plan to set fire to something you're not used to burning. Coal, for instance, burns hotter than wood but heats more slowly and takes longer to warm up a space. Coal also produces more carbon monoxide than wood, and more creosote (the dark, sticky flammable residue that builds up when you burn wood or coal). This difference could damage the air intake and exhaust system of a wood stove or fireplace, make the stove inefficient, or even cause a fire in the chimney. Burning cardboard, paper, or other garbage may produce toxic fumes, especially if materials are painted or glued. Plywood and other treated lumber commonly used may also contain adhesives or other additives that can create toxic smoke when burned.

If you have a small space to keep warm but no stove or fireplace, one last-ditch option is to build a fire outdoors and use it to heat up bricks, rocks, or something else that radiates heat. Then, bring the hot bricks or rocks into your living space. Put a blanket over the hot rocks and sit or lie right on or next to them, like you would with an old-fashioned hot-water bottle. This won't heat up an entire room, but it could warm up a smaller sleeping or sitting space. Before ceramic pots were invented, people also boiled water by heating up rocks and dropping them into a leather bag of water. Again, this is a lot of work, but it's better than freezing or succumbing to carbon monoxide poisoning.

Make sure you're wearing appropriate clothing. Yes, we know this sounds like something your parents would say when you asked them to turn up the heat, but "Go put on another sweater" is a valid suggestion. Getting warm might take more than one layer, but what (and how much) you're wearing is where you should start. In places like the Andes mountains in South America, many rural people have no heat in their houses even though it drops below freezing every night. Their main strategy to stay warm is to wear warm clothes.

Your next line of defense is insulation. Do what you can to keep the heat inside your home. This might include actual, commercial insulation, or it could be as simple as covering windows with heavy curtains or a blanket.

Keep your living space small—at least the part you want to keep warm, like where you sleep and will spend the most time. It is not uncommon, even now, to see people partition off part of a house (especially an old one with high ceilings and little insulation) to keep in the heat, while the rest of the house gets cold (note that these ideas also work to keep smaller spaces *cool*). Close doors or hang up decorative blankets or tarps (alas, they don't make decorative tarps) to cordon off part of your house or apartment and focus the heat or cool air in one area. Don't forget pets and plants that might need to be in the heated (or cooler) parts too.

Keeping Cool

According to a story in Bloomberg in August 2025, there are fourteen million households without air-conditioning in the United States. There's no doubt that those of us fortunate enough to have AC can't imagine going without, especially as the hot days (and, more dangerously, hot nights) increase. So what to do if you don't have it? As with the "Keeping Warm" scenario, one of your first moves should involve your clothing. Change into something light and loose, made from a fabric that breathes and won't feel clammy: cotton, linen, nylon, or silk. Or if your housemates aren't home, your neighbors can't see in your windows, and you're not the shy type, make like a banana and peel.

Next, look for a spot in your house or apartment that naturally doesn't get a lot of sun. Bonus points if it's large enough to sleep in. Block it off from the rest of the space with a large sheet or a tarp and block out whatever sun may come in using curtains or shades.

Third, try to promote airflow by opening doors and windows to create a cross breeze. You can use a portable neck or manual hand fan, although they mainly just feel good in the moment and won't really lower your body temperature. If possible, time your activities to avoid the heat and sun. Taking a shower, or simply getting wet, can help keep your body temperature down, and it feels good too. Also see chapter 12.

Let There Be Light

Obviously, generating light will be more of an issue when it's dark outside, which is why you should lay in a sufficient number of flashlights, lanterns and/or candles, and batteries to get you and your household through. You are probably going to be dependent on battery-powered light sources. There are crank flashlights that work pretty well, but they are typically far less powerful than battery-powered lights. Depending on whether the power goes down when the weather is hot or cold, a wood fire might produce light—even a tiny one in a bowl or on a non-flammable surface. Remember, even a small fire produces deadly fumes, so make sure you are in a place with ventilation. There are also solar-powered lights, like those on a garden walkway or floodlights for illuminating an entryway. These could be used in many emergency situations, even adapted to use inside instead of out. You have to keep them in direct sunlight for five to ten hours for most lights to fully recharge, but even an overcast day or a shady location will charge them to some degree.

Cooking

If your stove runs on gas, cooking won't be an issue. If it runs on electric and the power goes out, you'll be happy you stocked up on canned goods and other nutrient-rich foods that don't require much prep. You could also use a camp stove that runs on propane or butane, supplies of which you should also have for backup. Cooking fires using wood are another option, but you might want to practice ahead of time. Cooking over a campfire is different from a stove—the heat is usually higher and harder to control. No matter what kind you use, be sure you have adequate ventilation where you are cooking.

Communication

Without electricity, most of our means of communication will not work for long. Landlines (for those who still have them) might last a while (not forever), and walkie-talkie batteries could be replaced or recharged, but most phone, text, and social media will be gone or limited. How did people communicate over long distances before the advent of electricity?

Snail mail via the U.S. Postal Service is an option, but it takes a long time to get a response. Actual human messengers are another possibility, but if the power outage was caused by a large disaster, this also may have limited utility. Next are signals—smoke, lights, or semaphores (i.e., flags) traditionally used by seafaring folk—but unless you are trained and practiced, this is probably not going to be a viable alternative for those of us who aren't sailors.

The only thing that really works when the grid is down is long-distance radio and satellite-based communication. Satellite phones and messengers need batteries but don't depend on the power grid as cellular phones do. The radios need power, but they don't rely on a complex system that needs electricity. Ham radio, VHF, GMRS, or even CB radios can reach a long way (worldwide for ham radio) using only batteries to do so. With enough batteries to recharge or replace, these would be one of the few options for long-distance communication in a grid-down situation. However, the people with whom you hope to make contact will need to have them too.

What You Need When You Need to Leave

The question of whether to stay or go is not always easy to answer, which is why you should have a plan in place rather than waiting until the last minute to figure things out. But if trusted authorities (or your Spidey-sense) tell you to leave, play it safe and evacuate even if it's voluntary. If there is a credible threat—from wild weather, warfare, or something like a chemical spill—you need to skedaddle.

But things don't always go as planned (see the Robert Burns quote from earlier). While you may envision tossing your go bag into the car, effortlessly gliding onto the highway, and arriving promptly at your friend's house in the next town over, if the emergency happens during rush hour or on a holiday weekend during the summer you may not be so lucky. It's smart to have prearranged with friends or family to crash with them in case of an emergency and have pretested routes out of town, but there is no guarantee you'll actually make it there. Trees may have fallen across the highway, or roads may be flooded and impassable. If you live in a populated area there may be enormous amounts of traffic, bringing exit routes to a standstill. Or your car could be low on gas or electric charge and not able to get you where you want to go.

In short, you should always be prepared with the basics you'll need to shelter, for at least a day or two, in the great outdoors. If the idea of communing in nature for that much time makes you uncomfortable, it may be because, according to estimates from the U.S. Environmental Protection Agency, the average American spends 90 percent of their time *indoors.* In other words, the more prepared you are to be outside, the "greater" the great outdoors will be.

Everything listed below should be included in either your go bag (see page 89) or your car (see page 104).

Protection from the Elements

- **At least one change of clothing,** including underwear and socks, because being able to slip into something *clean* during an emergency will feel like a luxury. Also, wearing damp clothing sucks, and hypothermia (which can be deadly) becomes an issue while you're out in the elements. Depending on the scenario, your clothes may get wet, dirty, or contaminated by smoke or dust, and not standing around naked while washing the other set of clothes can be good for your health as well as your mood. If there's the possibility of encountering cold weather, also consider packing some thin, insulated long underwear. It doesn't take up much space and can be worn in all but the hottest temperatures.
- **Duct tape.** It's true: It has unlimited uses.
- **Mylar emergency blankets.** They reflect a lot of body heat, do a really good job for their weight and bulk, and are small and inexpensive, so pack a few in case someone else needs one.

They will not insulate you from the ground but that's what the foam pad (listed below) is for. If you are using one of these emergency blankets and do not have a sleeping pad, you will probably have to sleep sitting up to keep the ground from absorbing all your body heat.

- **N95 masks** for every member of your family.
- **A sleeping bag and foam ground pad.** A down sleeping bag is warmer for its weight, more compressible, and longer lasting than synthetic, but it's not great when it's wet, so opt for one with a breathable waterproof shell. A ground pad is essential in cold weather. If you don't have one, find something to lay underneath your bag for insulation—pine needles, dried leaves, cardboard, bubble wrap—almost anything is better than nothing.
- **Fifty feet of string, thin rope, paracord, and/or zip ties.** These are useful for many things, including making a shelter with a tarp.
- **Lightweight waterproof tent, a hammock with a rain fly, or even plastic sheeting or a small tarp** (see page 49, "How to Build an Emergency Shelter").

Poor Air Quality

Breathing, as you know, is essential to life, yet a new analysis found that in 2024 only seven countries and 17 percent of global cities had air quality that met World Health Organization guidelines for harmful fine-particles (PM2.5) pollution. Emergencies, from certain terrorist attacks (e.g., 9/11) to wildfires, can affect air quality, with smoke from wildfires being especially dangerous and transient, particularly if you live in an urban area. Burning vegetation is bad enough for your lungs. Burning plastic, treated lumber, and other toxic materials make the smoke potentially more hazardous, which is why it's extremely important to include an N95 (or equally impregnable) mask in your go bag (more on page 89).

Stuff to Start (and Stop) a Fire

- **Cotton balls or some other kind of tinder.** Unless you do it on the regular, it's harder than you think to start a fire, even with a lighter (see page 52, "How to Start a Fire"). The weather may be wet and cold, and your fuel might be damp. You can find natural tinder all over the place, like twigs or pine needles, but it's so much easier if you have something in your pack that will start a fire with just a spark. Cotton balls are about the easiest, and if you take one and pull it apart to make it fluffy, it will catch fire with a single spark. Or coat them on one side with petroleum jelly, leaving the other half dry to catch a spark, and they will burn for a few minutes.
- **Ferro rods or fire starters.** These metal sticks, which often come tethered to a scraper, create a ton of sparks that can light tinder like cotton balls. They last forever and won't get ruined by water.
- **Fire extinguisher,** in case things get out of hand.
- **Lighter.** While a regular Bic will work, there are others that are more powerful and longer lasting (and not much more expensive), like little butane-filled lighters with stronger flames. An old-fashioned Zippo will work if it has fluid, but the fluid evaporates even when you don't use it, and you might find that your emergency lighter is out of gas when you need it.

- **Plants and shrubs,** including eucalyptus, cypress, rosemary, and cattails, which all catch fire easily and burn for a long time. Bonus! Cattails will also keep bugs away.

Stuff to Keep You Hydrated and Fed

- **Camp stove and a few portable propane tanks** (one-pound green cans are available at the grocery store). Don't store these in the car, especially during hot weather, but have them ready just in case.
- **Cookpot,** lightweight, covered, for cooking food or sterilizing water.
- **Fishing kit** (if you have line, hooks, and sinkers, you usually don't need a rod).
- **MREs (Meals Ready-to-Eat),** precooked meals in a pouch that retain their full moisture like canned food but are less heavy to transport and have a much longer shelf life. Also consider freeze-dried and/or dehydrated foods for traveling light and packaged items that don't require refrigeration, like granola bars, cereal, nuts, or emergency calorie rations (calorie-dense food bars that you can buy in stores that sell outdoor equipment). Pretest these and include the ones you like, as you will have enough to worry about without gagging from the taste of your rations!
- **Water,** one gallon per person per day for drinking, washing, and cleaning. A metal bottle is better than plastic because you can use it as a vessel to boil water for cooking or if you need to purify/decontaminate it. Look for a single-walled bottle rather than a double-walled or insulated one as those have an air space between the walls like a thermos, making it much harder (if not impossible) to boil water. If your water bottle is plastic, include a metal cup or pot that you can use to boil

water in. Also have a collapsible water bag or canteen if you need to clean water for a group of people.
- **A means of water filtration and/or purification** to make any water source drinkable (see chapter 4).

Stuff to Keep You Clean

- **Composting camp toilet** or a large bucket that can be used in lieu of a toilet (see page 55 for how to create a makeshift toilet) and a portable toilet seat. Liquid bleach, lime (calcium hydroxide or calcium oxide), or kitty litter (seriously, and not for the kitty) for the makeshift toilet, plus a folding trowel for burying waste.
- **Water for washing:** Most of the water you have will be consumed, but it is important to maintain a certain degree of hygiene (both for mental health and to prevent disease), so you will need some to wash your hands and your dishes. Like all washing when water is limited, you want to get wet, soap up, then rinse off. With a little practice, you can wash your hands with less than a cup of water, and a plate or cooking pot with a cup or so.

Stuff to Keep You Comfortable

- **Comfort food:** something portable that doesn't require preparation, like candy, granola bars, pastries, or a sandwich.
- **Insect repellent.**
- **Pillow,** inflatable or small-sized for camping. You can probably improvise a pillow with spare clothing, but it would likely be less comfortable.
- **Work gloves,** medium-weight, rubber-palm. In many cases during and after a disaster, you (or someone tougher and

stronger) might be dealing with rubble, wreckage, or debris, and sturdy gloves can keep you (or them) safe. They are light and cheap and will protect your hands.

What about bringing and using alcohol, weed, or other recreational drugs? While it may be tempting—and many of the above are known to help with anxiety, insomnia, and fear—this is probably not the best time to indulge. Put simply, in the midst of escaping a disaster and having to keep yourself alive, you'll want to be in full control of your senses and ready to act at a moment's notice.

How to Navigate the Great Outdoors

If there's a campground close by that's not affected by the emergency you're fleeing—and not already overflowing with your neighbors—this is a good first choice for setting up outdoors. Campgrounds often have running water, bathroom facilities, and even showers, so it can be a relatively simple option to hole up there for a few days. If your only options are more rustic, here are some tips for temporary outside living.

How to Pick a Good Campsite

Look for a flat area that offers natural protection from sun, wind, rain, and other weather. Be aware of what is above you. Avoid pitching your tent right under dead or dying trees as you could get hit by falling limbs should there be a storm or excessive wind. (More than a hundred people a year die from falling trees and limbs in the United States alone.)

While having a nearby water source can be a bonus, know what is upstream and don't choose a site where water accumulates or that's prone to flooding. As we saw with the 2025 tragedy in Kerr County, Texas, water can rise incredibly quickly, and flash floods are deadly. Also keep in mind that some water, like a fast-moving stream or a rapids in a river, makes a lot of noise, which could make it hard to hear people approaching (like rescuers). And remember, the rain that creates a flood might have fallen far away from you, farther up the watershed.

Keep an eye out for anthills if you are in warm areas, as well as plants with thorns, poison ivy, or other greenery that will make your life miserable.

How to Build an Emergency Shelter

1. Tie one corner of a tarp or piece of plastic to a tree or post, about knee high if possible.
2. Stake or weigh down the other three corners using tent stakes, wooden stakes you make from tree limbs, or something heavy like rocks.
3. Place a stick or a backpack under the tarp in the middle to keep it raised. This gives you a diamond-shaped shelter, with one side raised off the ground, but not too high.
4. Use dry leaves or another tarp to create a floor to keep you dry and insulated.
5. Climb in from the corner you tied to the tree or post, and you're good!

How to Protect Yourself from Insects and Other Critters

Let's start with the most obvious and ubiquitous pests we encounter outdoors: insects. Insects tend to be an issue only in warmer weather and/or climates. That said, in early October 2025, the historically mosquito-free nation of Iceland confirmed its first sighting of the species *Culiseta annulata,* which scientists have attributed to a warming climate. So unless you live in Antarctica, the only continent in the world believed to be pest-free, you may want to read on.

Whether it's because you ran out of the commercial stuff or you just prefer to avoid synthetic chemicals like DEET—a neurotoxin and the active ingredient in many insect repellents that has been linked to blisters, headaches, shortness of breath, seizures, memory loss, stiffness in joints, and skin irritation when used in high concentrations—there are many repellent options made from plant-based ingredients that are effective at deterring bugs (and depending on where you live, some of the plants they're made from can be foraged). Note that effectiveness can vary depending on the environment and the type of insects you're dealing with, and you may have to reapply natural repellents more frequently than chemical ones. But come the heat and the high grass, you'll be glad you stashed a couple of these natural options in your go bag.

- **Apple cider vinegar** has a pungent odor that mosquitoes find unpleasant.
- **Citronella oil,** derived from lemongrass, is one of the most popular natural insect repellents and works by masking scents that attract insects.
- **Clove oil** contains eugenol, which repels mosquitoes, flies, and other insects. Note: Clove oil is also great for pain associated with a toothache.
- **Geranium oil,** especially when combined with citronella or other oils, is a potent insect repellent.
- **Lavender and cinnamon oils** have a scent that is unpleasant to mosquitoes and other insects, making them good natural repellents.
- **Oil of lemon eucalyptus** (OLE) is an EPA-registered active ingredient in many insect repellents and combines great protection with a yummy fragrance.
- **Peppermint oil** has a strong scent that repels mosquitoes, ants, spiders, and other insects.
- **Tea tree oil** has both antimicrobial and insect-repelling properties, effective against mosquitoes, ticks, and flies.

- **Thyme and basil oil** are effective repellents for flies and mosquitoes.

Before using any essential oil, do a patch test on a small area of skin to ensure you don't have an allergic reaction. Always dilute essential oils with a carrier oil (like coconut, jojoba, or olive) to avoid skin irritation. To create your own spray, combine a few drops of essential oil (like citronella, lavender, or eucalyptus) with water and a bit of witch hazel or rubbing alcohol in a spray bottle.

> "When you don't have insect repellent, use your clothing and environment to keep you safe. I worked in the rainforest and other places in the tropics for decades and almost never used insect repellent. Insects were the worst during the evening and at night, when the sun was not too hot for them. I usually wore long pants and often a long-sleeved shirt, which provided a lot of protection. I also lived in places where we cooked on wood-burning stoves, and the smoke kept many insects out of the house. Screens and clothing did the rest. Think of insect repellent as the last line of protection when your clothing doesn't do the job.
>
> —Chris"

What about other common critters? Many animal-human encounters involve animals looking for food and people who have left something tempting outside, often garbage. Trash cans and dumpsters can attract just about any omnivore from bears to seagulls. Sometimes these encounters are harmless; if we are camping and have some leftover chicken bones, the raccoons are welcome to them. But when it comes to bears, stray dogs, or mountain lions, we'd rather they keep their distance. So keep the area around your campsite clean. Food and other smelly things like toiletries (who doesn't love a lemon-scented body lotion?) can attract animals that have much keener olfactory senses than we do. Keep food wrapped in airtight containers or plastic bags and store it away from where you are sleeping. If bears are around, don't store food in your car as they can smell it and may break in. Bears are incredibly strong and could easily disable a vehicle by ripping out wires or bending metal.

While you're outside, it's best to avoid the local wildlife, even if they seem cute and friendly. More animals are out at night than during the day, so try to minimize your movement after the sun goes down. A bite or scratch from an animal—many of which carry rabies—can get infected and quickly become a problem you do not need. Medical help may not be available during a disaster, and in the case of rabies the lack of it could be fatal.

How to Start a Fire

1. First, find a safe place to build your fire. You need a dry location out of the wind and rain (or a platform of dry branches). Situate your fire where it will not spread to any surrounding vegetation, especially during a drought. If you have a tent or tarp, make sure the fire is far enough away to not melt or set fire to your temporary home.
2. Make sure the ground where you will start the fire is relatively dry and free of snow. If the ground is wet, create a dry area for building your fire by putting some branches, rocks, or dry sand on the wet ground.
3. Gather a big pile of tinder. This could be newspaper or clean paper bags; cotton balls or cotton makeup remover pads (fluff them up to make them easier to light); small twigs, grasses, and leaves; even store-bought tinder—the stuff that lights easily. You use tinder to start the fire and help keep it going.

4. Place your tinder in a pile on the ground. You will need a lot more than you imagine—so gather quite a bit before you light it. Surround it with small sticks or twigs—and we mean *small,* like the width of a pencil lead; don't cram everything together, leave lots of air space. Put some larger sticks—the thickness of a pencil—on top of that pile. Twigs from pine trees (or other conifers) are especially good, as are pine needles. If the twigs make a good cracking sound when you break them, they are likely to be dry enough to work well. Leave a space in the pile of twigs so you can get to your tinder with your lighter or match.
5. Light the tinder. Good tinder should start with a single match, easily. Cotton balls start with a spark (Chris always uses cotton balls for tinder). When the smaller sticks begin to catch fire, add larger pieces of wood in a pyramid or teepee shape. The exact shape is not important, just that there is lots of open space for air to get in.
6. Once the fire is blazing, add more wood as needed to maintain the fire. Keep it as small as possible to accomplish what you need (warmth, cooking, light) so you don't use up all your fuel right away.
7. Sing a camp song. Look up at the sky and the stars. Take time

to appreciate the people who are on the journey with you. You can view this as a hardship or a new experience. We encourage you to choose the latter.

8. Always put out a fire thoroughly with water and be sure to tamp down any sparks. This is important! Fires can be very hard to start, but if conditions are right, they can re-spark and quickly spread.

How to Make a Waterproof Fire Starter

1. Cut a four-inch-long strip of two-inch-wide waterproof duct tape.
2. Smear a wad of cotton with petroleum jelly, leaving a little bit of your cotton dry.
3. Fold your cotton into the duct tape and seal on all four sides.
4. To use your fire starter, cut off a corner of your duct tape package, pull out a bit of the cotton, and light it (the cotton/petroleum jelly combo will both extend burn time and increase heat output).

How to Set Up an Outdoor Kitchen

Whether you are cooking on a camp stove or over an open fire, you need someplace to locate your fire source that is flat, sturdy, and secure. And you need somewhere to sit and eat, even if it's a log or a five-gallon bucket. Remember: Keep your food in a receptacle that prevents animals from getting into it. To deter small animals, like rodents, you don't need much—a sturdy plastic or metal receptacle with a snug-fitting lid will do. For bears, you need something specially constructed to keep the smell from escaping and attracting them, so locate your kitchen (and food) away from where you are sleeping.

How to Make an Outdoor Toilet

If you don't have access to bathroom facilities, you can either haul a camping toilet with you or make a composting toilet.

A camping toilet is a smaller version of a porta potty with a toilet seat and removable container lined with a bag to collect the waste. When you're done, take the bag or the whole container to a disposal site away from food and water.

To make a composting toilet, do the following:

1. Look for an area to locate your toilet that is secluded, is downhill from sources of water, and, if possible, has a nice view (reading material is optional).
2. Dig a hole about three feet (or a meter) deep or line a five-gallon bucket with two heavy-duty trash bags or commercial liners.
3. Center a toilet seat, if you have one, over the hole. Chris has taken dozens of groups of students and tourists to remote areas, and a toilet seat makes a big difference to people who are not used to pooping in the woods.
4. Use toilet paper if you have it, newspaper if you don't, or some leaves (but be sure you know your plants, so you aren't inadvertently wiping with a poisonous variety!).
5. Cover the waste with just enough of the dirt from the hole you dug to cover it completely. Or use lime (calcium hydroxide or calcium oxide, not the fruit used in tequila), dirt, and ash, or a cup or two of kitty litter, after each bowel movement. Don't use bleach, which can react with urine to produce toxic gas that can kill the beneficial bacteria that are breaking down the waste.
6. Keep hand sanitizer and/or baby wipes nearby.

7. When the hole fills up, cover it thoroughly and dig another. If you've used a bucket, once it's full, twist and tie the bag tightly so it doesn't leak and take it to a disposal site away from food and water.

A final, more permanent option (and thus probably not practical if your outdoor situation is temporary) is to build an outhouse. Dig a large and deep hole in the ground, top it with a toilet seat, and make sure you're surrounded on all sides for privacy. This is an endeavor best started before you need it. As this option is not portable, make sure to locate your outhouse an appropriate distance and elevation away from food and water sources.

Note: For those without a penis who prefer the ease and safety of being able to pee standing up, may we suggest a female urination device (FUD), which, as the name suggests, helps direct urine away from the body while you are standing up to urinate. Forget about penis envy and look into getting one of these babies. It's perfect for:

- When toilet facilities are unavailable or unsanitary
- When clothing or physical issues prevent squatting or sitting to urinate
- Outdoor recreation and occupations
- Gender affirmation and safety
- Medical reasons

How to Set Up an Outdoor Shower

You'll need access to a hose for this makeshift shower, or you can purchase a solar-powered pressurized shower with a foot pump and add it to your in-case-of-evacuation stash.

1. Use a large black plastic bag (the dark color will better absorb the heat from the sun's rays).
2. Poke a dozen or so tiny holes over a small area (the size of a saucer) on the bottom of the bag or attach a shower head (if

you happen to have one) to the bottom of the bag with duct tape. You can buy commercial versions of the bag with the nozzle attached and a loop for hanging, but this DIY version works fine too.

3. Fill the bag with water but position it so that the fluid does not run out of the holes or shower head. Raise those areas or tie them off temporarily.
4. Close the bag and set it in the sun to heat. Depending on the temperature and sunlight, the water can get really hot, so be sure to test before using.
5. Hang the bag in an elevated position from a tree branch or tall structure above your head. Gravity will provide the water pressure.
6. Listen to the birds. Gaze at the clouds. Sing a song.
7. Use the water sparingly. Of course, you could skip most of these steps and simply scoop water (heated or not) from a bucket and pour it over yourself, a method used all over the world where there is insufficient water pressure for a shower.

How to Tell Direction Without a Compass

The sun rises in the east and sets in the west, of course, but it does not travel directly overhead unless you are near the equator. In most of the Northern Hemisphere, north of the Tropic of Cancer, it is always in the southern half of the sky, which means that around noon the sun should be to the south. At night, you could look for the North Star (Polaris), but it is faint and not always easy to find. Instead, look for the Big Dipper. The three stars in a row are the "handle." At the end of the "handle" are four stars arranged in an irregular rectangle that make up the Big Dipper's "bowl." If you draw an imaginary line between the two stars that make up the outer side of that rectangle (farthest from the handle) and continue it about five times the distance between the two stars, you will find the North Star (hence the song "Follow the Drinking Gourd" that led enslaved people north to freedom). In the Southern Hemisphere, you would use a different but also easily identifiable constellation: the Southern Cross. Look toward that and you are looking south.

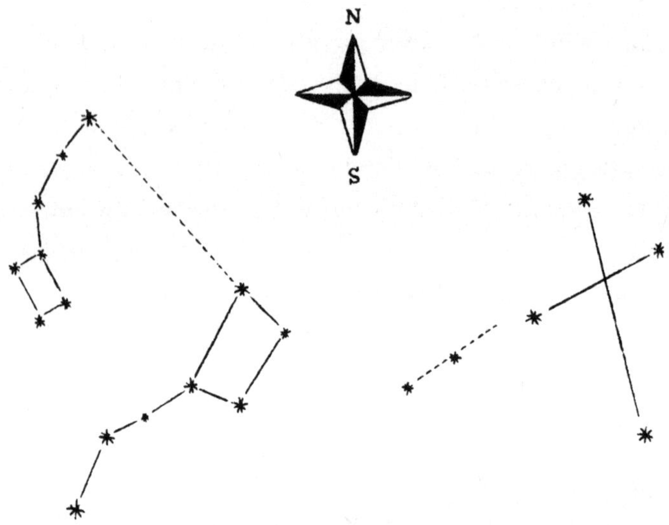

The moon is also a good indicator. If it is not full or new, draw an imaginary line from one "horn" of its crescent to the other and follow that line down to the horizon. In the Northern Hemisphere, the place where the imaginary line meets the horizon is south. In the Southern Hemisphere, it's just the opposite: Where the imaginary line meets the horizon, it's north.

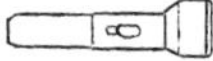

In the next chapter we discuss the importance of water, also known as "the liquid of life" because without it humans, and most organisms on earth, wouldn't be able to survive. It kind of makes wasting it as we sometimes do seem pretty stupid, no?

4. Water

Forewarned, forearmed; to be prepared is half the victory.

—MIGUEL DE CERVANTES, *DON QUIXOTE*

You can survive *three days* without drinkable water.

Sure, some people have survived much longer than that, but if you are even somewhat active, a day without water can cause debilitating dehydration. We are all familiar with the symptoms of mild dehydration—dry mouth, dark pee, maybe a headache—but most of us have probably not experienced severe dehydration, which is a whole other ballgame. By the time you get confused, start hallucinating, and lose muscular control, you are in serious trouble.

How Much Water You Need

According to the U.S. Geological Survey, the average American uses between eighty and one hundred gallons of water every day for drinking, cooking, toilet flushing, bathing, and lawn and garden care. Excluding the lawn and garden care—as they will probably not be making the top five list of concerns should an emergency hit—a normally active person needs about three-quarters of a gallon (or three quarts) of fluid daily, from water and other beverages. The absolute minimum is one quart per person per day. We get fluid from our food too (up to 20 percent), so if you're not eating much, you may need *more* than the minimum quart of water per day. While experts do recommend sipping rather than gulping water, in most cases rationing does not work (except maybe in the movies). Our bodies need a certain amount of water to function, and a sip now and then is not enough to make a difference, dehydration-wise.

The most common recommendation is to store at least one gallon (four quarts) of water per person per day for drinking and sanitation (that's three quarts minimum for consumption and one quart for hygiene), multiplied by at least three days. Given the average estimate of eighty to one hundred gallons of water used daily that we cited above, this recommendation seems inadequate, but it clearly does not include water for laundry, flushing toilets, or anything resembling a long, hot shower. Looking at recent disasters, where infrastructure is wiped out by flood or fire for weeks or months, three days' supply might not be enough to last until service is restored and water is running again. Storing enough water for a week or two per person (seven gallons per week per person) would be better if you have the space. The water you store does not have to be bottled; it is a lot cheaper to store the kind that comes from the tap so long as it is filtered and disinfected. Tap water also often contains added fluoride to prevent tooth decay and is regulated by the EPA.

Water Requirements per Person, per Day*

4 quarts = 1 gallon

Absolute minimum	Suggested minimum	Better	Best
1 quart	3 quarts	1 gallon	1 gallon-plus

***We also get up to 20 percent of our water needs from food.**

Be sure to take the following into account:

- Children, nursing women, and sick people may need more water.
- A medical emergency may require additional water (for cleaning a wound, etc.).
- If you live in a warm climate, more water may be necessary. In extremely hot temperatures, water needs can double.
- Never ration drinking water unless ordered to do so by authorities. Drink the amount you need today and try to find more for tomorrow.
- Minimize the amount of water your body needs by reducing activity and staying cool.
- Don't drink carbonated or caffeinated beverages instead of water as they dehydrate the body, which increases the need for drinking water.

Storing Water

Assuming you are going to store at least one gallon of water per person in your household per day for three or more days, you'll want to consider a few things regarding types of containers:

- How easy they are to clean
- How heavy they are when full
- How easy they are to pour from when full
- How well they seal

- How easy they are to stack or otherwise store
- How durable they are for extended use
- Whether they can be repaired

At the first sign of trouble, deep-clean and fill your bathtub(s) and other containers like pots and pans with water from the tap (this is not long-term storage, obviously, so use this water first).

Store-bought gallon jugs are inexpensive and fit in lots of places. Many people routinely buy cases of single-serving water bottles, which also work but cost more. Chemicals from the degrading plastic can leach into the water over time (say within a year), so keep them away from sunlight and heat and rotate in new bottles regularly. Food-grade plastic is a good choice, and grades 2, 4, and 5 are the best. Look for that number inside the recycling symbol (the triangle made of arrows) on the container. Commercially bottled water in the five-gallon jugs for water coolers is a good option if you have more room. Store these in the original sealed container in a cool, dark place. If that place happens to be your shoe closet or your home office cabinet, that works too.

The best water storage containers are durable, light enough to carry should you need to bug out, stackable, and made from food-grade materials like high-density polyethylene (HDPE), which can withstand a wide range of temperatures, is resistant to corrosion, and has non-leaching properties. Stainless steel, which is noncorrosive and resistant to bacterial growth, is perfect for storing water for extended periods. Glass also works since the containers will not leach chemicals and they're easy to clean, although they're also heavier and more fragile than plastic and stainless steel, meaning you'll have to worry about breaking them.

It's helpful to write the fill or buy date somewhere on the container in permanent marker so you know how long you've had it. As noted above, properly stored water doesn't go bad and should taste fine for two or more years as long as any degradation of the container doesn't contaminate it. Improperly stored water can have microbial growth, which can cause illness, so make sure everything is clean and the water is purified.

Before filling, thoroughly clean your containers with dishwashing soap and then sanitize them with a solution of one teaspoon of unscented household chlorine bleach and one quart of water.

Whichever type of container you choose (and you could choose a mix based on your needs), use lids that seal securely to prevent contamination from insects, dust, or other pollutants. Store as many containers as you can. Most people are used to water flowing freely from the tap. That will probably not always be the case, and it's easy to forget how much you drink out of your bottle on the daily.

Water from a municipal water source (meaning your tap) can be bottled unless you've received a notice that says otherwise, but if you are on well water or have a private water system, purify it first (see page 67). Water that has not been commercially bottled should be replaced every six months.

Note that stored water can taste stale as oxygen levels decrease over time. To preserve freshness, add one teaspoon of ascorbic acid powder, a.k.a. the purest form of vitamin C, per gallon when the water is first stored. Ascorbic acid might even increase the water's shelf life as it inhibits bacterial growth.

Sourcing Water

If you did not store enough water or the water that you did store is gone, then you'll have to look for alternative water sources in or around your house or apartment building. Here are a few ideas:

- **The tank on the back of your toilet?** Sure, there are a few gallons in there that are drinkable unless a toilet-cleaning chemical has been added.
- **Don't forget your freezer.** Ice will keep food cold during a power outage and can be used as drinking water once it has melted.

- **Have a water heater?** It will typically hold from thirty to sixty gallons of drinkable water, especially if it has been in constant use. There should be a spigot near the bottom of the tank where you can access it. In some cases, you might need to open the hot water tap on a sink to let air in as the water drains out. If the water heater has been sitting for months unused, you should purify the contents (see page 67) as there may be contaminants present. The risk is higher with hot water (or formerly hot water) than with cold water, as chemicals from the pipes and tank dissolve better in hot. Likewise, since the water was heated, bacteria could grow in the tank (and may not die off when the water cools), and there may be sludge and sediment that should be filtered out.
- **If you have a sump pump** in your basement or crawl space to keep the space dry (or drier), the pump itself is usually located in a shallow well into which water drains and then is pumped out to keep the water table below the surface. In the absence of an operating pump, the well will fill with water if there is enough in the soil. It will not be clean, but it is a source of water, like a creek or a pond, to be purified.
- **You might be able to drink the water in your pool,** depending on what chemicals are in it. Chlorine only? It's probably okay. Algicides? Chemicals to keep the water clear? Avoid it.
- **You can drink from the water hose in your RV,** but don't drink from a garden hose as it may contain lead or bacteria.

And here are a couple of strict don'ts:

- **Don't drink water from the radiator in your home.** Unlike the water in your water heater, the radiator water may be treated with anticorrosion chemicals.
- **Don't drink water from the radiator in your car.** Most cars outside of the tropics will have antifreeze in the system, which can kill you.

Once you've exhausted the water sources in and around your home, you may need to extend your search. Some water sources may be on private property (ponds, wells), and you should get permission before entering the property. Most navigable waterways are public. If you are on a public road or other place where you have permission to be, there should be no legal issue with collecting water.

- **Surface water,** from rivers, streams, and lakes, including ponds and reservoirs, might be the easiest source of water to gather, although it must be purified before you use it. Do you know where to find the natural bodies of water near you? You should.
- **Rainwater.** Outside of surface water, rainwater is your best source of potable (drinkable) water. To collect rainwater before an emergency, you could place fifty-five-gallon (or so) drums under your gutters (or elsewhere). This water must be purified as it will have drained over unclean surfaces and will potentially be contaminated by whatever it encountered. Note: Rain may be an unreliable source because of increasing instances of drought.
- **Well water.** In many rural areas, most water comes from wells. Generally, wells have an electric pump that brings the water up to a home or a holding tank. Losing electric power could mean losing water in this situation, unlike in a city, where water pressure is provided by gravity from a storage tank or tower that has enough water for a day or more. Some wells have gasoline-powered pumps or alternative sources of electricity provided by, for instance, a solar-charged battery or a windmill. Hand pumps are also available to pump water from wells up to around three hundred feet deep, which covers most wells, but many are deeper than that.
- **Municipal pipes.** Even when you lose service, there will be some water in the pipes. Accessing it might be difficult, and there probably won't be much there, but it's better than nothing. Find a low access point, like a basement faucet, and run a

siphon hose down into the pipe. If you find some residual water, suck it into the hose and try to lower the other end of the hose as much as possible into a container. Gravity should continue the siphoning process. If you can't lower the hose sufficiently for gravity to do its thing, you might have to try to pump the water up from where it has collected using a siphon pump that employs suction to move the water.

- **Snow.** Look for the clean white kind. Since it will not have drained over dirty surfaces like rain does, snow should be mostly clean, but you should still purify it if you can.
- **Humidity.** Yes, that stuff in the air that makes your hair frizz does have another purpose. If water condenses on something cooler than the air, like a window, a piece of fabric (also known as a fog catcher), or dew on the grass in the morning, this can be used for drinking. In some places, water from the atmosphere is a principal source of water, but collecting it usually requires special conditions and equipment. It is possible to harvest the moisture in the air, but it usually requires a lot of work.

Tip: If you are running low on water and don't have a filtration system, pop a piece of hard candy in your mouth or, if nothing else is available, a smooth, clean pebble—large enough that you won't swallow it. This won't keep you hydrated, but it will stimulate the flow of saliva and keep your mouth moist. You'll feel less desperate and function better until you find water.

Purifying Water

You've collected water from your local stream; now what? You'll want to filter, boil, or otherwise purify it depending on how you're going to use it. Following is a complete list of possible purification methods.

Filtration. Filtering water removes impurities by trapping them, which, depending on the type of debris, may be only your first step. In the absence of a commercial filter, you can pour water through finely woven fabric (a cotton T-shirt will do) to eliminate large debris (no one ever asked for a cool glass of water with a side of bird poop).

Modern camping water filters that look like thick straws use filtering microtubes too small for most debris to get through, although some viruses and smaller compounds and dissolved heavy metals may not be removed. Unlike when you use some chemical purifiers like iodine tablets, you don't have to wait to drink after it has been filtered. These small filters are great for one or two people, but they are not very useful for purifying large quantities. For that, you want a high-capacity filter.

High-capacity filters are often gravity fed. They work by pouring water into an upper chamber and letting gravity pull it through a filter into the lower chamber. They don't require electricity or complex installations and can clean water from rivers, lakes, hot water heaters, and swimming pools. They can remove bacteria, protozoans, chlorine, and heavy metals like mercury and lead, just like the smaller camping filters that usually work by pumping it through the filter instead of using gravity.

Filtering with charcoal blocks debris by passing water through activated charcoal, which attracts and traps contaminants via their electromagnetic charge. There are commercial charcoal filters, but you can also make your own. In a container that will drain, add small rocks on the bottom, then pieces of black charcoal from a wood fire (not the charcoal you buy for a barbeque grill, which may have contaminants), and finally a layer of sand. Sand physically blocks larger, insoluble things in the water and charcoal captures organic and mineral impurities. The small rocks at the bottom prevent the charcoal from coming out of the drain holes. This will not remove most bacteria nor all heavy metals, so after filtration be sure to boil well. Note: Some heavy metals can only be removed via reverse osmosis or ion exchange filtration, which are not DIY projects.

Ultraviolet pens and/or UV lights—from personal-sized lights you can carry while backpacking to industrial-sized units that need a power source—can kill bacteria, viruses, fungi, and protozoans. Note that these types of filters are on the pricey side.

Or you can just use the sun! Solar water purifiers can be portable, are inexpensive (and easy to DIY), and effectively remove pathogenic contamination, but you need direct sunlight for six to eight hours. Water stored in a clear container and left in direct sunlight for at least six hours will be effectively purified (that is, enough of the pathogens will have been killed that you have a low probability of being affected by them). Many factors affect how purified the water gets using this method (how sunny it is, the type of container, and the angle of the sun, for instance), so this should be a better-than-nothing solution. A glass container would be ideal, but most people end up using plastic bottles. If it's cloudy or you live in the northern latitudes where the UV index is lower, let the water sit outside for a couple of days. The World Health Organization has endorsed this method for areas in which clean water is hard to find. Adding a pinch of salt can help remove suspended dirt in cloudy water, and lime or lemon juice can greatly reduce the number of bacteria that survive during this process.

Reverse osmosis pushes water through a semipermeable membrane to remove impurities and contaminants including dissolved solids, heavy metals, bacteria, viruses, nitrates, and many chemicals. These filters are expensive and require water pressure to function. Most use a booster pump, which requires electricity, so these might not be available during an emergency in which the power is also out.

Boiling. The widespread practice of disinfecting water via boiling dates to 1858, when the method was recommended to fight cholera outbreaks. Boiling will kill bacteria, viruses, and parasites like *Giardia* but does not remove other types of contaminants, such as carcinogens or toxic chemicals. How long do you boil? The rule of thumb is to bring your water to a full rolling boil for at least one minute—longer at high altitudes because water boils at a lower temperature when the ambient air pressure is lower—and then allow it to cool for about thirty minutes. Some containers might not be suitable—glass could shatter, plastic could melt—so take care to let the water cool as needed. If you are able, boil large quantities of water in advance so you aren't tempted to use it hot and risk scalds or burns. Store cooled water in a clean and covered container.

Chemical treatments. Bleach, iodine, and water purification tablets are effective at killing bacteria but not great against viruses, cysts, or protozoans. Determine the volume and clarity of the water you're purifying before you start. If it's cloudy, filter it through a clean cloth first, then add the appropriate number of tablets based on the dosage instructions (usually one tablet per liter or quart). Mix well and wait the recommended time (usually thirty minutes) before drinking.

- If using **chlorine bleach,** use eight drops per gallon of clear water (double that for cloudy water) and let it sit for a minimum of fifteen to thirty minutes.
- If using **iodine,** use five drops of a 2 percent solution of iodine per gallon of clear water and let it sit for a minimum of fifteen to thirty minutes. Double that for cloudy water.

Distillation. You can use virtually anything that contains moisture, including mud or vegetation, to distill water. This method can also be used to treat salty or contaminated water. The classic way to distill is to dig a small hole in a sunny place, put the water source (salt water, mud, vegetation) in the hole, and place a container in the center of the hole to catch the liquid as it condenses. Cover the hole with plastic wrap and weigh down the center of the plastic with a rock or something heavy so the condensed water on the plastic runs down to the center and drips into your container. Alternately, you can secure a plastic bag around the source material, like a leafy branch of a tree. The sun will cause water in the leaves to evaporate and condense onto the plastic, after which you can carefully remove the plastic bag containing the water, that evaporated. If this sounds like a lot of work for a little water, it usually is, but it

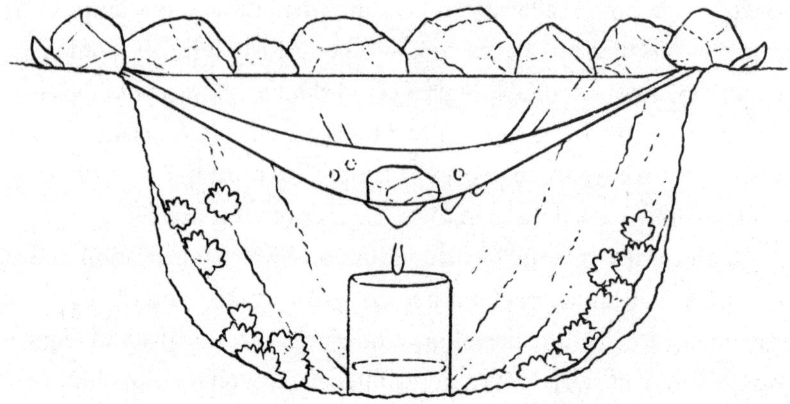

is infinitely better than nothing. Like some of these other techniques, it is not really a substitute for a more substantial water source.

What Those Water Notices Mean

Most of us take the presence of clean running water for granted right up until the moment the tap stops working. Whether your water source is depleted because of drought or tainted by lead in the pipes or a chemical spill, you may at some point be under a locally issued water notice. Here's what the warnings mean.

"Boil Water"

This means it's not safe to drink or use your water without boiling it first because the water supply has a microbiological contaminant that can be rendered safe only by boiling.

Here are the guidelines to follow if you're under a *boil water* notice:

- Use boiled or bottled water for drinking (for people and pets) and in baby formula. For more specific information on pets, contact your vet.

- There's no need to boil water for showering, bathing, shaving, and washing hands as long as you use soap and scrub well and take care not to swallow any. Avoid having water come into contact with nicks, open wounds, cuts, or blisters. Limit time in the bath or shower to minimize contact with the water. If you plan to handle food, use bottled or boiled water.

Note: *People who are immunocompromised or have chronic illnesses should use boiled, then cooled water to bathe; sponge bathing is advisable here.*

- Hand-wash dishes with previously boiled water. Otherwise, rinse your dishes for a minute in a diluted bleach solution (one tablespoon of unscented bleach per gallon of water) after washing them with dish detergent. It's fine to use your dishwasher as long as the hot wash is at least 170 degrees Fahrenheit and includes a full dry cycle. If you aren't sure about the temperature of your specific dishwasher, employ the diluted bleach mixture mentioned above after dishwashing. If you happen to have a commercial dishwasher, it's okay to use as long as it is a National Sanitation Foundation–certified washer.
- It's fine to use a washing machine for laundry as long as the clothes are fully dried before being worn.
- Wash fruits, vegetables, and other ingredients with previously boiled water.
- Use preboiled or bottled water for brushing teeth.

"Do Not Drink"

This means the water supply is considered unsafe for drinking, *even after boiling.* Boiling water kills microbes but does not remove chemicals or toxins that are not alive. Boiling water contaminated with a chemical might release some of that chemical into the air, but it will not remove it all.

Here are the guidelines to follow if you're under a *do not drink* notice:

- Do not drink tap water (this applies to people and pets) or use it in baby formula, even if it is boiled. Use bottled water to make baby formula and for all your other drinking needs.
- Using lukewarm tap water to shower, bathe, shave, and wash hands is safe as long as you use soap and scrub well, take care not to swallow any water, and ventilate the area. Avoid having water come into contact with nicks, open wounds, cuts, or blisters. Limiting time in the bath or shower can help minimize contact with the water. If you plan to handle food, use bottled water.

Note: *People who are immunocompromised or have chronic illnesses should use boiled, then cooled water to bathe; sponge bathing is advisable here.*

- Use bottled water for washing dishes. It's fine to use your dishwasher as long as you use the air-dry setting. The heat and drying have results similar to boiling.
- It's fine to use cold tap water to wash your clothes. If your clothes dryer does not vent to the outside, don't use it, and dry your laundry indoors.
- Use bottled water for washing fruits, vegetables, and other ingredients and for making ice—don't use automatic ice makers.
- Do not use swimming pools or hot tubs.

"Do Not Use"

This means you shouldn't use the tap water for *any* home activities, including drinking, bathing, handwashing, washing dishes or clothes, and food preparation. Use only bottled water or water that was stored prior to the notice. (Aren't you glad you're prepared?)

Once you've squared away your water supply, your next concern is storing food. You can survive three weeks without food. And while Mahatma Gandhi survived twenty-one days of starvation, that is not necessarily a goal for which you want to aim.

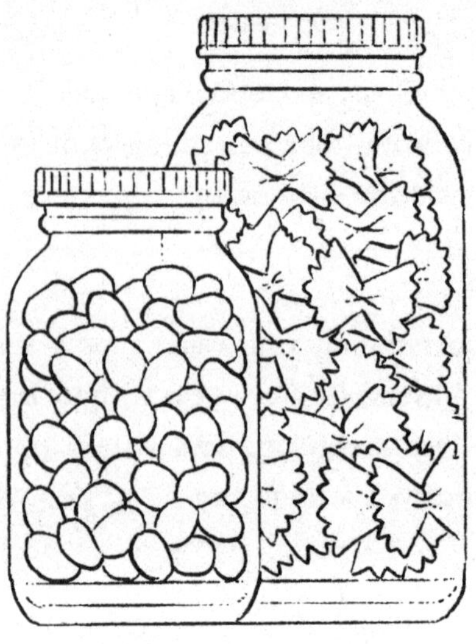

5. Food

Chance favors the prepared mind.

—LOUIS PASTEUR

You can survive *three weeks* without food.

That's what we hear. Really, you'll live for much longer than that, but after a couple of weeks you will be weak and not able to function very well. You'll be hungry but okay if you miss a few days of eating, but if you won't have access to food for longer than that, you want to be prepared. Also note that depending on the severity of the situation, the government, emergency services, and/or other organizations may be offering food to those in need, but those options aren't unlimited, and you don't want to count on them (especially these days).

Before the great shutdown of 2020, most city-dwelling folks took it for granted that they could drop in to their local grocery store any time of the day or night to buy anything from a bag of Cheetos to a frozen vegan pizza. And while there were shortages in some places during the early stages of the pandemic (anyone trying to find ingredients for making comfort food was certainly out of luck), most parts of the food chain weren't terribly affected. But that might not be the way things play out next time. If stores are closed, you can't get out (because of flooding or closed roads), you don't want to leave (hello, pandemic), you don't feel like waiting in long lines (hello, unprepared), or you think there may be food shortages, we suggest you stock up now, mainly because most serious disruptions won't give you a two- or three-week heads-up before occurring.

What should a dedicated stash of food consist of? Consider that one person's stocked kitchen is another's empty nightmare. Is your pantry packed with mostly fresh, healthy food and snacks for a family of four? Or are you single and dieting and have only crackers and apples? Seeing how you may potentially be getting less exercise than normal during an emergency (which could lead to an increased possibility of depression), having food that is healthy, easy to prepare, and yummy is a wise decision. Stock a mix of what you and the other members of your household usually eat, along with backups that are especially formulated to last, like freeze-dried foods or military Meals Ready to Eat (MREs). In an emergency, you do not want to have to get used to something unfamiliar or deal with heartburn or extra pounds. Finally, don't forget things like coffee, tea, and sweets that might make a huge difference in your mood. In one sense, your morning coffee and afternoon chocolate are not absolutely necessary, but then again, they might be.

Some Surprising Facts About Chocolate

My old neighbor and homeopathy adviser, Mirjana, always kept a stash of dark chocolate around "just in case" (and as she grew up in the former Yugoslavia, "just in case" meant

something serious). And while the sweet stuff may not be a food you think of when stockpiling for the future, given its lesser-known attributes, along with its rising cost and scarcity (due to, you guessed it, climate change), maybe it should be.

—Amy

- The tannins in chocolate help fight tooth decay.
- Dark chocolate contains flavonoids that help regulate your small intestines, which can help prevent diarrhea and cholera.
- Dark chocolate supports heart health and lowers blood pressure.
- Dark chocolate contains caffeine and can boost your energy.
- Chocolate contains tryptophan, which can promote relaxation and reduce tension.

How Much Food You Need

Living in a suburban or rural area may give you the advantage of more space to store bulk foods, but it's possible to build a nice food stash wherever you live if you think creatively. While staples like rice, pasta, and dried beans are long lasting and relatively inexpensive, keep in mind that preparing these types of foods also requires you to have access to water and heat. Frozen, canned, and freeze-dried foods tend to be more expensive, but they give you more flexibility (and variety) if water and fuel are also in short supply.

When putting together your stash keep the following in mind:

- Most adults can function relatively well on 1,500 calories a day for extended periods of time. Larger people require more (up to about 10 percent or so). If you have the space, store at least a two- to three-week supply of nonperishable food to help you avoid the possibility of fighting your neighbor over the last can of beans at your local Trader Joe's. You can live a long time without food, of course (see page 74), but being hungry affects everything from physical to cognitive ability (they don't call it *hangry* for nothing), so it's best to have at least a little something stored.

- Choose foods you enjoy eating. Now is not the time to forgo treats and/or comfort foods because, if your days are possibly numbered, why the hell not eat what you want?
- Remember to keep any special dietary needs in mind (hello, peanut and gluten allergies).
- Avoid processed meals that contain a lot of sodium and/or food that will make you thirsty (even if you have laid in a generous supply of water).
- If stored in mylar bags (airtight, light-proof, and tough) with oxygen absorbers (little packets of iron powder and salts that bind to oxygen, similar to the desiccant packages we find tucked into new clothing and shoes) and sealed in buckets, some foods, including most beans, wheat berries, lentils, pasta, oats, and rice, can last for fifteen to twenty years. Freeze-dried foods can be edible for up to thirty years.
- Depending on your interests and skills, freezing, canning, drying, pickling, curing, and/or smoking your own food may also be an option. And until the food distribution system collapses, homemade jams, jellies, and sauces also make great gifts!
- Stockpile seeds. Keep them in an airtight container in a cool, dark place. When you run out of food, you may need to have the option of growing more.
- In addition to being almost-forever foods, honey, salt, and sugar can help make your other food taste better.

Foods That Can Be Stored for a Long, Long Time

Like your water, your stash of food should be consistently rotated to keep it fresh. Store it at room temperature (or as close to it as possible—not in an attic in the summer, for instance) and keep it out of the sun.

Here are some foods that have a shelf life of six months or more:

- Canned goods like tuna, beans, and soup will last for years (if not decades) if not damaged. But be aware that the contents in swollen cans can be deadly.
- Dried beans. Kept dry, out of the sun, and protected from bugs or rodents, these will last a year.
- Flours (wheat flour, cornmeal). Kept dry and protected, they will last at least six months.
- Honey. This lasts forever if kept free from outside moisture. It may change color or become crystallized and still be fine, but it can also grow mold or bacteria, so it must be stored properly (in a sealed container).
- Jarred goods, from sauces to soups, should last a year or more.
- Jerky. Lasting a long time is its entire raison d'être. Commercial jerky, unopened, should last at least a year past the sell-by date on the package. Homemade jerky, even if stored in airtight containers, won't last as long; assume two to three months.
- Lard or vegetable shortening should last at least six months if opened, longer if not.
- Nuts in their shells can last many months on the pantry shelf. Without shells and stored in an airtight container, nuts will last at least six months. Roasted nuts, without a

shell, will last about a month. Dried nuts with no shell will last three months to a year. Storing nuts with the shells on in a dry, sealed container would allow them to last a year or so.

- Pasta (dried) is good for at least a year past the sell-by date.
- Peanut butter, or any nut butter, lasts at least a year past the sell-by date.
- Rice (dry). White rice typically lasts a year or longer, while brown rice should be good for six months if kept dry and free of bugs or mold.
- Salt. This lasts forever. Seriously, the salt on your table is already millions of years old. It's more like a rock than food.
- Sugar. Like salt, it can be stored indefinitely if kept dry and free of pests.
- Vegetable oil stored in glass bottles. Oils high in saturated fats and oleic acid content, like coconut, palm, and sunflower, could last two years. Those with high levels of monounsaturated fats, like olive oil, are the next most stable, and last up to two years if unopened. Oils high in polyunsaturated fats, like corn and canola, are the least stable and should last six months to a year if stored out of sunlight in a cool place.

Thanks to preservatives, most foods on grocery store shelves—if unopened and stored out of the sun and extreme temperatures—can last for months or years.

Food Storage and Safety

While some foods can be stored at room temperature—think fruits, grains, nuts, seeds, and highly processed snacks—without electricity or a cold source, most other items can quickly become unsafe. The USDA recommends that perishable food left out for more than two hours should be thrown away.

For nonrefrigerated foods, the lower the temp, the better. Bacteria can grow rapidly in food that's been kept above refrigeration temperatures, which is anything above 40 degrees Fahrenheit, so it needs to be stored properly even in cool weather. If you eat food that hasn't been stored correctly it can make you very sick (which is a bad idea at any time but worse when medical assistance may be slow-to-never coming). Thawed food from your freezer is usually safe to eat if it is still "refrigerator cold." And it can be refrozen (should you get power back) if it still contains ice crystals.

It is worse for temperatures to oscillate between hot and cold than for food to be kept at a slightly higher-than-optimal temperature. Too hot is bad, but going suddenly from cold to warm is also not ideal. Make sure the place where you store your emergency food is both climate controlled and consistent (sheds, attics, garages, and crawlspaces are not ideal places to put your stash). And take into account possible power outages, floods, or heat waves.

Tight on space? Think cool, dry, dark places like closets (bedroom and hallway) and/or pantries that are part of your living area. You can even utilize the space under your bed so long as the temperature remains relatively consistent. And while you may not love the idea of sleeping on top of three months' worth of canned beans, in an emergency you are much more likely to have access to your main living area than to an off-site storage space.

Food Storage Dos and Don'ts

DO choose foods that can be stored for several months to a year or more.

DO keep food stored where you can easily rotate it as expiration dates loom; the aim is to use the older stuff first and buy new to replace it.

DO use smaller containers that can fit in small spaces. Bags—while fragile—are also more flexible and adaptable to small areas than cans or boxes.

DO think linear: Stack food low (under beds) and high, and use a ladder if you need it.

DO keep food in tightly covered containers and out of direct sunlight.

DO keep cooking and eating utensils clean.

DO throw away any food that has come into contact with contaminated floodwater.

DO throw away any perishable food (such as meat, poultry, fish, eggs, or leftovers) that has been at room temperature or above 40 degrees Fahrenheit for two hours or more.

DO throw away any food that has an unusual odor, color, or texture.

DO use ready-to-feed formula if you have an infant and you're not breastfeeding. If you must mix infant formula, use bottled water—or boiled water as a last resort (see pages 68–71).

DO keep the refrigerator and freezer doors closed as much as possible (if you lose power, the fridge will keep food cold for about four hours if it is unopened).

DO keep refrigerated foods at 40 degrees Fahrenheit or colder (the definition of "refrigerated") and frozen foods at or below freezing for proper food storage. It's pretty easy to identify below-freezing temperatures (the food is frozen and hard), but you should use a thermometer to occasionally check the temperature of the refrigerator, as it's harder to tell that it is sufficiently cold to inhibit bacterial growth.

DON'T eat foods from cans that are swollen, dented, or corroded, even though the product may look safe to eat.

DON'T eat any food that looks or smells abnormal, even if the can looks okay. Remember, when in doubt, throw it out.

DON'T assume you're prepared because you have what you need in a second location. What if you're not there when an emergency strikes? Bottom line: You can always find room for the stuff you (literally) cannot live without (like food and water).

Grow Your Own

After your canned, freeze-dried, and otherwise surplus food supplies have run out, if grocery stores still aren't an option, you might need to produce your own food. Growing fruits and veggies and even medicinal plants (see page 148) can supplement the food you have or, depending on how much you're able to grow and how many people you need to feed, can be a complete food source. And contrary to what you may think, you do not need acres of land to do it. But you *will* need to already have plants and/or seeds in the soil when a long-term emergency hits, as some produce can take months to grow.

Feeling a little daunted? Turns out fewer than 2 percent of Americans know how to grow their own food, which is a steep drop from the Depression years, when approximately half of Americans kept vegetable gardens and perhaps a chicken or two to avert starvation. These days, what with giant supermarkets, food delivery services, and an abundance of restaurants, not so much. Maybe this is why almost every apocalyptic movie includes a scene where the protagonists go from (abandoned) house to (abandoned) house checking the cupboards and pantries for food or backyards for a live chicken.

Because they tend to have more space, people in rural, and even suburban, areas may garden or practice agriculture to a greater degree than those who live in towns and cities. This familiarity with farming or gardening can come in handy in a long-term catastrophe in which normal supplies are disrupted. But even if you've never cultivated a thing in your life, if you have just a small sunny window, you can grow your own food. Keep in mind that, unless you are buying seedlings or larger plants at a nursery, you will need viable seeds to start your garden, whether it's a few containers on a porch or a bigger plot in the yard. Sometimes you can get seeds from the food you eat, but sometimes you can't. Some modern crops are genetically engineered to produce nonviable seeds, meaning you must buy seeds from a seed company (sounds unfair, doesn't it?). Even if the seeds you have access to are potentially viable, you may need to pick them at the right time or treat them in a certain way so they remain so. In an emergency, you may not have access to those resources, so if you think you want to grow your own food, start now—and stockpile some additional seeds just in case.

Even if you don't have room for a backyard garden (or a catastrophe happens in the dead of winter), it is possible to supplement your food stash with fruits, veggies, and herbs grown in containers on a small patio or balcony, or even inside on a windowsill (or hydroponically; see below). Look for compact or dwarf varieties of lettuces and kale, radishes, cherry tomatoes, peppers, spinach, and herbs like basil, parsley, chives, mint, thyme, and cilantro. To see what grows best in your area, check the USDA Plant Hardiness Zone Map and choose plants that thrive in your geographic location. To maximize the space you have, think vertically in terms of raised beds, trellises, wall planters, and hanging planters. And be sure your planting area receives enough sun; most vegetables need at least six to eight hours of sunlight per day.

Make a Hydroponic Garden

One way to grow food with minimal water (and minimal space—even a countertop will work!) is to create a hydroponic garden. The concept is simple: Nutrients for plants are provided not by soil but by water, which enables the plants to grow 30 to 50 percent faster than their soil-based counterparts. Also, you don't need to venture outside to reap what you sow, which could be a plus in some situations. A hydroponic system provides a controlled growing environment where you don't have to worry about pests, unpredictable weather, or contaminated soil.

The easiest and most popular plants to grow hydroponically include lettuces, dwarf tomatoes, peppers, herbs, dwarf strawberries, and spinach, but other crops can be grown, too, including green onions and bok choy. It's possible to DIY a hydroponic garden, and many books and websites will tell you how to do it. But if you want to make things easier (and at this point, why wouldn't you?), consider purchasing a hydroponic growing system that comes complete with pods, LED grow lights, and a pump to circulate the water.

At this point in the book, your most basic needs are covered: protection from the elements, water, and food. The next chapter deals with getting your act together—or in this case your essentials—and taking them on the road.

6. In Case of Evacuation

It would be some advantage to live a primitive and frontier life . . . if only to learn what are the gross necessities.

—HENRY DAVID THOREAU, *WALDEN*

While sheltering in place is the preferred way to ride out some cataclysms, it's not always recommended, and in many instances evacuation will be mandatory. The sheer number of people who live and work in America's largest cities (and even the suburbs, where research shows about two million people moved between 2020 and 2022) means you want start thinking about an evacuation plan *before* you're told to go.

When we plan for emergencies in our heads it usually involves being preternaturally calm while gathering family, pets, and go bags, tossing them into our fully charged and stocked EVs, and heading leisurely, as planned, to a friend's house a few towns over to crash in their spare bedrooms. Reality is usually not so accommodating. Chances are that you will have less time than you think, the kids may be in different locations, the car may be only halfway full of gas or the battery not fully charged, and a helluva lot more people will be on the road than you expect.

So here are the main questions you should have asked—and answered!—before you have to evacuate:

- **When will you go?** If it's a weather-related emergency, know the differences between a *watch,* an *advisory,* and a *warning* (see part three). This will help you determine your plan. If you are facing civil or political unrest, trust your instincts and historical precedents.
- **Who is evacuating with you?** This should include everyone in your household; if there are older people, those with mobility challenges or medical requirements, and/or pets for whom this could be difficult, plan ahead for these situations too. Your plan should also include the possibility of people being in different locations when the emergency happens (school, work, the gym, running errands), so have a preplanned meeting place, preferably out of harm's way, or a plan B.
- **What is your communication plan?** This would include what to do when evacuations are recommended but not mandatory. Everyone should be on the same page ahead of time. It is worth noting that many of the disasters happening now are unprecedented, so arguments like "We survived Hurricane So and So" or "This area never floods" are no longer valid. (See page 119.)
- **Where will you go?** Do you have relatives or friends you can stay with if you must leave your home? Contact them now to have an agreement in place—and if you're able to, offer your home to them in case of an emergency where they live. Know where your community shelters are located. If you have a second home you can escape to, is it stocked with the essentials you will need (water, food)?

- **How will you get to your destination?** Do you have a car? Is it fully gassed or charged? Even if the distance you plan to travel isn't that far, you may encounter traffic. Do you have a second route planned if the first is impassable? Do you have a bike? Are the tires inflated and is it otherwise safe to ride? Are you fit enough to get to where you need to go (assuming you won't have to fight off people who are panicking)? Is your destination reachable via public transit? Is public transit still running? Or do you plan to fly? Do you know how you'll get to the airport if a rideshare or cab isn't available?
- **What will you bring?** Some disasters, like most hurricanes, have days of warning, but for others, like tornadoes or flash floods, you get only minutes. With those things in mind, keep your go bag packed (see page 89) with the minimal essentials you'll need to meet the Rule of Three: water, food, and shelter (see page 24). But if you think you have an hour or two to spare, remember that people who received the same warning as you are likely already heading out, which could mean more traffic or, worse, getting stuck in harm's way. If you're traveling by car, you should have a prepacked stash of additional supplies in your vehicle (see page 104). If you're traveling by bike or public transport, you'll have to make do with what you can carry. Remember, the aim is always to get you and your loved ones, including pets if you have them, out safely. But getting out with the right supplies is just the first step—most likely there will be a much longer road to travel. At any rate, use the information in this book to plan ahead. That way you won't waste time—if you have it—figuring out what to take and how to take it.

Know the answers to these questions *before* the hurricane hits your house or the wildfire wipes out your Wi-Fi. And keep in mind you may not have the luxury of choice when it comes to where you'll be when you're told to evacuate. You may well be in your vehicle, at school or the office, or running errands when an emergency strikes. If you can't stop at home to collect your go bag, you should also think about what you can keep in your car (or at the office, or anywhere else you spend a lot of your time) so you're ready whenever and wherever disaster strikes.

> "On 9/11, my daughter-in-law Kelly was eight months pregnant and working in her office in midtown New York City. When the city effectively shut down after the World Trade Center was hit, she had to *walk* out of Manhattan across the Fifty-Ninth Street Bridge to catch a train back to her home in Long Island. That is a long walk even when you're not pregnant. Fortunately, Kelly kept a pair of comfortable shoes and a water bottle in her desk drawer, which made her trek out of the city a tiny bit easier. Use past experiences to your advantage and think about how you can be better prepared for the unexpected.
>
> —Amy"

If you've been paying attention to what's happening in the world and have gathered the necessary items for even short-term survival (FEMA recommends assembling a kit of basic supplies to last three days), the last thing you want to think about is evacuation. Dorothy was right: There's no place like home. But in a number of scenarios—floods, hurricanes, and fires—we (and local officials) suggest that you are safer being away from the affected area. And in most cases it's hard to predict whether you should stay where you are or run for the hills, so it's best to be prepared for both.

Like the contents of a handbag, briefcase, or wallet, what is contained in a go bag varies with its user, but this is what we recommend.

What to Pack in a Go Bag

A go bag is what you grab when you must leave immediately. It should contain what you need to ensure that you can meet the needs of the Rule of Three: shelter, water, and food.

Let's start with the bag itself. Choose something made from rugged but light material, such as nylon. Make sure the straps are sturdy and the fasteners of good quality so you don't end up with an overly heavy bag that won't zip. Look for something with lots of pockets and compartments.

Fully packed, your go bag should weigh *no more than 15 to 20 percent of your body weight* (20 percent is the maximum if you're in good shape, and by "in good shape," we mean you work out multiple times a week). If you think you'll have to carry your bag any distance (versus just throwing it in the back of your car), lean toward a functional (as opposed to fashionable) backpack with good hip and sternum support and a waist belt.

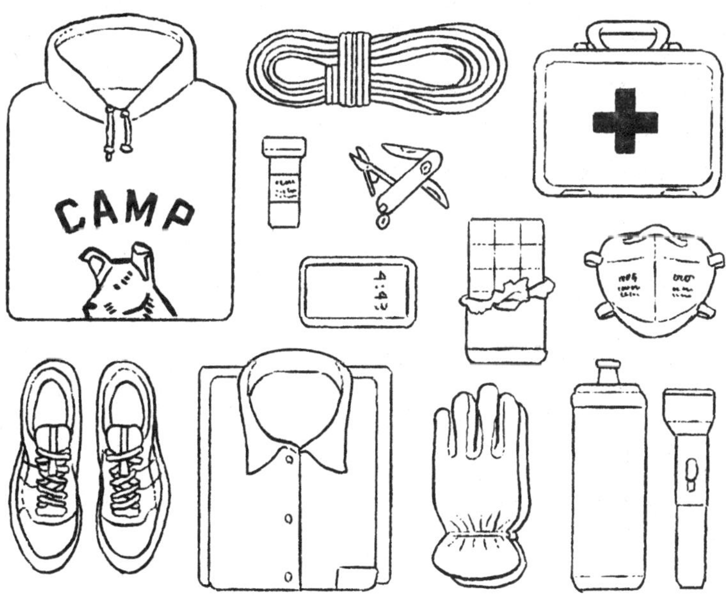

Don't wait until you have to carry your packed bag to make sure you can. Give it a test run (or walk) to make sure you can carry it easily. If not, remove items that are of less importance or duplicates of what others in your party already have until you can carry the bag.

Keep frequently used items like a hat or rain poncho in easily accessible places, keep related items together, and store smaller items in clearly marked plastic bags. In addition to your clothing and toiletries (more on this below), you'll want to keep important documents (or copies of them) in a waterproof bag inside your go bag (see page 89).

Include an itemized list of what's in your go bag in the bag itself, so you can rotate contents with expiration dates as needed.

Every member of your household who is able to carry one should have their own packed go bag. Here's what to put in it.

The Basics

A go bag is not the same as a camping backpack, but depending on the emergency you might be caught outside for a night or two or ten. Severe cold might require more than you can pack in a go bag, but with the basics listed below, you can make it through most weather.

- **Cash in small bills,** some loose change, debit and/or credit cards.
- **Your clothes.** When an emergency is unfolding you should choose clothing that enables you to survive out in the elements for several hours—and ideally overnight.
- **Emergency blanket.** Those Mylar or plastic sheets really keep you warm and pack down to nothing.
- **Gloves.** They can make life easier and more comfortable, and they really protect your hands from the elements.
- **Important documents/information:**
  - Banking information.
  - Deeds and titles to home and car.

    - Driver's license, passport, birth and marriage certificates.
    - Green card or visa.
    - Insurance and medical cards and policy info.
    - Pen, pencil, a waterproof marker, and a blank notebook.
    - Printed list of friends and family with contact info.
    - Thumb drive with important info from your computer.
- **A multitool,** like a Leatherman or a Swiss Army knife, to cut with and to open cans in an emergency.
- **Nylon string, thin rope, or paracord** (e.g., multistrand military rope). In conjunction with a poncho, tarp, or even a plastic garbage bag, you can rig a roof or shelter that helps protect you from the elements.
- **Waterproof plastic bags** to keep other items dry as needed.
- **This book!** Even if you've already read it, you won't remember everything, and having access to useful tips and information will give you some control over your situation. We made it as small and packable as possible for this reason.

Sanitation, Hygiene, First Aid, and Makeup

In addition to whatever daily products you use, don't forget these key items and any special requirements for pregnant women, small children, pets, and people with disabilities or significant medical issues:

- **Baby necessities,** if relevant, like diapers, wipes, blanket, favorite toy.
- **Brush and/or comb.**
- **Chlorine liquid bleach,** unscented. For disinfecting purposes: Dilute nine parts water to one part bleach. For water purification: Use sixteen drops per gallon of water.
- **Contact lenses, case, and solution.**
- **COVID/virus test kits:** can be found at the pharmacy or grocery store.

- **Deodorant/antiperspirant.**
- **Disposable razors.**
- **Dry or other shampoo and conditioner** or hair products as needed, including ties, scrunchies, clips, a scarf or bandanna, or other ways to tie your hair out of your face.
- **First aid kit** including instructions and containing:
    - Allergy medication (antihistamines).
    - Ammonia (calms bug bites).
    - Antibiotic cream.
    - Anti-itch cream (cortisone).
    - Antifungal cream.
    - Bandages and Band-Aids (adhesive and elastic of various sizes, including butterfly).
    - Burn gel.
    - Digestive remedies (antacids, antidiarrheal, antinausea)—because the last thing you need when your world is falling apart is nausea and heartburn.
    - Eye drops for irritation due to smoke or dust.
    - Insect repellent containing at least 40 percent DEET or 20 percent picaridin or a natural alternative (see pages 49 and 50).
    - Instant hot and cold gel packs for sprains and strains or achy muscles.
    - Latex or other thin gloves.
    - Medical tape and sterile gauze pads.
    - Oral thermometer, preferably unbreakable (the old-fashioned kind with no batteries).
    - Oral rehydration, Pedialyte, or equivalent electrolyte drink powder (to mix with water for avoiding dehydration).
    - Pain medications (ibuprofen, aspirin, acetaminophen, arnica).
    - QuikClot (stops bleeding; Taylor Swift is never without it).

    - Sterile suture kit.
    - Topical lidocaine (anesthetic).
    - Tourniquet.
    - Vaseline.
- **Hand sanitizer and/or antibacterial wipes** containing at least 60 percent alcohol.
- **Makeup and/or perfume/aftershave:** If putting on lipstick and/or aftershave makes you happy and is part of your normal routine, then you absolutely should include those items among your essentials.
- **Multipurpose soap.**
- **N95 or other face mask** to reduce inhalation of germs and/or dust, at least one for each person in your party. A full-blown respirator with replaceable filters would be better (but probably wouldn't fit in a go bag), and any dust mask could make a big difference.
- **Nail clippers** and/or small pair of scissors.
- **Prescription glasses.** Pack at least one extra pair; the worse your vision, the more backups you should have on hand.
- **Prescription and/or alternative medications/remedies** (see page 94 about stockpiling medications) and any vitamins or supplements you take regularly (now is not the time to catch a cold or worse). Be aware of expiration dates if you take easily perishable drugs—a stockpile of expired drugs might not do you any good.
- **Safety pins.**
- **Sanitary napkins and/or tampons.**
- **Sunscreen** (can double as moisturizer in a pinch).
- **Toilet paper** (remember how it felt to run short during the pandemic!).
- **Toothbrush, toothpaste, dental floss** (because it might be hard to get to a dentist, and do you really want to handle dental work on your own?).

- **Small towel:** This is a multiuse item that can wipe off dirt (or worse), be used as a tablecloth or seat, or be used to dry your hands.
- **Tweezers** to remove splinters (or stray hairs, no judgment).

How to Stockpile Your Prescription Medications

Most doctors prescribe medications for a particular illness and a specific time period. Physicians have gotten in trouble for writing scripts for drugs that aren't needed or are requested "just in case." In an emergency, you may not have the luxury of visiting your doctor or local pharmacy, so it may be wise to keep some extra medication on hand, especially if it's of the lifesaving type.

- Educate yourself beforehand. For instance, is it possible to take a smaller than prescribed amount? Some medicines don't work this way, but you might be able to stretch yours out by minimizing the dosage.
- Fill your prescription(s) as soon as your doctor, pharmacist, and insurance allow so you always have extra on hand.
- Fill your prescription(s) for the maximum amount of time allowed (usually three months for uncontrolled meds and one month for controlled meds).
- Multitask. When taking a trip outside the country, see a doctor and fill your script. You can save a lot of money filling prescriptions abroad and build your stockpile at the same time. Note that the legality of this tactic depends on where you live, where you travel, your prescription, and the particular medication.
- Tell your doctor that you are concerned that you may not have enough of your meds in an emergency and ask

if they will help you build a backup supply. (Note: If you're on a controlled medication, your doctor's license could be at risk if they fill more than a month's worth, so don't be surprised if they don't help in this case. But it can't hurt to ask.)

- Research and stock up on alternative (i.e., herbal or homeopathic) remedies that can replace your prescription medication in a pinch.

Clothing

Many of us start our day by putting on clothes that make us feel like our best selves. And while that spirit remains important, our best selves ultimately want to *survive*. Since what you're wearing will be your first line of defense, what you pack in your go bag—at minimum one complete change of clothing, including socks and underwear—should be somewhat utilitarian and seasonally appropriate. Don't forget a hat (it will help keep you warm and protect you from the sun) and a rain jacket (just in case).

Hypothermia occurs when a person's core body temperature drops to under 95 degrees Fahrenheit. Keep in mind that while it may be cold for some parts of the day where you are, strong sunlight and increased exertion could make it feel warmer. In short, the best defense against the cold is the ability to pile on. If you might have to evacuate, choose lighter or more breathable layers you can take off or add to as needed. The more extreme the cold is where you live, the thicker or more insulating each layer should be. Many outer layers have zippers or vents to regulate body temperature without removing layers entirely. These work really well.

For bugging out in cold weather, pack the following:

- **Moisture-wicking base layers:** long-sleeve shirts, thermal tops and bottoms, leggings, socks, and underwear. Your base layers help keep you warm and dry by wicking sweat away from your skin. Suggested materials include Merino wool and synthetic fabrics like polyester or nylon. Note: Make sure whatever fabric is directly against your skin is comfortable, as itching and scratching can quickly make a bad situation worse.

- **Insulating mid-layers:** sweaters, vests, and jackets. Your mid-layers help you retain heat by trapping warm air close to your body. Suggested materials include fleece, down, or synthetic insulation such as Primaloft or Thinsulate.
- **Protective outer layers:** water-resistant, waterproof, wind-proof shells and jackets. Your protective layers shield you from wind, rain, and snow, keeping you and your inner layers dry. Suggested materials include wool, microfleece, nylon, and Gore-Tex.
- **Footwear:** lined, water-resistant boots or sturdy shoes. You want shoes or boots that cover your ankles (that's where you lose a lot of heat as the blood vessels are near to your skin's surface) and have thick soles, which will insulate your feet and make them feel warmer. If you pick thick-soled platform shoes, make sure you can walk in them comfortably.
- **Accessories:** hats, gloves, and scarves. Wool, fleece, or knit hats or beanies are great for trapping heat (don't forget the earflaps!), and while it's a fallacy that we lose most of our heat through our heads, we do lose enough to matter. Include insulated mittens or gloves to keep your hands warm and a wool or fleece scarf to protect your neck and face from the elements.

Love the One You're With

If you are dealing with cold weather and are unable to shelter in place, your next job after wearing the right clothing should be finding a source of warmth, be it a fireplace or the person standing next to you. A resting human generates about one hundred watts of heat—more if it's during or right after physical exercise—which is enough to slightly warm a small space but not sufficient to heat an entire room. To effectively share body heat, you don't need skin-to-skin contact. Covering yourselves with a blanket or sleeping bag, even fully clothed, will help you keep each other warm. And while the other person may not be your cup of awesome, in most cases they're a better option than freezing to death.

In general, a healthy human can withstand a wet-bulb temperature (which combines temperature and humidity) of 95 degrees Fahrenheit before being unable to regulate their internal temperature by sweating. But far below that temperature, humans can get in real trouble with heat. In hot weather it's important to wear clothes that are breathable and lightweight and that help keep you cool. But remember that temperatures can fluctuate quite a bit, so just because it's hot at high noon or cold in the evening doesn't mean it will stay that way.

For bugging out in hot weather, pack the following:

- **Lightweight and loose-fitting clothing:** pants, shorts, short- and long-sleeve shirts, jacket, socks, and underwear. You want clothes that allow for air circulation and prevent sweat from sticking to your body (tight clothes can trap heat and sweat). You will stay cooler in sunny weather by covering up with a light layer rather than exposing your skin to the sun. People who live in the Sahara, for instance, are typically covered from head to foot, and part of that has to do with staying cool.
    - Choose clothes made with UPF (ultraviolet protection factor)-rated fabrics, which are specially designed to block UV rays. The higher the UPF rating, the more protection the fabric provides. For example, a UPF 50 fabric

blocks 98 percent of UV radiation. Tightly woven fabrics, including denim and canvas, offer a good level of sun protection (although they could be hot). Cordura is a high-strength fabric made from nylon that is often used in protective gear and outdoor apparel. While it's a soft, breathable, and natural fabric, cotton can also hold moisture (like sweat), which may not be ideal if the temperature drops. While linen has a tendency to wrinkle, it has a crisp, cool, and airy feel and more moisture-wicking properties than cotton. Finally, moisture-wicking materials like polyester blends or nylon are designed to pull sweat away from the skin and are good in warm weather.

    - While Amy's go-to color choices are black or black, light and pastel colors better reflect sunlight and will help keep you cooler compared to darker colors, which absorb heat. That said, tightly woven dark fabrics offer better sun protection than lighter ones.

- **Footwear:** Choose footwear made from breathable materials like canvas or mesh. Avoid closed-toe shoes made from synthetic materials that don't breathe and so trap heat and moisture. Sturdy shoes are better than flimsy ones, and footwear that offers protection (like closed-toe shoes) is more advisable than something like sandals, which offer little protection if it's wet or raining. In warm weather, wet feet do not present a hypothermia hazard, but they can nevertheless be uncomfortable and lead to fungal infections, which are icky even in nonemergency situations. Shoes that keep your feet dry, or from which water evaporates quickly, like canvas tennis shoes, are good choices.
- **Accessories:** Wraparound sunglasses look badass and protect your eyes from UV rays. A lightweight scarf or shawl can help protect your neck and shoulders. A loosely woven (think straw) and breathable wide-brimmed hat can protect your

skin from the sun without making you too hot. When it's really hot and sunny, you absolutely need a hat. People who work outside regularly rarely do so bare-headed. Also, sunscreen, sunscreen, and more sunscreen.

For evacuating in wet weather (hurricanes, tornadoes, and rain), be sure you have (or are wearing) the following:

- **Waterproof boots** (as high as you can get 'em).
- **At least one change of clothing** (including underwear and socks) because wearing damp clothes sucks and is deadly should hypothermia become an issue while you are out in the elements. If you must go several days without access to another change, keep one set dry and wear the wet set when there's a good chance that it'll get wet again. It's no fun putting on damp clothes, but it's better than having no dry clothes at all.
- **Rain poncho** with hood, or other durable waterproof outer shell layer.

What to Put in Your Child's Go Bag

If they are old and/or strong enough, kids can carry their own go bags (but unless you're sure of their packing skills you should probably supervise the assembling). Assuming you're traveling together, they won't need some of the things that you already have packed in your own bag. Some necessary items:

- A second set of clothes (reference list above), allowing you to wash or dry the clothes they're wearing, keeping in mind that the need to dress up for a social occasion during an emergency is unlikely.
- Copies of their birth certificates.

- Laminated index cards with their name, parents' names, home address, health and/or allergy issues, and contact info for friends and relatives.
- Medications, if relevant.
- Snacks, preferably heavy on the protein and light on salt (which would make them thirsty) and sugar (which after the initial rush would make them sleepy).
- A favorite toy or book because, well, they're kids.
- Water bottle, filled.

If you have a baby, also pack:

- Antigas medicine (simethicone).
- A baby blanket (babies are more susceptible to cold and heat/sun).
- A baby carrier to allow you to walk easier and free up your hands. Some front carriers are just fabric that can pack up very small.
- Baby food and/or formula and bottles, enough for three days (keep in mind if you're nursing that stress could prevent your ability to do so; bring formula and bottles just in case).
- Diapers and wipes.
- A pacifier if they use one, as it can soothe and stave off hunger.

Communication and Navigation Essentials

Ah, the joys of today's technology when a lousy sense of direction or a bad memory no longer has the power to affect an otherwise fulfilling life. But what happens when your cellphone—which also acts as your phone book, GPS, and meditation app—no longer has a charge? Accurate and up-to-date information is incredibly important to have in an emergency but may be harder to access than we expect.

It's especially important to keep your tech dry on the road—and according to the World Health Organization, the most common natural disaster is a flood. So be sure to include a handful of plastic bags in your go bag along with the following (listed in alphabetical order):

- **Analog watch** (with hands). This can help you keep track of how long, and thus how far, you have traveled. Also, it can help you determine direction. How? Point the hour hand at the sun and find the place on your watch dial that is halfway between where the hour hand is now and where it would have been at noon. That halfway point will be south if you are in the Northern Hemisphere and north if you are in the Southern Hemisphere.
- **Binoculars.** You may want to see something while maintaining distance.
- **Cellular phone,** preferably fully charged.
- **Compass.** Avoid the tiny ones that fit in a small survival kit as they are often unreliable and may be hard to use or see (sometimes size *does* matter). One exception is a ball compass, the type that looks like a sphere, often with a safety pin to attach to your pack or shirt. These work well and are so cheap that you could throw in a couple for backup. Of course, it will help if you have a destination and a paper map. Or you can navigate by using the sun (see above).
- **Extra batteries** for all devices. Rechargeable batteries would be best; maybe you'll have access to a solar charger or another opportunity to recharge.
- **Hand-cranked or battery-operated AM/FM NOAA Weather Radio** with tone alert (which enables the user to find out more about an impending hazard immediately) and shortwave bands (which can be used for communication over very

long distances). Any radio is better than none, but weather radios give you access to a lot of information easily.

- **Laminated paper road maps** of your local area with at least two possible escape routes highlighted and maps of nearby states in case of statewide evacuation.
- **Signal mirror and/or signal flares.** Mirrors are better: to signal rescuers or to make your presence known. Sunlight reflected by a mirror can be seen for miles. Flashlights and flares can't do that.
- **Portable solar charger and power-charging cords** for devices. Look for a power bank that's at least 10,000 mAh, which should be enough to recharge a smartphone twice. (Note: Be sure to recharge the one in your go bag every three to four months so it's fully charged when you need it.)
- **Two-way walkie-talkies** are widely available, but make sure your group has the same band so you can communicate with one another. Most of the inexpensive ones use Family Radio Service (FRS), and almost all of them will work for only a mile or so in real-world conditions.
- **Whistles.** If you lose cell service or battery power, a whistle can help alert emergency rescue crews to your location. It takes much less energy to use a whistle than to yell, and depending on your situation, energy may be in short supply. Having a bright bandanna or scarf to signal people is also a good idea.

Tip: Landline and cellular phone systems are often overwhelmed during and following disasters, so you may need to use text messages or social media to keep friends and family updated (which for many of us is known as "business as usual").

Personal Items

Yes, there are many items such as family photos, your kid's preschool artwork, your grandfather's gold watch, or your grandmother's wedding band that are important to you—but arguably not as important as your life and safety. If the piece has intrinsic value, it should be stored in a safe in your home or off-site in a safety deposit box, as it may attract the wrong kind of attention if you bring it with you. If it's mainly something of sentimental value and isn't too cumbersome, by all means take it, as it may offer strength and comfort when you need it.

How to Evacuate with Pets

If you're evacuating with pets and they're mammals, their needs will be similar to yours, so be sure to pack a separate go bag for each that contains adequate food and water along with any medications, treats, leashes or harnesses, portable carriers/crates, poop bags/litter, toys, and favorite comfort items. Just like you, your pets may need to make some adjustments. If that means sleeping on a pile of leaves in an outdoor camping situation instead of their own cushy beds, so be it. Some pets, like fish, can't be easily taken with you, and if you think they may suffer

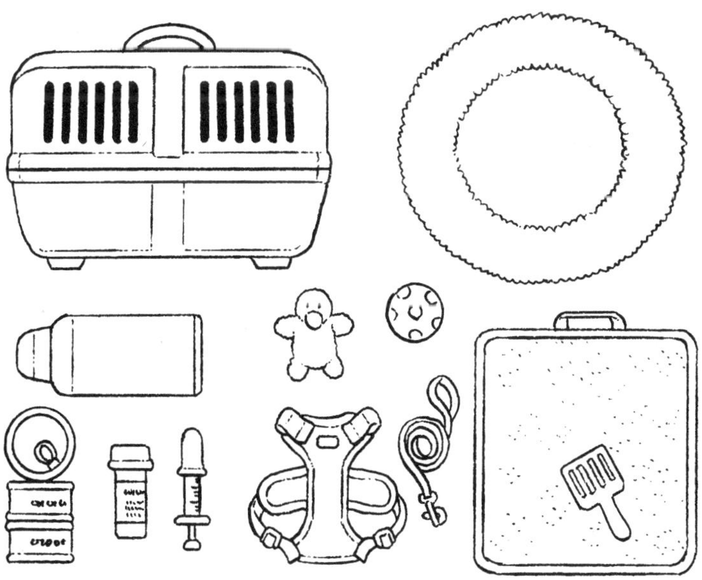

and starve, you may be faced with some hard, unpleasant decisions (the assumption being that if you're leaving, your neighbors will be doing the same).

How to Evacuate Without a Motor Vehicle

Many situations make evacuating in your personal vehicle impossible or inadvisable, which is where having a bike or scooter comes in handy. If neither is available and you have to travel on foot, consider your fitness level, your ability, and how much you can carry. Will you need to sleep outside for a while? An emergency blanket and a plastic tarp can make all the difference, and those should be in your go bag. If you have mobility issues or an injury, leaving on foot may not be possible and you should plan for other options such as grabbing a ride with a family member, friend, or neighbor.

How to Evacuate by Car

Beyond the make and model, hybrid or EV, exactly how much do you know about your car? A 2016 survey by CheapCarInsurance suggests that knowledge once considered routine by drivers is . . . not so routine anymore. A full 60 percent of people don't know how to change a flat. And while watching a tutorial on YouTube seems like a reasonable option, it may be impossible to do if you don't have internet, your device is not charged, or water is quickly submerging your vehicle. To put it bluntly, in an emergency scenario, you can all but assume AAA is not coming to save you. If you drive a car, you need to know how to jump-start it in case your battery dies, check the oil and coolant levels to keep it running, and check the proper tire pressure (and fill your tires with air if they're low). Even electric vehicles (EVs), which tend to be more reliable than internal combustion engines, can overheat because of battery defects or inadequate cooling systems.

Newer cars (those made after 1996 or so) have sensors and check engine lights to alert the driver to many things, but they do not yet have the ability to change a flat tire. If you have a hybrid vehicle, note that their engines are more like internal combustion engines than EVs. And because your EV's battery takes up so much space, yours may not come with a spare tire—a fact you should probably know before that "Yikes, we have to flee!" scenario.

Learning how to do basic car maintenance takes study and practice. You may not be able to fix much on your own if you have a newer car, which is mostly run by computer. Older cars, made from the early 2000s or prior, may be easier to repair, but they also require more maintenance than a newer one. Most of what you will be dealing with in a relatively short evacuation period (a day or two) will be failure to start, overheating, and/or flat tires. Learn what causes these issues, how to diagnose the problem, and what can be done by a nonmechanic on the side of the road. Make sure you have the tools you need (see the next page) as you do not want to be fixing your car for the first time while trying to evacuate. Make it a habit to keep your car as close to full of gas as you can—or, if it's electric, fully (or mostly) charged—because the nature of most emergencies is "Oh shit, I didn't see that coming."

In addition to your family and pets, go bags, and other essentials, it's helpful to keep the following items either in your car or stored nearby in an emergency kit, ready to throw in your trunk if you must leave. The list (broken up by need) may seem long, but the items it contains will fit in almost any car with a trunk or cargo area. (Those of you bugging out in your Lamborghini might have to improvise.)

As an archaeologist, I work in a variety of places, from farms to forests and cities. Following is a list of tools that I keep in my truck, which can be used to fix the vehicle and get it unstuck and through gates, fences, or other obstacles. In an emergency, you might need to do all of those things. If I am going on a road trip, I will also put my go bag in the car.

—Chris

”

Stuff to Fix Your Car (and Related Items)

- **Air compressor,** twelve-volt. These tiny compressors that plug into your car's lighter socket will inflate a tire, but not very quickly. They can be used to reinflate tires for highway driving after the air pressure has been lowered for off-road use (a common practice to get better traction, but you would not want to drive on the pavement with low tire pressure). If you had a flat and fixed it, you can use the compressor to reinflate your tire. If you have a slow leak, you can check it every morning and pump it up. If you can't get one of these, a bicycle pump will work, but be prepared to pump it for a long, long time.
- **Basic tool kit** (see page 112).
- **Car jack.** One may have come with your car, but you can easily buy one if not. Make sure it will fit under your car when the tire is flat and practice using it. Not every place on your car will support its weight or be stable, so learn where to place a jack before you need to know. Keep a metal plate or piece of board handy on which to set the jack—large enough that the base of the jack doesn't sink into the ground—should you have a flat on the shoulder of the road or on a dirt road or off-road area where the ground may be soft.
- **Emergency triangles or flares** that can be set out at intervals behind your car should you need to pull off the road. They can be either reflective or the battery-powered, flashing kind and will (hopefully) keep other drivers from hitting your car

in the dark. In nonautomotive emergencies, they could be used to make it easier for rescuers to find you.

- **Emergency work lights.** These are like flashlights but more powerful and designed to sit on the ground or hang somewhere where they can illuminate a large area. They are small, cheap, and often battery-powered.
- **Engine oil and coolant.**
- **Fire extinguisher.**
- **Fix-a-Flat or similar.** These are cans of sticky, rubber-like liquid that you put in your tire just like air to seal small leaks. The can is also supposed to reinflate the tire, but you (should) have a compressor, so no problem.
- **Flashlight or headlamp** with extra or rechargeable batteries. Find one that is sturdy, has various settings, and uses AA batteries or larger. Flashlights that use AAA batteries do not last nearly as long. That said, carry at least one extra set of batteries. A headlamp is probably more useful, so that you can use your hands while you wear it. Other lighting options: hand-cranked or solar-powered lanterns and flashlights.
- **Folding shovel** in case you have to dig your car out of snow or mud. A full-sized, long-handled shovel may be more efficient, but a folding one takes up very little space.
- **Fuses.** Your car probably has dozens of fuses, for everything from headlights to the ignition. Get some spares. A blown fuse can strand your car or leave you with no lights or gauges.
- **Gas can (to carry the fuel), siphon, and funnel,** in case you need to put fuel in your car outside a gas station. Never carry a full gas can in your car; transport it on the roof or somewhere outside of the passenger compartment.
- **High-visibility vest.** This is small, light, and cheap and makes a big difference between being seen and not, especially if you happen to be standing on the side of a road at night. Chris wears one all the time while conducting archaeological

fieldwork in the United States—if anybody sees him wandering around and doesn't know what he's doing, a hi-viz vest makes him appear more official and less suspicious.

- **Hose clamps.** These are the metal rings that tighten down with a screwdriver, commonly used to hold radiator hoses in place, hence the name. They are multiuse and take up little space.
- **Jump-starter battery pack,** which is better than jumper cables as it won't damage the computers on modern cars and doesn't require another car to function. Cables are cheaper and won't lose their charge, but you need someone willing to provide the "jump." In addition to the fact that some fear the cables will damage their car (and they could), they may also be too busy trying to head out of town to escape the same thing you are.
- **Nylon tie-downs or tow rope,** either with ratcheting straps or the kind with a buckle that only tightens until released. We're not talking about stretchy bungee cords—those are far too weak to hold anything heavy in place. Nylon tie-down straps can be used to fasten stuff to the roof of your car, secure any number of things, and serve as a rope to pull your car out of a jam if stuck.
- **Snow brush/scraper** if you live in, or plan to drive to, an area where there could be snow.
- **A socket set** with a selection of sockets that fit your vehicle (some are metric, some imperial, and there are sets with both), a ratcheting wrench, and an extension or two. Almost any car repair beyond a spare tire will use a socket wrench.
- **Spare tire(s).**
- **A tire iron or lug wrench.** Your car probably came with one or the other, but they are typically short-handled and don't provide much leverage to remove stuck lug nuts.
- **A tire plug set,** should you run over a screw or nail. These are not very easy to use but they work.
- **Windshield washer fluid.**

Tip: Store small items in a container so you don't have loose tools rolling around your trunk.

Stuff You May Need Along the Road

- **Books, games, and puzzles.** Think small so as to not take up too much space. Or you can always go old-school with a lively game of I Spy or a sing-along.
- **Crowbar, wrecking bar (a crowbar but longer), or sturdy pry bar** to apply leverage, break a lock, or pry apart a wooden fence to drive a vehicle through. Look for a claw on the end that can pull nails.
- **Food.** Plan for at least a three-day supply of food per person. You are after calories more than nutrients for the short term, and we suggest calorie-dense food that you *actually like.* Anything that is comforting or familiar may offer a mental boost. Also consider freeze-dried and/or dehydrated foods, for traveling light, and packaged items that don't require refrigeration, like granola bars, cereal, nuts, or those commercially available emergency ration bars. Don't forget the baby food (formula, bottles) and/or pet food, if relevant. And finally, whether your taste runs to chocolate bars or licorice, include treats. *Never miss an opportunity to savor the things that make life worth living!* Store nonperishable food and water in a tub or chest on wheels (light enough to lift), and shove it into the car on your way outta Dodge.
- **Machete** to cut trees and branches (almost as good as an axe, and much easier to use for the inexperienced person). A machete can also cut weeds, grass, and briars, and it even works as a knife.
- **Mylar emergency blankets.**
- **Nonmotorized transportation.** Think about if you had to travel ten miles or more but could not go in a car or public

transportation. Depending on the shape you're in, ten miles on foot could take four or five hours. Traveling more than twenty miles would be a multiday trip. On a bicycle, you can easily ride ten miles in an hour on pavement (depending on how hilly or windy it is). Even a scooter (or rollerblades!) can dramatically increase your range if the conditions are correct. If you are physically able to ride a bike or scooter, consider getting one. You may not keep any of these modes of transport in your car normally, but consider tossing them in in an emergency.

- **Pepper spray**, to keep away lions and tigers and bears (oh my).
- **Reusable or paper towels, plates, cups, and eating utensils.**
- **Siphon pump**, which uses suction to move liquid. This usually comes with a length of hose on each end, for moving something like fuel from one place to another. You can find this at any auto parts store.
- **Tarp** (one or two), preferably lightweight and eight by ten feet or larger. A cheap tarp can be used as a ground cloth (if you have to get under your car), a shelter, or a means of keeping something dry.
- **Spare toilet seat** to rig up outdoors just in case; this can make a big difference to somebody who is already dealing with too much.
- **Water.** Unless temperatures routinely go below freezing, keep some water in your car. More is better. It can be used to fill the radiator in an emergency too.
- **Wire or bolt cutters** (heavy-duty) to cut through chain-link fence and other thick wire. A bolt cutter will do all of that and can cut through most padlocks, nails, or bolts, but it is bulkier.
- **Wool blanket or small sleeping bag.** To really stay warm if you are stuck in your car alone in frigid weather (see page 96,

"Love the One You're With"), you will want something beyond a Mylar emergency blanket. A sleeping bag or blanket takes up more space but can be a lifesaver. You can use the blanket as a seat cover or spread it across the floor of the cargo area and you will hardly notice it's there.

- **Rubber-palmed work gloves** are inexpensive. Get more than one set if you can, in case one pair gets wet or lost.
- **Zip ties** of various sizes hold things in place and keep them from rattling around.

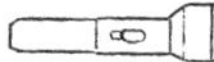

The next chapter is all about tools, including (and arguably the most important gadgets in an emergency) those that enable us to communicate.

7. Tools for the Home and Methods of Communication

Why don't birds prepare for speeches? They like to wing it.

—UNATTRIBUTED JOKE

Back in the day it was the ability to create and use tools that first distinguished intelligent humans from beasts. Tools to make fire, tools to hoist heavy objects, and the little metal wrenches you get from IKEA to help you put together a bookshelf—hence their appearance in multiple chapters of this book.

Your Tool Kit

In a crisis, knowing which tools you have, where they are, and what they do can literally be a lifesaver. Even if you don't know how to use all of them (and that's where knowing your neighbors comes in handy), you should have the following in your home in case of an emergency. (Note: Previous chapters have listed tools to keep in your go bag and car. There is some overlap.)

- **Duct tape.** It sticks to most things that aren't wet or oily.
- **Electrical tape.** This sticky, black tape was made for sealing wires and will stick where other tape won't.
- **A portable fire extinguisher.** There are different types for different types of fires, but an ABC-rated fire extinguisher is best for your home. It works on ordinary combustible material like paper and cloth, flammable liquids like grease, and electrical fires. Get a bigger one with at least five pounds of fire suppression agent in it. These will be about eighteen inches tall and five or six inches in diameter. Keep one in or near the kitchen, but not right by the stove where a fire is likely to start and might impede access.
- **Some type of fire starter** (ferro rod, waterproof matches, lighters). For everyday use, a lighter is the best, but a ferro rod (those sparking rods that survivalists use to start fires) will last nearly forever and work when wet.
- **Waterproof flashing** and plastic sheets to seal up doors and windows, as necessary.
- **A flashlight and/or headlamp and extra batteries.** Several are better than one. Small ones are nice, but larger lights with bigger batteries typically last much longer. Your phone has a flashlight, sure, but a dedicated one is better and won't use up your phone's battery.
- **A sixteen-ounce-head claw hammer.** The claw on the back allows you to pull nails out as well as hammer them in.
- **A section of hose** for siphoning a liquid, like gas from a tank. To siphon, get the flow of liquid started by sucking on the hose until the liquid starts to move. It then continues moving down the hose using gravity. This hose should be clear, so you can see what's happening inside, and should have an

inner diameter of around one-half inch. A section about six feet long is a good compromise between having a good reach and being pretty easy to start the liquid moving. Alternately, a siphon pump to move liquids through a hose can be handy. Available at auto parts stores, siphon pumps use a squeeze bulb or lever to create suction. These are commonly used to fill kerosene stoves or to fill a boat's gas tank from a gas can.

- **A sturdy utility knife** with at least a two- or three-inch-long blade. If you have a folding pocketknife, one with a blade that locks open is much safer than the kind with no lock. A fixed-blade knife, one that does not fold, is typically stronger and more durable than a folding knife but is bulky and may cause concern as it looks like (and can be) a weapon. A box cutter–type knife that uses replaceable blades would also work. Even a kitchen knife works in an emergency, if you have a sheath to keep it in so it doesn't get dull or damaged in the tool kit. EMT shears can work as a general cutting tool, but a knife will be more flexible.
- **Nails and screws,** a variety from small sizes (like you use for hanging a picture) to larger ones (three inches or so) that can be used to build something.
- **Fifty feet of parachute cord or rope.** Parachute cord, commonly called paracord, is made of a braided sheath that surrounds seven smaller cords. This is strong for its size, and you could deconstruct it to use the inner strands if thin string is needed. It's important to have a means of tying things together and/or suspending things.
- **Pliers:** (1) Needle-nosed pliers, with a built-in wire cutter. These are good for reaching into tight places, holding things in place, or removing snap rings and other fasteners that are commonly found on cars. The wire cutter does just what its name suggests. (2) A variety of vise-grips, a.k.a. locking pliers

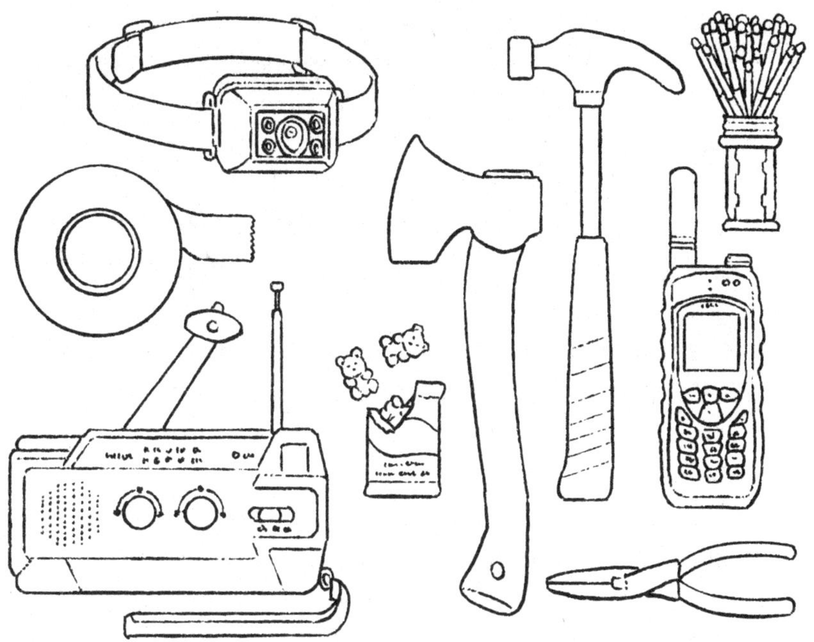

that can be used to clamp things together temporarily, or to grip a bolt or screw if you don't have the proper tool.

- **Saws:** (1) A hacksaw with thin blades and very small teeth used to cut metal. Be aware that the teeth wear out quickly and you'll need replacement blades. (2) A handsaw to cut wood or plastic. Look for folding versions that take up less space, and get one with aggressive teeth to cut through wood quickly.
- **Standard-length screwdrivers,** both flat and Phillips head. If you have the space, add large and small sizes of both types, as well as long and short versions with medium-sized blades.
- **A shovel,** long-handled, not short; your back will thank you. A pointed shovel (for digging) is better than one with a flat edge (for shoveling loose material) for general use.
- **A shutoff or backwater valve,** which allows you to close off the incoming sewer lines. This isn't really a tool, but it's something that you can install in your home.

- **A Sillcock key** to open Sillcock valves. These are used by commercial buildings, city parks, highway rest stops, and campgrounds to keep unauthorized users from tapping into their water supplies. In an emergency, you may not be able to ask someone to do this for you.
- **A socket set** with a ratcheting wrench and several sockets of different sizes. They make installing and removing bolts much faster and easier.
- **Spray can of WD-40.** This has a million uses, from lubricating and protecting metal from rust to quieting squeaky or noisy moving parts.
- **Rubber-palm or leather work gloves.**
- **Wrenches:** (1) A set of box or open-end wrenches. These are like sockets but can fit into smaller places. A standard set of six or eight wrenches would cover most of what you need. (2) A medium-sized adjustable crescent wrench. If you have space, also have a smaller one and a larger one. (3) An adjustable wrench that opens and closes when you turn the knurled wheel. Cheap ones can be frustrating, but even the cheapest one works better than nothing. Bonus points if you get a larger one that opens to at least 30 mm (or 1.12 inches) for propane fittings.

In addition to the basic tools listed above, people who live in apartments or other multistory structures should include:

- **A fire escape kit,** consisting of at least a fire mask and a fire- or heat-resistant blanket. (The latter will help you get out of a burning building, not fight fires.) Inexpensive versions of these can be bought for under $100. Make sure your apartment has more than one exit. Fire ladders and escape ropes may also be suggested, but their need and appropriateness should be determined on a case-by-case basis.

And people who live in areas where there are lots of trees that could fall or break and cause problems should include:

- **A machete** for cutting limbs of small trees, grass, or any vegetation.
- **An axe,** which works better on big trees.

There are infinite tools and gadgets you might use, but the ones listed above give you the best bang for your buck (and storage space).

The Toilet Stopped Flushing. Now What?

Most cities generate water pressure by pumping water up into tall water tanks and letting gravity do its thing. This system will provide a typical suburban house with water pressure, even without power, until those tanks are empty. In a high-rise apartment building, however, gravity is never sufficient to get water to the higher floors. Electric pumps are constantly in use to get water high up in a tall building, and there may or may not be a way to do that without power. In an urban context, you might find yourself without water very quickly if the power goes out, while suburban or rural folks would still have it. In short, living in a high-rise doesn't just mean you have to get along with other people. It also means that, in the event of a power outage, flooding, or a system-wide collapse, you may have to deal with other people's sewage.

The solution to this possible problem is a shutoff or backwater valve, which allows you to close off the incoming sewer lines to your apartment (note that once these are closed, you can no longer flush your toilet). In an apartment situation you'll need to ask your landlord or homeowners' association to install it. If you own your home, you'll probably have to hire a plumber to install it or be really skilled at following online videos to DIY. While a valve can be a bit on the pricey side (especially for a renter), once it's in place it will close automatically when sewer lines overflow, avoiding a potentially shitty situation (pun intended).

If it's winter and you have lost heat, the water in the toilet tank or in the line running to the toilet could be frozen. This also happens when you no longer have water to fill up the tank, in which case you don't have a lot of options. If you have plenty of water, you can flush a toilet by dumping a bucket of water directly into the bowl. If you don't have a lot of water, or if it's frozen, you would be better off looking for an alternative.

If it's dangerous to go outside because of the cold, radioactive fallout, chemical spills, or wild animals, use a bucket inside the house and dump it outside later. This waste makes great fertilizer, too, so maybe dump it in a place where it can be composted (see page 141) or mixed with other soil for the garden.

Other essential tools when an emergency strikes are those with which we communicate. You will want to be informed of what's going on around you and be able to change plans should the unexpected happen. Old-fashioned landlines had backup batteries that lasted several days after the power went out (newer systems for landlines may not), and modern cell towers have generators with fuel for a week to a month that automatically kick in when a loss of power is detected. Both of these systems rely on physical infrastructure, either copper lines or fiber-optic cables, that can be damaged. Walkie-talkies have very limited range, and radios with a range of hundreds or thousands of miles, like VHF or ham radios, require special training and sometimes licenses to use. All methods of communication have a potential downside, so let's focus on your specific needs—to stay informed and keep track of loved ones—along with some strategies to meet them.

Communication in a Crisis

Establish a crisis communication plan with your family, friends, and others you are responsible for *before* a crisis happens. Will you communicate via cellphones, text messaging, or calls to a landline? In certain emergencies it may be more important to do other things—such as getting out of harm's way—prior to communicating. For instance, if a hurricane is coming, phone service is out, and evacuations have been ordered, it might make more sense to move first and try to establish communication later. (We know it can create stress and anxiety, but nearly everybody would want their loved ones to stay safe and then communicate, not the other way around.) Assign specific roles to each person: For example, who is the point of contact for out-of-town family members, who is the email contact, who handles social media? Assign someone to check a certain meeting point or walkie-talkie channel.

Make a (paper) list of everybody in your group with whom you will try to communicate and their contact info (phone number, email, and social media handles). In the heat of the moment, it might be easy to forget someone. Maintain a (digital and hard copy) list of local emergency contacts, authorities, and utility companies. If your cellphone is lost, damaged, out of charge, or otherwise not working, you will want to be able to call from another phone, and chances are you won't have those numbers memorized. Write 'em down; lists are good!

Set a prearranged meeting point if communication fails or is delayed, with protocols for when to use this option. Pick a place everyone knows that can be approached from many directions and seems likely to be available during a crisis (for instance, don't choose the beach if a hurricane is the likely emergency or a river if your area is prone to flooding).

Use multiple communication channels. Don't rely on a single method of communication; use a combination of phone, text, email, walkie-talkie, and social media for redundancy (more on methods of communication follows). And in a crisis, focus on sharing important information—your location, safety status, and emergency updates—rather than the latest viral video. This allows people to get the critical information quickly, and minimizing chatter frees up the airwaves, so to speak, for others trying to get a hold of emergency services and/or loved ones.

Methods of Communication

In his book *Profiles of the Future,* science fiction author Arthur C. Clarke wrote (and Steve Jobs later paraphrased) that "any sufficiently advanced technology is indistinguishable from magic." And what with the advent of tech like cellphones, email, and texting, he has a point. But disruption to a satellite or cellphone tower can make it all disappear (like magic!). Even if you don't expect to use them, enable emergency and community alert systems. We're not saying that you're going to *need* all the communication methods outlined below. But then again it wouldn't hurt to be familiar with them just in case.

Following is a list of various communication methods. Some of these only receive information, like an emergency radio, and some are two-way communications, like a telephone or walkie-talkie. Don't rely on just one of the following. The more options you have, the better.

- **Automated Messaging Systems:** Text or email alerts can provide rapid updates regarding weather, safety measures, quarantine protocols, or the location of services.
- **Cellphones (SMS, Calls, Apps):** Solar chargers and power banks allow you to keep your cellphones and other communication devices charged during power failures. Newer cellphones might have a satellite option for emergency calls and nonemergency texts that can work during a cell-service out-

age or power blackout. Check your phone and see what satellite capabilities it has and how to use them.

- **Community Alert Systems:** Reverse 911 systems allow local authorities to send out alerts to homes and mobile phones, including evacuation orders or shelter-in-place instructions.
- **Emergency Alerts and Radio Stations:** Enable notifications from official apps like FEMA or Red Cross to receive updates during emergencies. Community radio stations may provide updates on curfews or local safety advisories.
- **Emergency Communication Systems:** Some homes or businesses may have emergency backup systems that use satellite-based communication, including phones or two-way radios.
- **Encrypted Messaging Apps:** Signal and Telegram offer encrypted messaging to ensure privacy when there is concern about surveillance or interception of communication.
- **Established Emergency Plans:** Many towns, organizations, businesses, and schools have preestablished emergency communication networks (e.g., group messaging apps or walkie-talkies) to quickly share information.
- **Mobile Apps:** Use apps like WhatsApp, Signal, or Facebook Messenger for voice and text communication. Some apps also allow you to send messages without using mobile data if there is a Wi-Fi connection.
- **Offline Communication Apps:** Bridgefy can allow offline communication between devices even when there's no internet connection. Decentralized messaging apps such as Bitchat operate without internet service using a Bluetooth Low Energy (BLE) mesh network that enables peer-to-peer communication by relaying messages through nearby devices, bypassing traditional infrastructure like cell towers or servers. They're perfect for those times when you need anonymous, off-grid communication.

- **Public Announcement/Warning Systems:** Authorities or community leaders may use public loudspeakers or sirens to communicate critical information, evacuation instructions, or safety alerts in the absence of digital communication or in areas of political or civil unrest.
- **Radio (AM/FM/NOAA Weather Radio):** Use battery-operated or hand-cranked radios to receive updates when the power is down or cell networks are inaccessible. NOAA Weather Radio should provide continuous broadcasts of official weather warnings and emergency information. But note that what are still free government weather forecasting and emergency alert services may eventually be privatized so that they are available only to subscribers who can pay for them, or downgraded and defunded to the point that they are no longer reliable or easily accessible. Readers may have to stay alert to this possibility and become subscribers to commercial forecasting services as the price of staying safe.
- **Satellite Messengers:** Satellite messengers, such as those from Spot and Garmin, are popular to use in remote areas to send emergency signals. Older versions might only send a message, but newer models can send *and* receive texts. They can be programmed to send messages to various phone numbers and emails, and some connect to your smartphone. These are relatively inexpensive, and some do not require a subscription to a service.
- **Satellite Phones:** In areas where regular cell service is unavailable, satellite phones provide a way to connect. They work independently of internet and cellular networks, making them reliable during cyber disruptions. The phone itself is not as expensive as a smartphone, but the separate service plans can be. Prepaid plans are usually offered, but the prepaid minutes often have an expiration date of three months to a year, so you have to buy them again whether you use them or not. Monthly

plans are not much more than a cellphone plan, but with limited minutes. These phones can send and receive texts but are not really a substitute for a cellphone as they typically only work outside with a clear view of the sky (contrary to what you might have seen in movies, you cannot place a call from a submarine or an underground bunker).

- **SMS (Text Messages):** Texting often works when cellular networks are overloaded, as it uses less bandwidth than voice calls. It can be the most reliable way to communicate during an active threat when phone lines might be jammed. Emergency services may use SMS alerts to inform people of evacuations or danger zones.
- **Social Media and Government Websites:** Use platforms like Bluesky, X, Facebook, or Instagram to share information with family and friends. Follow local news or official police/government social media accounts for real-time updates on the situation.
    - Public health information is provided by federal agencies such as Centers for Disease Control (CDC) and the National Institutes of Health (NIH). But during a health crisis, governments sometimes interfere with the messaging of public health agencies. If agency staffers and directors are reporting political efforts to suppress scientific results and censor science-based policy recommendations, and if independent medical and scientific organizations are questioning those agencies' credibility, you may need to consult other sources: for example, the Center for Infectious Disease Research and Policy (CIDRAP) at the University of Minnesota, a global leader in addressing public health preparedness and emerging infectious disease response; the World Health Organization and sources from other countries like the European Public Health Association (www.eupha.org); the American Public Health Association

(www.apha.org); medical associations like the American Medical Association (www.ama-assn.org) and the American Academy of Pediatrics (www.aap.org); research and medical institutions like the Mayo Clinic, the Cleveland Clinic, and the Kaiser Family Foundation (KFF); and your healthcare provider.

  - During civil unrest, X or Facebook can be useful for both receiving updates and sharing your status. Just be aware that analyses indicate that upwards of *60 to 80 percent of users on X* are bots. Hashtags like #StaySafe, #getmethehellouttahere, or #Protests can provide local updates. Assume that everybody can see all of your online activity and act accordingly. Understand who owns and controls these apps, and who they are aligned with. If you need to keep something confidential, use an encrypted messaging app like Signal.
  - Be cautious of misinformation (see page 126), which tends to spread faster and farther during health crises in particular, when, as noted on the previous page, even government sources may be unreliable because of political interference, pressure, and defunding. Check health information against the websites of independent research and medical institutions that attempt to educate the public and back up their claims by linking to peer-reviewed studies.

- **Telecommunications:** Use Skype, Zoom, or Google Meet for remote communication with loved ones, colleagues, or emergency personnel.
- **Walkie-Talkies/Two-Way Radios (e.g., CB/GMRS/FRS):** In rural or isolated areas, walkie-talkies are useful for short-range communication when cell towers are down. There are several types of two-way radios, including inexpensive walkie-talkies with a maximum range of a few miles (using FRS, or Family Radio Service, channels); Citizen Band (CB)

radios for short-range communication; GMRS (General Mobile Radio Service) radios, which are similar to CB radios but permitted to broadcast with more power on some channels; VHF radios (like those on boats, which can broadcast a long distance); and more powerful (and complicated) ham radios, which can communicate across the globe. Each type of radio uses a different set of frequencies (although some walkie-talkies use VHF frequencies). If you want to use your radio to communicate with another, the two radios have to share a band. These devices can work when internet access is down.

Two main factors influence range: power output and antenna height. For handheld radios, the greater the power (measured in watts) and the higher you are (or your antenna is) in elevation, the longer the range. Walkie-talkies tend to have a range of a mile or less when down on city streets, a little farther from high rooftops, and sometimes longish ranges when in rural areas. From mountain peak to mountain peak, with nothing in between, a walkie-talkie can transmit twenty miles or more. CB radios in vehicles tend to go a little farther (five to twenty miles on average) because of the long antennas, and GMRS radios a little farther than that. Ham radios are much more powerful, but they require a license to use (yes, even in an emergency), and their long-range ability depends on having a tall or high antenna, often seventy to well over a hundred feet.

In an emergency where you do not have access to your home or vehicle, walkie-talkies are probably your best bet for communicating with family that is close by. For communicating with the authorities, CB or VHF radios both have emergency channels (channel 9 for CB, 16 for marine VHF). Walkie-talkies don't have an official emergency channel, but channel 9 is sometimes used in that way. Note that this is not the same frequency as CB channel 9. For emergencies, two-way radios are the choice of first responders and emergency personnel and are probably the best way to communicate if you understand the range limitations.

Things That Disrupt Communication

- Overloaded Networks: In major crises, mobile networks may become congested, making it hard to connect.
- Power Outages: If the power goes out, consider having backup power sources (portable chargers, solar chargers) to keep your devices running. Keep your devices charged. Like making your bed or wearing lipstick, this is something that you either do or don't do. If you're the type that tends to forget, invest in backups. Also, remember that a long-term power outage, one lasting more than a couple of weeks, might deplete the backup sources that power cell towers.
- Communication Blackouts: Governments may shut down mobile networks or internet access during political unrest, limiting communication. Use offline apps (e.g., Bridgefy, Bitchat) for peer-to-peer messaging, as anything broadcast over the airwaves or internet could be intercepted. Face-to-face may be the way to go for some communications if you really need to keep them confidential.
- Vulnerabilities to Digital Systems: Cyberattacks could target communication infrastructure. It's essential to have backup systems in place (e.g., satellite communications).

Where to Get Reliable News

In his Substack newsletter, *How Things Work,* journalist Hamilton Nolan wrote, "News is just true information about the world. The act of producing that information—investigating it, uncovering it, observing it, reporting it, analyzing it, considering it, drawing conclusions from it—is journalism. There is and will always be a demand for journalism for the same reason that there is a demand for information itself. In order to live, in order to do stuff, you need to know stuff." But because most of today's media outlets are run by Big Business with the intention of spreading propaganda and making money, and because media outlets may succumb to political pressures, the process of knowing stuff—*true* stuff—is purposely way harder (and more expensive) than it should be.

Having access to accurate data is always important, but never so much as during a crisis. Rumors, mistakes, and misinformation can be widespread, and you need to know how to tell truth from fiction. Remember, your life could depend on knowing what is happening and how to navigate the disaster. On 9/11, there were reports on major news channels that a bomb had detonated at the State Department and that hundreds of planes were missing. This turned out to be false and highlighted the fact that the truth is hard to come by when things get chaotic.

Another factor making accurate information hard to access: artificial intelligence. According to a September 2025 article titled "AI Misinformation Is Threatening Emergency Communications," by Ethan Beaty in the *Bulletin of the Atomic Scientists,* "AI is not only making misinformation more convincing but also making it available at a moment's notice. From natural disasters and humanitarian emergencies to nuclear incidents and geopolitical crises, anyone with a smart phone can add to the confusion. Because emergency communication is almost always a race against time, the damage done can be serious, even if corrections eventually arrive."

These are the outlets where you're (most) likely to find accurate information:

- **Local emergency managers** are responsible for communicating with the public about disasters and rescue and response efforts and coordinating between different agencies. If you live in a large city, the emergency management department is often a separate agency. In smaller communities, fire chiefs or sheriff's offices may manage emergency response and alerts. They usually rely on an SMS-based emergency alert system, so sign up for those on their website. Many emergency management agencies are active on Facebook, so check there for updates as well. Also note that while larger cities may offer multiple languages, most emergency alerts are only in English.

- **Local television news** from verified sources will have live updates during and after a storm.
- **Social media.** These days it's getting harder to tell truth from fiction, but make sure as best you can that the news you're getting is from verified sources. We don't mean people who bought a checkmark for their account, but rather accounts that are the official social media source of a particular group, like a university or a government agency (though political interference may make even government agencies suppress scientifically backed information; see page 123). This may take a bit of research, but it's worth the effort.
- **Weather stations and apps.** The Weather Channel, Apple Weather, and Google should have updated information on major storms, but you should not rely on them for up-to-the-minute advice. The National Weather Service (NWS) offers information and updates on everything from wildfires to hurricanes to air quality (though see page 122 on political attempts to privatize weather services). Go to weather.gov and enter your zip code to customize your homepage. The NWS also has regional and local branches where you can sign up for SMS alerts. If you're in a rural area or somewhere that isn't highlighted on its maps, keep an eye out for local alerts and evacuation orders, as NWS may not have as much information ahead of time.

In some ways the next chapter, concerning money and bartering, is a natural to follow this one. You can't barter for what you need if you can't communicate, which is also an extension of how getting through an emergency reinforces the value of community. Like holidays with family, how well things go sometimes comes down to letting the more important factors, such as love and connection, take priority over trivial ones. It's a key point to remember—especially when cows and trees go airborne—that we're all in this together.

8. Money, Bartering, and Other Valuable Things

Trust is the raw material from which all types of money are minted.

—YUVAL NOAH HARARI, *SAPIENS*

In the “old” days parents advised their kids to always carry an extra twenty dollars in case of emergencies. Today, with the advent of debit and credit cards, Venmo, and Zelle, dollars and coins hardly change hands. Little thought is given to what happens when systems go down, which is exactly what happened in February 2024, when a nationwide outage of cellular service made it impossible to make calls or for many credit card machines and ATMs to access the internet. No connectivity meant that transactions couldn’t be approved. Some people couldn’t even post updates to their Instagram accounts. (The horror!) Later that year, after the North Carolina floods, businesses in the affected areas couldn't accept credit cards because of the lack of electricity, cell service, and internet. They requested cash only. And on an otherwise normal Saturday in Seattle, when Amy and her husband were waiting in line at a Playa Bowls, the cashier announced that their system had gone down and they were only taking cash. The line melted away faster than the polar ice caps.

All of these situations caused substantial disruption but were ultimately temporary and short-lived. The lesson? We don't need to be in a postapocalyptic situation to have to barter or trade for goods. There are many circumstances in which we may lose access to our money, or it may decrease in value. And what is "money" anyhow but a mutually agreed-upon form of currency decorated with dead presidents? The paper is just paper, and the coins are just whatever metal coins are made from these days.

A loss of value, referred to as a currency crisis, usually occurs because of runaway inflation. This has happened many times in the past. In 1923, after World War I, prices in Germany doubled every few days. Then it got worse. A loaf of bread that cost 250 marks in January cost billions (yes, billions) by the end of the year. In Zimbabwe in 2007, people carried currency in wheelbarrows as prices doubled daily. In Venezuela, inflation was nearly 1,000,000 percent in 2018. In cases like these, bartering—at least for some items—becomes the norm.

"

In 1990, Peru was suffering from hyperinflation of more than 7,600 percent. I traveled there from Bolivia to see the archaeological site of Machu Picchu. The site is reached by train, and tickets could be purchased only with cash. The local bank didn't have large bills, so I settled for the largest they had. I walked to the train office to buy three tickets with more than a thousand bills in my pockets (all of my pockets!). People spent any money

they got immediately, often on a foreign currency that would hold value. This was a full-blown currency crisis. A new currency was subsequently introduced a year later.

—Chris

”

Accessing your money during a crisis may be difficult. In the aftermath of a disaster (or, as above, on just an unfortunate day in February), power and internet service may be disrupted. Banks also rely on power to keep track of accounts, so in the case of natural or human-caused disasters, you might not be able to access your money or credit.

Another issue to consider is that prices may be much higher than usual. Price gouging, while often illegal, is quite common (think toilet paper during COVID, hotels during the 2025 California wildfires, airline tickets during the holidays, etc.). Prepare to pay more for *everything,* especially essentials (food, water, generators) that others may not have had the foresight to stock up on.

Keep a cash stash. With so many people living paycheck to paycheck, the question becomes how much extra, if any, you have available to put aside. Depending on the crisis, you may not need to cover expenses like mortgage, insurance, or credit card payments (though don't plan on this), but you will likely need enough to cover (the presumably jacked-up prices for) food, water, electricity, household supplies like toilet paper, and—should you be unable to shelter in place—the cost of travel and lodging. If you can't afford to put a chunk of just-in-case money aside, add "withdraw cash" to your to-do list when you see a possible emergency on the horizon.

If you run out of funds, the banks are closed, and ATMs are down, there are some cash alternatives to consider. Do you still have your diamond engagement ring, your big-screen TV, and your husband's designer watch? While these types of items are considered valuable in the world we're currently living in, you can't eat a watch or drink a diamond. In an emergency, you can sell them, but count on getting very little in exchange for your expensive stuff. What does hold its worth will depend on the nature and scale of the disaster and how much time passes before things return to the way they were. If the road back to normalcy is short, people may be willing to trade for things that will be valuable when the disaster passes. If the return to normalcy is a long way off, value may be directly related to an item's utility. A bag of tools, some nails, or a winter coat might have more worth than your (virtual) bitcoin.

The ABCs of Bartering

Trading something for goods or services without using money is called bartering, a practice as old as humanity itself. In the apocalyptic stories we have read or watched, it is common for money to have lost its value and for bartering to become the standard financial interaction. In real life that often happens because of war (when a certain currency loses value), some other kind of economic collapse, or hyperinflation. If something like that does happen, what can you trade or barter? What's at the top of people's "most wanted" lists will depend on the situation, but in most cases following a catastrophe, those who have not prepared in advance will be most in need of the necessities (water, food, etc.).

Bartering is not a zero-sum game, meaning ideally both parties should gain something from the transaction. Every situation is unique, but there are some fundamentals on how to barter effectively.

- Be fair in your trading. Pushing your advantage to wring as much as possible out of your trading partner can come back to haunt you. People may not want to trade with you or you might be shunned by the community as a price gouger taking advantage of the suffering of others. A win-win is better overall than a win-lose situation.
- Don't trade where you live. Find a neutral site, such as a parking lot or gas station, so you have some control.

- Goodwill goes a long way. You might get more in the long run by being generous and charitable. Giving may yield better returns than trading and may enable you in turn to get a good deal the next time.
- Having people owe you can come in handy too. Giving gifts to create a sense of obligation is a time-honored tradition. At the very least, it might make it easier to ask for help if you have helped others.

> "I lived or worked in several small villages in the countryside of Honduras, where people grow their own food and rarely have much actual money. In my experience, most bartering is food for food (for instance, a chicken for some corn, if you don't grow corn). The other most common trade is labor for food or raw materials (clearing brush and trees in exchange for cut wood, for example). Once, I traded an old transistor radio for a duck. Most often, I gave things away and received gifts back. I liked that type of exchange because everybody felt good about it, it built goodwill, and it made me less of an outsider and more a part of the community.
>
> —Chris"

What People Will Want (the Basics)

Simply put, the top items on people's list will be the basics that they do not have access to or that they didn't (as you did!) stash in advance.

- **Water.** In many places, water is plentiful, although one needs to think no further back than to November 2024, when every state but Alaska was in drought. Items used to purify water would also seem to merit the most wanted list especially if fuel to boil water is in short supply.

- **Food.** It doesn't make sense to barter your food unless you have extra. Most food takes up a lot of space, and we use a lot, so bartering might involve things that we use in small quantities but that are important, like salt. Coffee (which, if stopped suddenly, can bring on wicked withdrawal) and sugar will also be desirable, especially as your local Starbucks and Dunkin' will have presumably closed.
- **Medicine.** Some medicines, like insulin, are lifesavers and therefore would be highly valued, but most of us do not have access to these without a prescription (see page 94 on suggestions for stockpiling medications). The medicines that we can reasonably buy, and that people will probably lust after (let's not be coy here) include painkillers like oxycodone hydrochloride (OxyContin), ibuprofen (Advil), and acetaminophen (Tylenol); allergy or cold medicines (Benadryl); diarrhea medicine (Imodium); and general antibiotics like penicillin (Amoxicillin). And don't forget antacids (TUMS) for heartburn, as you'll probably be ingesting foods that you're not used to eating.
- **Toilet paper and feminine hygiene products.** How quaint it is to think back to the TP panic of 2020! Sure, people for thousands of years made do without toilet paper and tampons, but we'd wager it may be a while before we are happy about having to do so again.

What People Will Want (the "Luxuries")

In the harder-core world of prepping, it is generally assumed that items like ammunition, tobacco, and alcohol will be in high demand after the basics of water, food, and medicine have been met. But stocking up on bullets and imagining that you will be able to trade them for the more essential things you need is probably a bad strategy. With a few exceptions, contemporary and historical cases show that ammunition will be in limited demand.

Following are some items we believe will be considered the new "luxuries."

- **Clean, dry clothes.**
- **Comfort food.** Ahhh . . . Double Stuf Oreos, chips, chocolate. These are probably not realistic to stock up on (except for the Oreos, which contain so many preservatives they could probably outlast humankind), but if you happen to have them people will probably want them.
- **Tobacco, alcohol, and weed.** Millions of people are addicted to nicotine. Anything that is habit forming (and we could include coffee here) is a bitch to withdraw from, especially when you are stressing about whether your neighbor may cook and eat you. If you are a social smoker (and that includes marijuana) or drinker, it would be nice to know you have the means to escape for a while when you're not actually fleeing. If you are hooked and don't plan on giving up your habit anytime soon, make sure you have backup. If you have extra, there's a good chance someone else will be interested too.

What People Will Need (a Hand)

In our day-to-day lives, we trade labor and expertise for money. And because of the way our society has developed—away from agriculture and more toward the technical—some kinds of expertise are more highly valued than others. But when a disaster strikes, knowing how to trade commodities from a plush office may be of less value than knowing how to rough it (see the 2026 movie *Send Help,* where the mistreated office worker and avid *Survivor* fan is also the only person who knows how to fish and build a fire when a plane crash leaves her stranded on a deserted island with her misogynistic, nepo-baby boss, making her the de facto leader). Practical skills may be the best things to trade after a catastrophe. This could be general labor, such as agricultural work, or skills from cutting hair to repairing clothing to fixing a flat tire to providing first aid. After a wildfire, you need contractors and construction workers to rebuild. After a flood you might need carpenters, engineers, or heavy equipment operators. Every situation will be different.

Now that we've explained what *really* keeps its value when things go sideways, the next chapter will address how to keep you and your loved ones safe—not from zombies, but from more mundane perils like sewage, garbage, illness, and injury.

9. Protecting Yourself and Your Family

The greatest victory is that which requires no battle.

—SUN TZU, *THE ART OF WAR*

While it may be an oversimplification to say fear is *the* main driver of humanity, evidence from psychology, neuroscience, and evolution confirms that it is one of our most powerful and fundamental motivators, exerting influence on our survival, decisions, and social structures. Fear of embarrassment. Fear of disease. Fear of violence. Fear of clowns. When all hell breaks loose, be it due to a natural disaster or a human-made one (which these days, one could argue, are almost the same thing), our first thought is how to keep ourselves, our friends, and our families safe. But safe from what? Few of us are actively concerned with invading zombies or aliens. More top-of-mind is navigating the next pandemic, the next uncontained wildfire, or a failing economic and/or political system. So it might surprise you to realize that protecting yourself from *other people* is just one challenge among many.

First on our list, especially with diseases multiplying faster than superhero movie sequels, is protection from germs via good hygiene. And while some say that "cleanliness is next to godliness," when you're trying to escape a hurricane or wildfire there can be a bit of wiggle room. But be sure to double-check your go bag regularly for sanitation, hygiene, and first aid essentials (see page 89) so you're packed and ready to go.

How to Deal with Sewage and Garbage

Looks like your germophobic cousin was right. Empires have literally fallen because of poor sanitation and disease. Many archaeologists point to disease as part of the reason for the collapse of Rome and of the Classic Maya, as well as the widespread decline of Bronze Age societies around the Mediterranean. At least some of the decline was due to how they handled their refuse.

As with those ancient civilizations, the impact of sewage and garbage disposal today is directly related to population density. In other words: More people equals more poop. If you have evacuated with a small group in a rural area, you don't have to do much besides keep sewage far away from your water source. If you are hunkered down in a town or city after a disaster where the usual sanitation systems are not working, you have to plan much more carefully. Given that nearly 60 percent of the world's population lives in urban areas (and that number is upwards of 80 percent in many countries), most of us are going to be somewhere with a lot of other people. And at some point we will all need to go to the bathroom.

Why worry? Aside from the obvious ick factor, sewage contains bacteria and viruses that make us sick. The exact bacteria in a particular area might vary, but common ones include those that cause diarrhea.

Much more than a nuisance, "the runs" can lead to dehydration, which can be especially dangerous for the elderly, children, and those with other preexisting medical conditions. Not to mention it uses up a lot of toilet paper. Other bacteria found in sewage include *E. coli, Campylobacter,* and *Cryptosporidium.* Sewage is also a vector for diseases including cholera, encephalitis, typhoid fever, and salmonella.

There are two main things to worry about with sewage. First is direct contact. Keep your hands, eating utensils, and clothing clear of sewage or surfaces that might have been contaminated. Wash your hands, utensils, and clothing as often as practical. Use soap, not just water. This makes a difference, as soap traps germs that would otherwise get through. Do not walk barefoot in areas that might be contaminated; in fact, err on the side of caution and wear shoes all the time if you can.

The other way that sewage can make us sick is through our water. This is harder to guard against because it involves complex and long-term processes, like bacteria seeping into groundwater. When effective sewage treatment systems break down, we can do a couple of things to keep ourselves safe.

- Keep sewage as far away from water sources as possible, and make sure it cannot leach down into the groundwater. Locate latrines away from any groundwater you are using, and downstream if possible. Line latrines with something dense. Plastic works best, but clay or some other impermeable soil also works.
- Always purify the water you drink or use to prepare food (see page 67). If possible, use purified water to wash utensils, although the drying and cooking processes—for pots and pans, for instance—will take care of contamination for the most part. This should be part of your routine anytime you are unsure of the cleanliness of the water you use. After any big disaster (wildfire, earthquake, flood, hurricane) that upends a

lot of infrastructure or when governments are not functioning (see Flint, Michigan), assume the quality of any municipal water system has been compromised.

There is also the psychological aspect of dealing with sewage. Put simply, it's disgusting, and nobody wants to live within the sight or smell of open sewers. Taking care of sewage doesn't just help our bodies, it helps our state of mind too.

Like sewage, garbage can harbor bacteria, viruses, and mold that can make us sick. Sewage might be worse in that regard, but in a survival or an emergency any additional stress or threat should be eliminated if possible. Treat garbage like a latrine: Put it away from water sources, out of sight and smell if possible, and take steps to keep the nastiness from leaching down to the groundwater that you might use.

Burning trash releases lots of toxins, can contaminate air and water, and contributes to greenhouse gases in the atmosphere. There are better ways to dispose of garbage. If folks are burning trash, at least remove the plastic and stick to burning cardboard, paper, and wood. But even these can contain paint, dyes, adhesives, and other materials that will contribute to pollution, so finding another solution—such as reusing food containers, envelopes, plastic bags, construction materials, and pieces of leftover lumber for new projects—is best.

What About Composting?

You can compost almost anything that was once alive, but the proportions matter, and compost can still contaminate groundwater (composting is one of those things we suggest learning about beforehand, and you can find more info about it on page 22). A compost pile should be mostly brown plant material (like dead leaves or dried onion husks, which are high in carbon) and a smaller amount of green material (like sawdust, wood shavings, or shredded paper, food scraps, grass clippings, and/or coffee grounds). Naturally occurring bacteria will break all this down into good organic soil relatively quickly, but even well-constructed compost piles can create problems for groundwater because of leaching. Building a berm—a narrow shelf, path, or ledge typically at the top or bottom of a slope—around compost piles can help reduce the amount of water that runs through the pile and decrease leaching, as can covering the pile with something to keep rain from draining through it. Lining a compost pit with plastic is generally not recommended because the plastic will also leach. A good compost pile that is protected from rain with an organic lining (wood, cardboard, even vegetation) should not be a problem for groundwater. So, compost that organic garbage!

Composting human waste, also known as humanure (we're not making this up, folks), requires careful management to eliminate pathogens. There are also some laws regarding this, so we are assuming here that (1) you are composting human waste where it is allowed or (2) we've reached a point where laws don't really matter so much anymore.

First, separate solids from liquids. This means you must have a toilet that traps urine. Heat is an important component in composting human waste, so you will need a bin that is insulated (straw or soil works, but there are special bins that are insulated to retain heat). You also need other components: basically the same greens (nitrogen-rich material) and browns (carbon-rich material) that you use for "regular" composting (see page 22).

Mix about 50/50 browns and greens and use that as a starter in your composting bin. Collect the poop for a week or so (in a bucket with a lid or other container), before taking it out to the compost pile. Dig a hole in the center of the compost and add the human waste. Cover it with wood chips or other brown (i.e., carbon-rich material) composting material. Make sure you have a big enough bin that it can start generating heat. Every week or two, add some more browns and greens to the mix while also adding in more human waste. Within a few months, it should have turned to compost.

Alternatively (and less "hands on"), a composting toilet can be used. This also involves collecting waste in buckets and then mixing it with carbon-rich materials. The mixture is then composted, either actively (requiring high temperatures to kill pathogens) or passively (requiring a longer decomposition time).

Note that one of the dangers from composting human waste is the possibility of spreading pathogens. To avoid this, let the waste completely break down into compost, then let it stand for several months until all pathogens have died. Many people recommend using humanure only on nonfood plants, but some Native American tribes used it for agricultural purposes. This approach, referred to as "night soil" management, helped to enrich the soil and improve crop yields.

Urine is different. You can just put it on crops, either straight or diluted. No problem.

How to Deal with Illness and Injury

No matter how healthy you are, an emergency scenario is more likely to cause illness or injury, whether it's as severe as a broken bone or as mundane as heartburn. These days knowledge of even the most basic first aid skills, like bandaging a wound, splinting a broken ankle, or treating minor ailments, is usually left to professionals. So if you don't already have solid first aid skills, consider getting some training in CPR or more advanced first aid or medical techniques. Although we recommend that you keep a basic first aid instruction booklet with your kit (see page 92), an emergency scenario is not the best time to figure out how to stanch a ruptured artery or apply a tourniquet, which is why we suggest learning more about first aid before you need to (see page 22).

The best way to deal with illness and injuries: Don't get sick or hurt in the first place. You may have seen survival shows where contestants take great risks, climbing trees to get a better view or scaling waterfalls to save time when traversing the wilderness. *Do not do things like this!* When you are experiencing an emergency situation, be extra cautious and conservative. Move slowly. Stay on the trails. Wear your helmet and safety gear. Take as few risks as possible. Something as simple as a sprained ankle can make life so much harder during a disaster. Drive slowly and defensively. Don't run with scissors. In these types of situations, it's better to be boring and safe. Getting kicked off the island is the least of your worries.

Home Remedies

In an emergency (or even just on a regular Tuesday), it is possible that the medical care you are used to receiving will not be available, and medicines might be scarce. People have used all kinds of approaches to healing and wellness over the 300,000 years of human history, and there are many ways of healing that depart from the standard biomedical pharmaceutical model that is used in most places in the industrialized world. If you do end up in a minor scrape without access to an emergency room, the remedies used by our grandparents and great-grandparents can still work in dire situations. Here are some of the oldies but goodies.

Saltwater Gargle

Salt has been scientifically proven to help draw water out of oral tissues while creating a barrier that blocks harmful pathogens. Gargling with saltwater blocks viruses and bacteria, reduces the chance of infections in the mouth and throat, and can relieve inflammation. It's good for colds, sore throat, sinus and respiratory infections, and dental health.

TO MAKE:

$^{1}/_{4}$ to $^{1}/_{2}$ teaspoon salt

1 cup warm water (not hot)

Dissolve the salt completely in the warm water, which will soothe a sore throat and more easily dissolve the salt. Gargle the warm saltwater in the back of your throat for fifteen to thirty seconds. Then swish the water around the mouth and teeth afterward. Spit it out once you're finished and repeat until the liquid is used up. Use one to two times daily for sore throats or as needed for oral hygiene.

Note: Avoid swallowing the gargle, as drinking too much saltwater can also have health risks, such as calcium deficiency and high blood pressure. Consuming too much salt can also dehydrate you. For this reason, children younger than six years most likely shouldn't gargle.

Apple Cider Vinegar

Apple cider vinegar (ACV) may have beneficial effects on the glycemic index and oxidative stress in individuals with diabetes and dyslipidemia. Although it won't cure type 2 diabetes, it may moderately lower blood glucose levels. ACV also contains probiotics, acetic acid, and other nutrients responsible for its health benefits. It can help kill pathogens, including Salmonella, *which has been showing up everywhere these days and affects an estimated two million Americans each year.*

To use: Replace your usual vinegar with apple cider vinegar in a salad dressing, use it to make homemade mayonnaise, or dilute one teaspoon up to two tablespoons in a large glass of water and drink daily.

Note: Too much vinegar can cause harmful side effects, including tooth enamel erosion and potential drug interactions.

Raw Garlic Honey

The main health ingredient in garlic is allicin, a compound also used in homeopathic remedies (see page 147) that may help to ease inflammation. It contains oxygen, sulfur, and other chemicals that give garlic antibacterial and disease-fighting properties. Chopping or crushing fresh garlic cloves releases more allicin than using the cloves whole. For maximum benefit, you'll want to use garlic when it's fresh.

Honey is naturally high in flavonoids and polyphenols, which are antioxidants that can help fight inflammation and balance the immune system. Honey also has antibacterial, antiviral, and antifungal properties. A combination of the two can be used to treat colds and coughs, boost the immune system, ease symptoms of asthma, fight inflammation, and balance the immune system.

TO MAKE:

6 to 8 garlic cloves, to taste
1 cup raw honey

Peel and slightly crush the garlic cloves and place in a sterilized four-ounce jar. Pour the honey over the cloves, ensuring they're fully covered. Seal the jar and let it sit for two to three days at room temperature to allow the garlic to infuse the honey.

Take one teaspoon of the garlic honey as needed at the first sign of a cold or to boost immunity.

Note: Store the mixture in a cool, dark place and use within a month. Adjust the garlic amount for a stronger or milder flavor.

Herbal Medicine

Herbal medicine is based on the knowledge that plants contain a wide range of bioactive compounds that can help treat illnesses or improve health, including alkaloids, flavonoids, terpenes, glycosides, and phenols. Some herbs are used to boost the immune system, while others may have anti-inflammatory, antioxidant, or antibacterial properties.

It has been estimated that as much as 80 percent of the world's population depends on medicine derived from plants. Scientific research has isolated numerous compounds from plants and developed pharmaceuticals from them. In fact, the main ingredient in good old aspirin comes from salicin, which is found in plants such as willow and myrtle—a good piece of knowledge to have when your local CVS is no longer open and your doctor is MIA.

Herbal medicine emphasizes traditional uses of the original plants (which you may be able to forage; see pages 21 and 22), using whole or parts of plants—leaves, roots, flowers, fruits, bark—or their extracts.

The best way to learn about herbal medicine is to study with somebody who really knows their stuff. And yes, *study* is the right word. It takes time and effort to learn how to identify plants in the wild and understand what each one is capable of treating. Milkwood.net is a good place to start—they offer lots of beginners' guides and permaculture courses. You can also check out your local health food store for resources.

Plant remedies can take many forms:

- Teas, made by steeping dried herbs in hot water
- Tinctures (concentrated extracts), made by soaking fresh or dried herbs (depending on the type of herb) in alcohol or glycerin
- Capsules or tablets of ground herbs
- Essential and/or infused oils for topical application or aromatherapy

In addition to foraging (if you know what to look for) and processing the plants you find, you can buy herbs in dried form or already processed into remedies in herbal shops, health food stores, or via online retailers. If you forage the plant yourself, the Potawatomi Nation (and other Native American practitioners) say you should ask permission from the plant before picking it, never take the first or last plant you see, and use what you take. If purchasing, buy from a reputable source and follow the directions for use carefully.

Here are some of the most common plant remedies:

- **Aloe vera** can be used to calm sunburn. Usually found in gel form at most pharmacies and health food stores.
- **Blackberry root** can be used to treat mouth sores.
- **Catnip,** made into a tea using the dried leaves and flowering tops of the plant, can be used for cold symptoms.
- **Chamomile** fights inflammation, is known for its calming properties, reduces digestive discomfort, and helps with sleep.
- **Dandelion leaves and roots** aid digestion (and make a great salad!).
- **Echinacea** is often used to support the immune system and reduce the severity of cold symptoms.
- **Elderberry,** both the flowers and fruits, stimulates the immune system and lowers fever.
- **Fern fronds and sometimes the roots** can be used to make a poultice to treat minor cuts and burns.
- **Ginger** is good for inflammation; it is also known for its antinausea properties and is often used for digestive issues and motion sickness.
- **Goldenseal,** particularly tea and liquid extracts made from the root and underground stem, fights infections, including cold and flu.
- **Hawthorne,** for which some herbalists advocate using the whole plant (leaves, flowers, and berries) to maximize the potential benefits, can help regulate blood pressure.

- **Lavender** is known for its calming effects and is often used to treat anxiety, stress, and insomnia.
- **Mullein dried leaves and flowers,** commonly used in teas, tinctures, and topical applications, help with respiratory distress.
- **Nettle's leaves (traditionally used for allergies, arthritis, and anemia), roots (for prostate health), and seeds (for kidney health)** are high in nutrients and great in soups or teas.
- **Peppermint** is great for digestive discomfort and for headaches.
- **Plantain** is both a medicinal herb (it helps stop bleeding) and an edible green.
- **Sage leaves,** made into a tea or an essential oil, can be used for aches and pains.
- **Turmeric** contains curcumin, which has strong anti-inflammatory properties and is often used for joint pain and arthritis.
- **White pine needles** soothe, strengthen, and heal the lungs and bronchia and ease joint pain; they are rich in vitamin C and tannins, and their resin is an antiseptic for boils and wounds.
- **Wild yam** roots and rhizomes (underground stems) can be made into a tea or tincture and are used for nausea.
- **Witch hazel plants** (the bark, twigs, and leaves) can be used as an antiseptic astringent good for treating chicken pox, diaper rash, poison ivy, poison oak, bruises, sunburn, dry skin, cold sores, bug bites, and small cuts. It also helps prevent infection and control minor bleeding. The astringent is readily available in drugstores.
- **Violets,** both the leaves and flowers, can provide pain relief, are anti-inflammatory and rich in salicylic acid, reduce edema, and relieve dry cough.
- **Yarrow** leaves are known for their antiseptic, styptic, and

antimicrobial properties, while the flowers are often used to induce sweating and reduce fevers.

Opium Tea

(adapted from Michael Pollan's book *This Is Your Mind on Plants*)

The flowers of the poppy plant have long been used as a painkiller for soothing mild aches and pains (e.g., toothache, earache, and sore throat), a mild sedative/relaxant, and an expectorant for coughs. And opium-based preparations, in addition to having powerful painkiller effects, have been used to treat or prevent maladies including dysentery, malaria, insomnia, anxiety, and tuberculosis.

Poppy tea, an herbal infusion, is made from brewing poppy straw or seeds of several species of poppy. The species most commonly used is Papaver somniferum, *which produces opium as a natural defense against predators. In the live flower, opium is released when the surface of the bulb, called the seed pod, is pierced or scraped. For the purpose of the tea, dried pods are more commonly used than the pods of the live flower.*

TO MAKE:

6 poppy pods
2 cups boiling water

Cut open and remove the seeds from the poppy pods. Crush the pods and pulverize the shards (e.g., in a coffee grinder), then steep the resulting powder in boiling water for about fifteen minutes. Pour through a strainer. Drink (and yeah, it tastes pretty bad).

Note: Poppy tea contains opioids, which is why it works as a pain reliever, but it can also lead to an overdose when combined with other opioids.

> Several years ago, I contracted malaria in Honduras. I didn't recognize it as anything other than a flu-like illness, but it was rough. The very day I first felt symptoms, my wife and I were packing up our family to leave Honduras. Our children were covered with bug bites after all the time playing outside in a rural area, so my wife went out and collected tree bark that would help soothe their skin. She boiled it into a tea and added it to their bathwater. Later, I learned that the bark was from the Quina tree, which produces quinine—the cure (and preventative) for malaria. Had I known I had malaria and what that tree was, I could have drunk that tea and possibly cured myself before I really got sick (it subsequently took me a couple of months to recover).
>
> —Chris

How to Keep You and Your Family Safe

If you've come this far, you know that the best way to relieve stress and protect your loved ones is to level up your prepping game: Stock up and rotate your supplies and stay informed. Knowing whose counsel to take and strengthening community ties are as important for your well-being and survival as the stuff you have stashed away. In fact, it's mostly a horror movie plot device that people turn into murderous beasts when disaster strikes. Don't get us wrong, we know people can be selfish, dishonest, and untrustworthy even in the best of times. But we have also seen, via actual historical examples, that disasters bring out the best of us, at least for a while. Sooner or later, we all return to our normal self-absorbed selves, but there is no evidence to suggest that we need to be more worried about other people after a catastrophe than we are on the regular.

In this section we discuss personal safety and self-defense. Combining physical skills with mental resilience and strategic thinking will give you a well-rounded approach to protecting yourself. What don't we include? Weapons, because carrying one might not be the deterrent you think it is. A pistol, taser, or knife will not prevent violence and could quickly cause a situation to escalate. When lethal weapons are involved, the chances that things will end badly are much higher. You might win nine out of ten times, but you *will* eventually lose. Violence is not a sustainable strategy for getting what you want or protecting what you have. And nothing you have is worth the risk, even your stock of food and medicine. Certainly not your pride.

Always be aware of your surroundings. Stay alert, especially in unfamiliar or potentially risky areas, or when fleeing a dangerous situation, evacuating to an unknown location, or camping out in the wild. Although it's easy to be distracted in the midst of an emergency (or, like, every day), try not to stare at your phone while walking or to wear headphones that cut off all sound. Be informed about what is happening where you are. This will help you avoid places, people, or activities associated with problems.

Make friends and allies and treat people fairly and with respect. This won't stop everybody, but it is a lot easier to justify bad behavior against someone who behaves like an asshole. Not making enemies is a good start.

Make yourself a valued part of your community, which can be an important source of information and support. And having a posse around could prove to be a deterrent for those whose motives are less than pure.

Walk with purpose while channeling your favorite action hero. If you appear alert and confident, you're less likely to be seen as an easy target. Also do what you can to *not* stand out. Whether it's a show of wealth, gear, or supplies, try to blend in and not advertise what you have. Excessive security signals that you're trying to protect something. That said, keep your valuables out of sight, keep the doors to your home and car locked, and be cautious of anyone lingering near your residence and vehicle when entering or exiting.

Avoid walking alone at night or in other potentially dangerous situations, especially in poorly lit or isolated areas. And if you must go out alone, always let someone know where you're going and when you'll be back. Carry a personal alarm, pepper spray, or other self-defense tools to ward off potential threats, and practice using what you already carry (keys, hand sanitizer, or your handbag) as a weapon if needed. The goal here is to immobilize an aggressor and get away as fast as possible. To quote the brilliant Monty Python, "Run away!" Disengage. Swallow your pride. Any violent encounter can be deadly (people die in fistfights).

Trust your instincts. If something about a person or a situation feels off, remove yourself as quickly and calmly as possible. Stress levels may be running high during an emergency, making normally chill people act in surprising ways. Taking classes in self-defense or martial arts can give you practical skills to protect yourself or your loved ones in a physical confrontation should the circumstances go there, but your best first defense should always be avoidance. If a situation feels like it's getting out of control, involve other people or, preferably, a single person (the bystander effect has shown that you are more likely to be helped by an individual than a group). This may mean telling someone else about your unease or alerting someone in a leadership position. In a worst-case scenario, this may mean screaming for help. If the situation is something like a robbery attempt that is fraught from the start, keep in mind that very few things, aside from friends and family, are worth risking your life.

> "
>
> I've lived among some of the poorest people in the Western Hemisphere, and in places where petty theft was rampant, seldom did people resort to violence. In other cases, especially in areas with long histories of oppression

and hopelessness, people did turn violent. I lived in Honduras and El Salvador when street gangs were both powerful and vicious, and it's easy to see the connection between that behavior and the particular, long history that created it. But that's not how people normally react.

—Chris

”

Depending on what you look like, there may be other variables to consider. Some groups are discriminated against, stereotyped, and marginalized in everyday situations, and a catastrophe will not magically alleviate those problems. In some cases, it could make them worse. For example, Black communities in New Orleans had less access to resources and support both before and after Hurricane Katrina. The sad fact is that people who aren't willing to give you a fair break because of your race or ethnicity in "normal" times may not be any more inclined to give you a fair break in an emergency. You can't change that, but you can be cognizant of how those tendencies affect you and others. Be aware of the problem, and if you can, try to be part of the solution.

In terms of threats, don't forget about (nonhuman) animals, even in urban areas or places not known for wildlife. Obviously, if you're in Alaska or the mountains in California, you may worry about bears or mountain lions, but even in urban settings it's worth thinking about animals and your safety during a disaster. Any large animal, such as a cow, horse, or deer, can be very dangerous in some situations (there are reasons why animals come accessorized with horns and antlers). Any sharp part of an animal, from a deer to a sailfish, should be respected. We know bull horns can do serious damage, but so can deer antlers.

Most large animals you might encounter will ignore you or even flee, but in certain circumstances they can get physical, especially if they are protecting their offspring or if you startle or corner them. Sometimes they kick or bite if you happen to find yourself behind them and they're not sure what you're up to. Animals' muscles and bones are much denser than humans', so they are stronger and tougher. An animal half your size, even without dangerous teeth or other accoutrements, can hurt you, so keep your distance.

Animals will also be affected by some disaster scenarios—such as the mountain lions that lived in the areas engulfed by wildfires in Los Angeles in 2025. Some animals may have been forced out of their territory without access to food or water, or you may encounter domestic pets who've escaped their threatened homes without their people. Like us, roaming animals may be confused, scared, or hungry and may behave in unfamiliar ways.

The size of an animal rarely equates to how dangerous it might be. Following is advice on how to deal with the ones you are most likely to encounter.

- **Rodents.** Rats and other rodents could be a problem after certain kinds of disasters. Trying to trap or kill any large group of rodents might prove impossible, so focus on protecting your food from contamination by storing it in airtight containers. Keeping an area clean, trying to limit access, and exposing hiding places can make rodents look elsewhere. A rat can do real damage to small children and infants by chewing on toes, ears, and noses. If rodents are prevalent, keep small kids close (as you'll probably want to do after an emergency anyway).
- **Bats.** Unless you are in the bat cave or the proverbial belfry where they live, bats will steer clear of you. When you do see a bat in your house or in another area where you don't expect them, you need to pay attention. They may not simply be lost; they could be rabid. Do not touch or get near bats in those situations. Not that those of us brought up on tales of Dracula and Nosferatu are likely to do otherwise, but avoid any bat

you may come across, especially if it's in an unusual place or it seems to be lost. If you wake up and there's a bat in your room, you are probably fine (or possibly stoned), but it is best to assume you've been bitten and that it probably wasn't by a vampire, although these days who knows? Bat bites can be very difficult to detect. Even if you can't find the bite, seek treatment if you can to prevent the development of rabies.

- **Raccoons.** Not only can raccoons be rabid, but they're also incredibly strong. They can do real damage to a person and can kill most pets, even dogs. Sure, they looked charming and cute in the *Guardians of the Galaxy* movies, but in real life you should keep your distance. If they come near you, they will be after food, so remove that temptation. Keep food and food waste stored and your area clean.
- **Opossums** are largely harmless, so unless you sit on one or pester it, it shouldn't be a concern. Nevertheless, they could pose a threat to small animals and can kill chickens and eat their eggs, so keep that in mind.
- **Dogs.** Ah . . . man's best friend, which makes them of special concern as they're so common. Some dogs have been trained to be vicious, and most are territorial and protective of their people. Larger breeds can easily kill a person, but even the smallest pups can cause problems if they bite, as they could be carrying rabies and other infections.
    - In some areas now, and potentially in many more after a catastrophe, you may find packs of feral dogs, either the domesticated kind that no longer have homes or those who have lived this way for generations. These packs can be aggressive, and even if the danger in terms of serious bodily harm might be relatively low because they are small or weak, simply being bitten by a dog from a feral pack would be bad news.

   - If you find yourself near a dog or pack that seems aggressive, try to intimidate them with noise and movement and by making yourself as large as possible. If a dog attacks, fight back as if your life depends on it, because it might. Go for the nose and eyes, using whatever weapon you have or can improvise. Carrying pepper spray could break things up quickly.
- **Farm animals.** After some disasters, you might find farm animals wandering loose. Treat them as you would any other large animal and stay away. Animals that seem docile and slow can surprise you in situations when they may be scared or hurt.
- **Other wild animals.** For the most part, wild animals will steer clear of people. The exceptions would be animals that eat the trash we produce (rodents, raccoons, seagulls, bears) or those that prey on our domesticated animals and pets (raccoons, coyotes), and consequently often hang around where people are. So keep your food and trash contained to not attract unwanted attention. In general, though, the large predators are not what we will have to worry about. And except for polar bears, they won't bother you if you leave them alone. Remember, when you see baby animals, mama might not be too far away, and you do not want to get between the two, so it's best to steer clear when you can.

Protecting Yourself from Insects

The danger from insects is not limited to those with bad reputations, like killer bees, murder hornets, and bullet ants. The most prevalent danger is from ticks, mosquitoes, and fleas that can transmit diseases like plague, malaria, dengue, Lyme disease, West Nile virus, leishmaniasis, and Zika.

To protect yourself from insect bites:

- Appropriate clothing is your first defense. Wear long-sleeve shirts and long pants, even in hot weather (see page 95). This single measure might be the best way to minimize bites.
- Use insect repellent. DEET seems to work best, but anything is better than nothing. If you'd prefer not to use a chemical, there are natural insect repellents such as citronella, lavender, cinnamon oil, lemon eucalyptus, clove, and garlic. (See pages 50 and 51 for a full list of natural insect repellents.)
- Avoid being outside in buggy areas at dawn and dusk, when insects are most active.
- Smoke from a campfire can help drive insects away. Just be sure the fire is contained and remember that smoke poses its own hazards.
- Fleas will always be in proximity to animals. Avoid petting or holding unfamiliar animals to minimize your exposure. Remove fleas on pets using a fine-tooth or flea comb, then drown the fleas in soapy water so they don't escape. This will help minimize the chances that a flea-borne illness will be transmitted to you. Bathing your pet regularly with soap and/or using natural insect repellents can also help remove and kill fleas.
- Stay out of high grass and other overgrown areas that may expose you to ticks and regularly check your clothing and skin.

> "I have worked most of my life in the jungles of Central America. I have seen jaguar tracks on top of footprints I made only moments before, and I've been in a sinking dugout canoe in a river where I could see crocodiles. Those animals never bothered me. On the other hand, I have contracted malaria and dengue fever (several times). Jaguars kill a few people every year. Crocodiles kill around a thousand. Mosquitoes kill over a million every year. It's the insects we need to worry about.
>
> —Chris"

You've maximized your storage space, stocked up on water and food, beefed up your wilderness game, and learned some interesting new skills. Next up come the scenarios for which you've gotten ready. So take a deep breath and think positive thoughts. From hurricanes and nukes to droughts and civil unrest, this is what you've been preparing for.

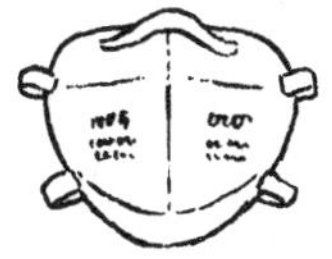

PART THREE

How to Handle Worst-Case Scenarios

Hoping for the best, prepared for the worst, and unsurprised by anything in between.

—MAYA ANGELOU, *I KNOW WHY THE CAGED BIRD SINGS*

Much like designer handbags and fancy ice cream, disasters come in many colors and flavors. To keep things simple, we have discussed them in alphabetical order so you don't get stuck thumbing through climate-related disasters when what you really want to know is how soon is too soon to flee a fascist dictatorship. First up are natural catastrophes (from droughts to wildfires) followed by the human-made ones, from civil unrest to nuclear events.

Keep in mind that preparedness is more akin to a *lifestyle choice,* like being vegetarian or taking a weekly Pilates class, than something you decide to do on the spur of the moment. In that spirit, pick one item a day, or even one a week—or, for something like keeping your vehicle well maintained or your devices fully charged, make it part of your routine. And while getting through an emergency always presents some challenges, we guarantee that it will be less stressful if you're prepared.

Regardless of the type of disaster that is likely to occur where you live, here are a few things you should do right now—and on the regular.

- **Enable emergency alerts** on your phone.
- **Keep your electronic devices fully (or mostly) charged.**
- **Keep a flashlight near your bed.**
- **Keep your vehicles well maintained** and filled with gas and/or make sure the battery is fully charged.
- **Know your evacuation zone,** which you can find through local government websites. Consult your local emergency management office if you rely on public transportation. Do this ahead of time. You don't want to try to locate this information after you've lost power and/or internet service.
- **Identify at least two different evacuation routes** (and have paper maps of the routes handy in case your mobile device doesn't work). Also have maps of nearby areas. Paper maps might be hard to find, but they won't run out of batteries.
- **Create an evacuation plan** that begins at your office, your kids' daycare, and anywhere else that's part of your regular routine, because emergencies tend to happen when we least expect them. Make sure your plan includes provisions for pets, kids, and anyone in your household with special needs.
- **Communicate your plan.** Make sure everyone in your household knows and understands what to do if you need to quickly evacuate, you cannot communicate with one another, and your main plan falls apart. Designate a meeting place outside the likely hazard area in case you get separated.
- **Know what your homeowner's insurance policy covers.**
- **Review your health insurance policies** to understand what they cover, including telemedicine options.
- **Document and store important files and keepsakes** in a safe lo-

cation. Take photographs of valuable property and store them with digital copies of important documents in a safe, off-site location.

- **Keep a packed, water-resistant go bag** for every member of your family (see page 89) and keep them easily accessible so you can grab them and go if necessary.
- **Write down important information** like phone numbers and addresses in case you can't access the contact list in your phone, because the days when people used to memorize phone numbers are long gone (and make sure you have an extra phone charger in your car or go bag).
- **Consider installing a security system** (and check reviews before purchasing) so that you can keep an eye on things if you have to evacuate.
- **Keep the batteries in your carbon monoxide detectors up to date.**
- **Know where the shutoff valves are** for your utilities, including power, water, and gas.
- **Keep your home's gutters and downspouts clear.**
- **Talk to friends or family** who reside in areas away from you about being able to stay with them in an emergency. Be prepared for them to possibly look at you like you're crazy for asking ("An emergency? What makes you think there will be an emergency?"). Humans are strange animals who prepare only for what they can see. Don't be put off if they think you're weird, or worse, a "doomer." (Remind them you're fun at parties.)
- **Practice makes perfect, people.** Drive the evacuation routes and identify shelter locations. Find the time to practice your plan with your family before the disaster finds you (yes, we know they probably won't want to, but try to make it fun).
- **Know where your local shelter is located.** In the event of a disaster, FEMA has traditionally supplied this info via text, phone, and the FEMA app, and has provided a large share of the funding for shelter

options, but if political efforts to drastically downsize FEMA or eliminate it entirely are successful, you may need to contact state and local social services, local emergency managers and fire departments, or nonprofits like the Red Cross or the Salvation Army. Discuss the latest Centers for Disease Control (CDC) guidance on the coronavirus (COVID-19) and/or other prevalent viruses and how they may affect your planning (but see page 123 about the potential need to consult the websites of independent scientific and medical institutions as well if federal agencies are being defunded or politically pressured). If you must evacuate to a public shelter, review the CDC's guidelines, and try to bring items that can help protect you and others from illness, such as hand sanitizer, cleaning materials, and two masks per person. Children under two years old and people who have trouble breathing *should not* wear masks.

10. Drought

Kind of like the loss of freedom, drought tends to creep up when one's attention is focused elsewhere. And while hurricanes and tornadoes can whip up far more drama, droughts have the distinction of being among both the costliest and the most far-reaching weather-related events.

In her Substack newsletter, *Radically Local,* Margi Prideaux, an author, wildlife advocate, and retired international environmental law negotiator, noted, "If you eat food grown by industrial agriculture, drought is already inside your life. You just don't see it yet. Dry ground does not grow crops. First, staples cost more. Then, as drought deepens, they vanish. The regions feeding you may already be starving of water. Some have already collapsed for this season. Others for this decade. Yet food keeps arriving, leaving you blind and complacent."

According to a study based on more than twenty years of NASA's Gravity Recovery and Climate Experiment (GRACE) satellite data, since 2002 the planet has been drying out much faster than ever before.

As droughts grow more extreme (and as new AI data centers, which are sprouting up like chanterelles, demand more water), farmers have increasingly had to turn to groundwater as a water source. This is unfortunate because around 2014 the NASA study also found that the pace of groundwater loss appeared to have accelerated and was growing by an area twice the size of California each year.

Historically, droughts have had huge impacts. One theory suggests that the collapse of the Classic Maya in the ninth century was largely the product of widespread drought that affected agricultural production. Drought may also have contributed to the decline of the Old Kingdom in Egypt around four thousand years ago. On a more recent and localized timeline, there have been at least three major U.S. droughts in the last hundred years. The first and second, the 1930s Dust Bowl and the 1950s drought, each lasted five to seven years and covered large areas of the country with significant impacts. The economic impacts of the third drought, the early twenty-first century drought from 1998 to 2014, are harder to calculate. And while they didn't quite bring down an empire, they weren't much fun for the people who had to live through them.

Although most of us probably assume a drought happens when an area doesn't get much rain (a.k.a. hydrological drought), that's only one common type.

There's also:

- Meteorological drought: When an area experiences dry weather patterns for a long period.
- Agricultural drought: When crops are affected by a lack of water.
- Socioeconomic drought: When a lack of water affects the supply and demand of economic goods.

Lack of precipitation (rain or snow that falls over a period of time) is only one indicator. Before a region is said to be experiencing a drought, other factors are also considered, such as the average temperature, the amount of water in the soil (soil moisture), the amount of water flowing in streams (streamflow), the level of water in the ground and in reservoirs, and the snowpack, or amount of snow on the ground. A study published in the June 2025 issue of *Nature* details how atmospheric evaporative demand has made droughts 40 percent more severe across the globe over the past forty years.

In November 2024, most of the United States, except for Alaska and Kentucky, was experiencing drought, the first time in recorded history when drought was so widespread. An article a month later in the *Bulletin of the Atomic Scientists* noted that "climate models paint an alarming picture of escalating drought risks in many parts of the world as temperatures rise. But as sophisticated as these numerical models are, they may actually be underestimating the true risks from prolonged dry spells in a warming world." Given the outcomes we're seeing already—increased wildfires, rising prices, ruined crops—this is pretty scary stuff.

Drought is felt in many ways. It could be devastating in areas where drinking water comes from flowing water, such as streams and rivers, whereas the same conditions could have much less impact in an area with lakes and reservoirs that would not dry up as quickly. Aside from being necessary for survival to most species, water is also required for growing—and transporting—food. Some droughts occur in seasons when no crops are being grown. But apart from seafood, food production almost always depends on rainfall, and that includes raising animals. At best, prices rise. In a worst-case scenario, food may not be available. Stop and read that line again. As impossible as it is for those of us used to opening fully stocked pantries and refrigerators to believe, *food may not be available.* Other impacts of long-term drought include water shortages, extreme fire danger, and ultimately malnutrition for both humans and animals, increased risk of infectious diseases, and psychosocial stress and mental health disorders.

Obviously, drought involves a lack of water, but its impacts go beyond that. The Los Angeles fires of 2025 have actually altered the composition of the soil in the burn area to a hydrophobic state, which means the soil no longer mixes with water, turning it hard, like concrete or asphalt. In subsequent rainstorms, the soil will be almost impervious to water, and rain rolls off previously burned areas in sheets, increasing debris flows and escalating the likelihood of flash-flooding.

Drought also affects animal behavior. As wildlife is forced to seek food and water farther from its usual territory, animals migrate into more populated areas, potentially into places they wouldn't normally inhabit. As resources dwindle, competition for food and water may increase between animals, including those of the human type—leading to more aggressive behavior all around.

Some droughts are completely natural, and others are influenced by activities like deforestation or human-caused climate change. Future drought will most certainly be made worse by AI data centers, whose water withdrawals compete *directly* with human drinking water, agriculture, and the ecological flows that keep rivers alive. According to a study by the University of California, Riverside, by 2027, AI data centers could consume 6.4 trillion liters of freshwater annually, enough to fill 2.8 million Olympic-sized swimming pools. Microsoft already draws 42 percent of its data-center water use from regions officially classified as "water-stressed." The Texas Water Development Board projected that data centers in the state will consume 49 billion gallons of water in 2025, and that's in the middle of a prolonged drought. That number is expected to rise to 399 billion gallons by 2030, nearly 6.6 percent of the state's total projected water use.

Minimizing the chance of drought involves years or decades of community-level action to avoid or correct the things that increase the likelihood of disrupting normal rainfall patterns. Obviously, none of that has happened.

If your region is susceptible to drought conditions, you probably already know a lot about saving water. But with weather patterns changing all over the world, drought is moving into areas where people aren't as familiar with the best practices. Here are some ways to prepare for a drought before, during, and after the fact. (Also refer to the prep list on pages 161–163.)

Before a Drought

- **Cut back on water use.** You won't be washing your car or watering the lawn in a drought, and you might need to limit things like bathing. Hygiene and cleanliness are critical to our physical and mental well-being, but most of us could take shorter or fewer showers and turn off the water when we soap up or brush our teeth.
- **Plant drought-tolerant plants;** ask for a list of native plants at your local garden center. And use mulch in your garden to reduce or substitute for watering.
- **Find and repair any leaks** in your home and yard. These might include drips from a faucet, a toilet that runs too long after flushing, or a broken sprinkler.
- **Invest in water-efficient appliances** such as low-flow showerheads and water-efficient toilets.
- **Store as much water as you can** for drinking and food preparation, and look for a source that might not dry up. A deep well would be ideal, or look for a larger creek, river, lake, or pond. This may mean a long walk or drive, as it does now for many people in areas with limited water. You will need containers that seal to transport. If we're on foot, five or six gallons of water is probably all most of us can carry, so use that figure to calculate how often you need to make that trip. (Also see chapter 4.)
- **Harvest any rainwater that does fall** for later nonpotable uses such as watering your lawn and plants or washing your car. The water gathered can be purified for drinking, but the juice

may not be worth the squeeze in terms of time and effort. For water purification tips, see page 67.

- **Prepare for no-water conditions.** While it is rare that water is turned off completely during drought conditions, this book is all about being prepared for "just in case." If you are in an urban area, you may have fewer alternatives to finding an additional water source, so plan them out in advance (see chapter 4). In a rural area, you could dig new wells. This is best done before a crisis, consulting a professional who knows how and where to dig (you can destroy an aquifer by perforating it the wrong way).
    - Sometimes, a hand-dug well may be an option. During or after a crisis, if the water table is high enough, old-school hand-dug wells can reach water. Unlike professionally drilled wells, these are limited to relatively shallow depths (maybe thirty feet deep). Even a shallow hand-dug well can be dangerous, as any hole over chest height can collapse and hurt or kill the person in it. This danger can be avoided by digging a well with sloped sides, rather than vertical. Sloping the sides by 45 degrees or so allows you to dig deeper holes, but that will require an enormous amount of digging. A ten-foot-deep hole with 45-degree sides would have a twenty-foot diameter at the surface.
- **Prepare for food shortages or increased prices.** Really severe droughts can cause famine, as in China in 1960 and Ethiopia in the 1980s. Since droughts are normally limited in the area they affect, in an ideal world, food from elsewhere would be brought in to help with the localized food shortage. In reality, factors related to politics, race, religion, or class can affect the speed and amount of relief offered to a stricken area. If you are caught in an area with little or no help, options can be bad

and limited. Stockpiling food might help, but this is a temporary solution. Gardening or growing your own food, via hydroponic or vertical farming, requires both preparation and equipment (see page 84).

During a Drought

- **Stay informed and follow any local restrictions** on water usage. Depending on the severity, these could include limits on overall water usage per household, designated days for watering lawns determined by your address, and financial penalties for noncritical use (such as washing a car) or overusage.
- **Conserve water.** Depending on the severity of the drought, this may mean not watering your lawn, not washing your car, taking shorter showers, and otherwise being more mindful about how you use water. For instance, reuse the water you cook with to sustain your indoor plants. Instead of running the tap while washing dishes, fill a bowl with soapy water and another with clean water and use those to wash and rinse. When you start to think about conserving water, you'll realize that we use so much unnecessarily that using less will not be as hard as you might think.
- **Prepare for hot weather.** Drought is often accompanied by extreme heat events (see chapter 12), so be ready for these possible occurrences too.
- **Prepare for wildfires.** Drought can also increase the risk of wildfires (see chapter 16), so be extra careful with outdoor activities, such as building campfires or driving off-road through dry grass, which can ignite from the exhaust.
- **Monitor your water bill** to find other areas where you can conserve.

After a Drought

- **Evaluate any damage** to your yard or garden and reseed or replant.
- **Consider planting drought-resistant vegetation** such as lavender, sedum, coneflower, catmint, rosemary, yarrow, and various succulents and ornamental grasses.
- **Continue your water conservation practices** even after the drought has passed, as this probably won't be the last drought, and saving water is a good daily practice.

As global warming increases, drought is becoming more common and lasting for longer periods with further-reaching consequences, so it behooves you to be ready.

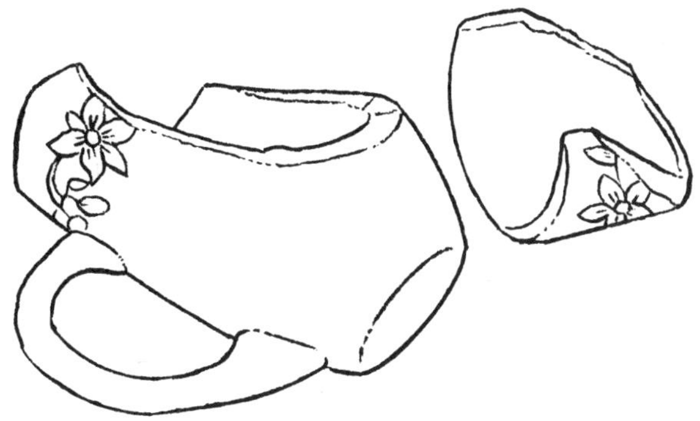

11. Earthquakes and Tsunamis

In terms of damage and loss of life, earthquakes are among the OGs of potential worst-case scenarios. In addition to the sudden release of pressure and tension that has been building in a fault—sometimes for decades—the secondary impacts of earthquakes, such as falling objects, downed power lines, gas leaks, landslides, and tsunamis, often go way beyond the damage of the actual quake.

For example, an earthquake in China in the fourteenth century killed more than 250,000 people by some estimates, leveled entire towns, and dramatically weakened the ruling power of the Mongol Empire. In 1692, an earthquake sank most of the city of Port Royal, Jamaica, at the time the most prosperous town in the Caribbean, which was subsequently largely abandoned. In 1755, a massive earthquake devastated Lisbon, Portugal, followed by a tsunami and a fire that consumed the ruined city. Around forty thousand people died, and the powerful Portuguese Empire never recovered. More recently, the Mexico City earthquake in

1985 changed the political landscape and, according to some, was the beginning of the end of more than fifty years of one-party rule. The 2004 Indian Ocean earthquake and tsunami changed building standards and tsunami warning systems.

These days, we have earthquake early warning systems that use sensors to detect seismic waves and send alerts before shaking arrives. Unfortunately, the early warning refers to seconds and not hours; still, sometimes that's enough to make a difference between surviving and not.

If your region is susceptible to earthquakes, you probably already know something about what to do when the earth starts shaking. The good news is that unlike climate change–driven emergencies, the frequency of earthquakes has stayed mostly stable. Here are some additional ways to prepare for an earthquake before, during, and after it happens. (Also refer to the prep list on pages 161–163.)

Before a Quake

- **Know what your homeowner's insurance policy covers.** While incredibly expensive, earthquake insurance is a specialized type of coverage designed to cover the cost of rebuilding your home and replacing personal belongings after damage caused by seismic activity. Standard homeowner's and renter's insurance policies typically do not cover earthquake-related damage, making earthquake insurance a consideration for individuals residing in areas prone to seismic events. If you are renting, be aware that renters can often face evictions after a disaster, so familiarize yourself with tenant rights in your state.
- **Research early warning systems.** Scientists can detect when conditions for an earthquake are more likely, but no model exists that can predict the time and place with any degree of accuracy. Still, some early warning systems and indicators can warn you a few seconds before strong shaking stars, and that can make all the difference.

- MyShake is an app managed by the U.S. Geological Survey, the system that powers earthquake early warnings in the western United States.
- Android Earthquake Alerts System uses networks of sensors to send alerts moments before strong shaking arrives.
- My Earthquake Alerts & Feed is an app that provides real-time alerts and information on earthquakes worldwide.
- Earthquake Network is an app used for global earthquake alerts and information.
- LastQuake is an app that provides alerts, news, and safety information.
- Your pets—and local wildlife in general—may become restless, agitated, and/or hide. The scientific reason for this is that they may be able to detect subtle ground vibrations and other environmental changes, such as the increased amount of charged particles in the atmosphere.
- Small tremors called foreshocks could occur.

- **Secure heavy furniture and objects,** including your water heater, which, according to Kathryn Schulz, in her *New Yorker* story "How to Stay Safe When the Big One Comes," is "basically a bomb in your basement: big heavy object, open flame, gas line." Bolt bookshelves to the wall and secure heavy wall hangings like mirrors and oversized pictures (which, by the way, you shouldn't hang over your bed).
- **Consider getting your home secured to its foundation.** This can be pricey but *is* cheaper than having to rebuild the whole house.

During a Quake

As soon as you feel the earthquake, do the following:

- Drop, cover, and hold on. This sounds like ineffective Cold War–era advice for a nuclear blast, but it's spot-on for an earthquake. When you first feel the earth start moving under your feet, drop down to the floor, cover your head and neck with your arms, and hold on to something sturdy until the shaking stops. If possible, get under or beside a sturdy, low piece of furniture that can provide protection from falling debris. Try to avoid being near heavy furniture, unsecured bookshelves, or anything hanging on a wall that could fall on you. Stay beside a wall (but away from windows) if nothing else is available. Do not try to crawl around to find a better spot. Do not run outside a building as falling exterior walls and facades can be dangerous. The old advice of trying to get in a doorway has changed as modern doorways are no longer constructed to be stronger than the rest of the structure, so getting low and under or beside something sturdy is your best bet.

- If you are outside when the quake hits, move away from buildings as fast as you safely can. Remember that cars on the street may not feel the quake as intensively as you do and could continue driving normally, so do not run out into traffic. Try to move away from anything over your head, including tree limbs and power lines. Slopes might give way and become landslides. If you are caught on a hillside, head for the top of the hill.
- If you're in a car, get out from under things like overpasses, trees, or power lines. Stop the car, stay in the vehicle, and get down low; this gives you the best chance of survival if something falls on your car and crushes the top. Remain in your car until the shaking stops.
- If you're near an ocean, start counting as soon as the shaking starts. If you get to twenty seconds and the ground is still shaking, that means the quake is likely a magnitude 7 or higher, so move as quickly as you can to higher ground when it's safe to do so because of the risk of a tsunami.

After a Quake

When the earthquake ends, the danger may not be over. Aftershocks, which are smaller than the main quake, can occur for days after the initial big event. These are hard to predict, but we can look at past patterns for some guidelines. Getting information from seismologists would be the best way to know what to expect in terms of aftershocks.

- **Be wary of anything that could fall on you or slide down a slope.** Buildings or other structures may have been weakened and can continue to collapse.
- **Watch out for downed power lines.** You can't tell by looking if there is electricity flowing through a wire. They don't always jump around and spark like you see on TV, so steer clear and assume any wire is live and can transmit dangerous amounts of electricity through the ground, water, or vegetation. If you are in a car and there are lines down around you, stay in place if you can and wait for help. Try to touch as little as you can of the car, including the doors and parts nearest to the outside of the vehicle. If your car is on fire or you must exit the vehicle, jump as far away as you can, with both feet in the air at the same time. Obviously, this is not a great option (or easy to do!), so use it only if you absolutely cannot stay in the car.
- **Beware of gas leaks.** Fires are very common after earthquakes, and broken gas lines are a major source of ignition. In the United States, many urban structures, including residential buildings, have gas lines, so do not try to light a cigarette post-quake to celebrate your survival. Newer construction and buildings in warmer climates might not have gas lines, but don't count on it. Note: Natural gas has no odor in its original state, but since 1937—after a leak at a school in Texas resulted in an explosion that killed nearly three hundred students and teachers—chemicals are added to make it smell like rotten eggs so leaks can be more easily detected.

- **If you are trapped in the rubble of a collapsed building, the most important thing to do is protect your airway.** If you can move, put cloth or a mask over your mouth and nose to minimize breathing in dust. Try to move and free your limbs. (Try to) stay calm and signal by tapping something or using a whistle (many backpacks have whistles on the chest straps, so being near one is not as unlikely as it sounds). Shouting can cause you to breathe in more dust, which is invariably toxic, so do that as a last resort. Wait for help. If you do try to extricate yourself, analyze the rubble you move and be aware of the possibility of further collapse.
- **If there is no tsunami risk (see page 179) and you are able, help the injured.** If you have first aid training (see page 22), use it. If not, simple things like covering injured people with blankets to keep them warm and putting pressure on bleeding wounds can help. Be sure to check children carefully for injuries, as well as people who might not be able to communicate effectively because of language issues, emotional shock, or neurodivergence.
- **Communicate with your friends and family and have them spread the word that you're okay.** Sometimes you can mark yourself "safe" from a particular disaster on social media. Understand that there may be circumstances in which you might *not* be able to communicate, and if so, try not to panic. It won't change anything. Do your part to help and try to be patient and calm even if you know people are worried about you or if you are worried about someone else.
- **Depending on the situation, you may want to evacuate the area after the earthquake** (if your residence is unsafe, for instance). See chapter 6. If you stay, be prepared to help. Listen for instructions on your radio or look for first responders or other trained personnel who can direct you. Remember, there are many ways to assist, and most of them are not heroic or

exciting. Going through lists of supplies, photocopying information, washing pots and pans, or unloading a trailer might be what is needed. Ask how you can help, and do what is asked, even if it seems mundane or boring.

Tsunamis

Tsunamis are large, long waves that result from earthquakes, landslides, volcanic eruptions, or other movement that is in proximity to the ocean. In the deep ocean, these waves may seem small, but as they approach the shore and shallower water, they can greatly increase their height, submerging and devastating coastal areas. They are dangerous only to those inside the inundation zone—roughly three miles inland in the area that's most likely to flood when an earthquake hits. On the North American Pacific coast the main source of tsunami risk is the Cascadia Subduction Zone, which extends seven hundred miles from Northern California to Northern Vancouver Island, Canada, while encompassing some of the most populated places along the coastline. Not all earth movement causes tsunamis, but strong earthquakes and volcanic activity both have the potential to form them.

Know in advance if your area is likely to be affected by a tsunami. Warning systems are in place in some areas, but if you feel a strong earthquake or other movement and are somewhere that could be affected (i.e., a coastal area), you should prepare to head for higher ground. Sometimes water retreats from the coastline as it is sucked into the oncoming wave. If the sea level suddenly drops, that's a warning that it could all come back as a tsunami.

Grab your go bag and leave on foot if possible since

roads and bridges might be damaged. If you can't find or get to higher ground, go to the top story of a sturdy building. If you can't find a building or if buildings are not safe, find something to climb (a tree, perhaps?) should water come.

A tsunami can come right away or hours to even days following the initial quake. You need information, so use your phone or the emergency radio in your go bag to hear or read updates.

If you are in an area that has suffered severe damage, get yourself out of immediate danger. Watch out for weakened structures, crumbling chimneys or walls, downed power lines, live wires, gas leaks, hazardous chemical spills, and other potential threats. You made it through the shaking part. You don't want to drown now.

12. Extreme Heat

Heat is the leading cause of weather deaths in the United States—ahead of hurricanes, floods, and tornadoes. There were 201,000 extreme heat events in the United States between 2019 and 2023—a fourfold increase from thirty years prior. The year 2024 featured the hottest summer on record in the Northern Hemisphere, 2.74 degrees above average. In fact, 2024 was the hottest year on earth out of the last 125,000 of them. Part of the reason for these staggering numbers is the occurrence of heat domes, stagnant high-pressure systems that trap hot air over a region like a cap on a carbonated wine cooler, creating prolonged periods of extremely hot and often humid weather. Both their occurrence and intensity have almost tripled since the 1950s because of the impacts of climate change. In fact, a paper published in *Nature* by Yann Quilcaille et al. in September 2025 shows that "climate change made 213 historical heatwaves reported over 2000–2023 more likely and more intense, to which each of the

180 carbon majors (fossil fuel and cement producers) substantially contributed." Despite that, oil companies continue with business as usual and the U.S. government and its federal disaster programs do not classify extreme heat as a catastrophe, which kind of sucks for a number of reasons.

This is how your body responds to extreme heat:

- Your heart must work harder to pump blood to just below the surface of your skin, where it can get cooler.
- Your kidneys work harder to conserve your body's water; when your temperature gets too high, it will ultimately cause proteins to break down and your enzymes to stop regulating your organs' function, which will lead to them shutting down.
- Heat stroke happens when your body cooks to the point of multiorgan failure.
- A recent study led by the University of Bristol states that long-term heat exposure can disrupt sleep.
- Last but not least, heat can alter our brain function, making us more violent, grumpy, and depressed, which may or may not have to do with the fact that smartphones will also overheat in triple-digit temperatures. And excessive heat combined with no access to TikTok can often lead to a volatile situation.

Just in time for some U.S. locations' increasingly endless and brutal summers, there's a new handy-dandy forecasting tool called HeatRisk. Created by the Centers for Disease Control and Prevention (CDC) and the National Oceanic and Atmospheric Administration (NOAA), HeatRisk combines public health data and weather forecasts to create a map of heat levels across the country, ranking them on a scale of 0 to 4 based on how dangerous they are. The metric integrates local weather, time of year, the forecast daily high and low temperatures, and the expected duration of heat. Each HeatRisk level corresponds to a color: The lowest level, green, indicates "little to no risk," while magenta signals the "highest" risk. There currently isn't a designation for "It's so hot you're screwed."

But it's not just the heat that can kill you. A measurement of the combination of heat and humidity called "wet-bulb temperature" reflects not only heat but also how much water is in the air. The higher the number, the harder it is for sweat to evaporate and bodies to cool down. The wet-bulb temp that marks the upper limit of what the human body can handle is 95 degrees Fahrenheit (35 Celsius). But any temperature above 86 degrees Fahrenheit (30 Celsius) can be deadly. To get to those wet-bulb temperatures requires only temperatures in the high eighties to mid-nineties with humidity in the 70 percent range. At temperatures of 100 degrees, any humidity over 50 percent can create dangerous conditions.

When your body gets too hot, you may experience a heat-related illness such as heat exhaustion or heat stroke. Such illnesses can be fatal. But heat exhaustion and heat stroke are preventable if you know what to look for.

The symptoms of heat exhaustion include:

- Cold and clammy skin
- Dizziness/fainting
- Excessive fatigue
- Headache
- Muscle cramps
- Nausea and/or vomiting
- Excessive sweating and thirst
- Weak rapid pulse

Treating heat exhaustion is as simple as:

- Moving out of the sun to a cooler location
- Removing or loosening your clothes
- Cooling yourself with a wet cloth or a cool bath or shower
- Drinking some water

Ignoring the symptoms of heat exhaustion could lead to heat stroke, also known as hyperthermia. The symptoms of heat stroke include:

- Body temperature of 104 degrees Fahrenheit or more (40 degrees Celsius)
- Confusion
- Dizziness/fainting
- A fast pulse rate
- Skin that is hot to the touch and red, dry, or damp
- Upset stomach, nausea, or vomiting

Heat stroke is a medical emergency, so call 911 immediately. In the meantime, move the person to a cooler location (if possible, out of the sun) and cool with a wet cloth, shower, or bath (just be careful not to drop them and/or to cause further injury). Do not force them to drink water or other fluids.

Extreme Heat and Kids

According to the United Nations, five hundred million kids will experience twice the number of extremely hot days as their grandparents' generation, with harmful consequences for their health. The fact is that extreme heat is harder on kids.

Children have a higher risk of heat stroke and illness than adults because their body temps rise three to five times faster. Extreme heat can disrupt sleep, affect mood, and hinder learning. Children are also more likely to ignore or miss symptoms of heat stress if they're busy outside playing, which can make the problem worse. Never leave a child in a vehicle unattended (this is a rule year-round but especially when it's hot).

Signs of heat-related illness in kids include nausea, weakness, cramps, headaches, and/or dizziness. Babies don't sweat the way older kids do; they may have flushed cheeks and feel warm and clammy.

If your region is susceptible to extreme heat, you probably already know something about how to stay cool. But with weather patterns changing all over the world, hotter temperatures are happening in areas where people aren't as familiar with the best practices. Here are some additional ways to prepare for extreme heat before, during, and after it happens. (Also refer to the prep list on pages 161–163.)

Before the Heat

- **Keep an eye on weather forecasts** so you know if and when an extreme heat event might be happening in your area. Enable alerts from the National Weather Service on your mobile phone; download an app from Accuweather, The Weather Channel, or the American Red Cross; and sign up for emails or text notifications from HEAT.gov and/or monitoring via a NOAA Weather Radio.
- **If you don't have AC, find a local cooling center** and be sure you have a way to get there. If your area doesn't have one, arrange to visit a friend or family member who has AC during the hottest parts of the day. If that's not possible, find out if your local mall or gym is air-conditioned. Make sure you have a place to go and cool down when it gets really hot (the National Weather Service records dating back to 1996 show that among heat deaths where a location is known, 62 percent of people *died indoors*).

- **If you do have AC,** make sure it's working. And if you have an alternate electricity source, a backup AC window unit can keep you cool while using less power than central AC.
- **Install double-pane windows** for energy efficiency.

During the Heat

Think you can just hit the beach and cool off? Not so fast. Proximity to water during times of extreme heat could make things worse because warming temps cause water to evaporate, adding humidity to the air (see page 183). Humid air traps more heat than dry air, and with moister air, your body's cooling mechanism, sweat, is less effective. These are some of the best ways to maintain a safe temperature.

- **Stay hydrated.** Water is usually sufficient, but you might need drinks containing electrolytes if you have lost a lot through sweat from intense physical activity, or from diarrhea or vomiting. Skip caffeinated and alcoholic beverages; they are diuretics and do not hydrate as well as nondiuretics. But depending on the water content, they are better than nothing. Fun fact: A drink made from crushed or chunked ice—be it a slushy or a milkshake—can drop your internal body temperature by about 1 degree Fahrenheit within twenty minutes.
- **Stay indoors with the air-conditioning turned on.** If you don't have AC, open the windows and use fans to get a cross breeze going (but close the window shades and curtains to keep out the sunlight). However, don't use fans when it's hotter than 90 degrees Fahrenheit (per the Centers for Disease Control) or 104 degrees Fahrenheit (per the World Health Organization). Keep interior doors open to allow for airflow throughout your home. Sleep where it's coolest, even if it's on the floor or in the basement.
- **If you need to be outside for work, try to avoid doing so during the hottest midday temperatures if possible.** According to

the Occupational Safety and Health Administration, almost half of all heat-related deaths for those who work outdoors occur *on the first day on the job,* and more than 70 percent occur within the first week. The lesson? Try to acclimate yourself to the heat slowly by gradually increasing your exposure. OSHA recommends that new workers work shorter workdays in the heat, starting with 20 percent of a workday's normal duration (e.g., no more than one hour and forty minutes if the usual workday lasts eight hours) and then adding 20 percent more for each subsequent day until the full workday time is reached (at the end of one workweek); individuals who are less fit or have medical problems may need a more gradual acclimatization of up to two weeks.

- **Dress accordingly.** Wear a wide-brimmed hat and loose-fitting clothes that don't chafe or itch. Clothing made from linen will provide good airflow and absorb moisture, while cotton may be softer on the skin but will soak up sweat. Light-colored clothes reflect light and are cooler than dark colors, especially black, which absorbs more heat. You could even don a cooling vest, which can hold multiple ice packs.
- **Take a *cool* shower** (a cold shower will make your heart race) and leave your skin and hair damp. Or put damp washcloths on your forehead, hands, and feet.
- **Stay wet when possible,** be it via a pool, a shower, or a water hose.
- **If you must go outside, stay in the shade** as much as possible.
- **A fan is better than nothing** if you don't have or can't afford AC (see the previous page for when not to use fans).
- **Be sure to check on your neighbors, friends, and/or family members.** Young and old people are more susceptible to heat-related distress, and some illnesses might exacerbate the problem.

Don't Forget the Sunscreen

While the glow of a suntan has been fashionable since Coco Chanel popularized it in 1923, tanning—and, to a much greater degree, sunburn—damages the DNA in your skin cells, leading over time not only to premature aging and (gasp!) wrinkles but also potentially to skin cancer (which, no surprise, has skyrocketed in recent years). Sunscreen protects you by preventing two of the sun's three types of UV rays, UVA and UVB, from penetrating the skin.

According to current statistics:

- One in five Americans will develop skin cancer by the age of seventy. And more than two people die of skin cancer in the United States every hour.
- Skin cancer is the most common cancer in America, and 6.1 million adults are treated each year for basal cell and squamous cell carcinomas, according to the CDC.
- On average, having had five or more sunburns in your lifetime doubles your risk for melanoma, one of the most common types of skin cancer and the fifth most common cancer in the United States (when detected early, the five-year survival rate for melanoma is 99 percent).

So, look for sunscreen with at least SPF 30 protection *and* broad-spectrum coverage that will provide protection against sunburn, UV damage, and DNA damage—and reapply often. Additionally, when the sun is at its strongest (which will vary depending on where you live and the time of year), seek shade, wear a hat, and cover up with clothing.

13. Extreme Rain, Flooding, and Landslides

Climate change has set the stage for more extreme rain events over recent history. Warmer air, capable of holding more moisture, results in intense, short-term rain episodes lasting a day or less. Intense rainfall like this causes flooding and, in some areas, landslides. According to FEMA and NOAA, flooding is the deadliest, costliest, and most widely experienced natural hazard in the United States, and is more severe due to climate change. As hurricanes fueled by warmer waters and a wetter atmosphere dump more rain, inland flooding has accounted for more than half of all deaths from landfalling U.S. hurricanes since 2013. But as we learned in 2024, hurricanes are not just a coastal problem. The rain that accompanied Hurricane Helene severely affected millions of people hundreds of miles from where it made landfall.

A study by Oliver Wing et al. reported in *Nature Climate Change* in 2022 shows a "locked-in" 26.4 percent increase in U.S. flood risk by

2050 *due to climate change alone,* meaning that even if dramatic decarbonization had been undertaken yesterday, we'd still be underwater (pun intended). That isn't great news, especially in light of new research by the Union of Concerned Scientists showing that almost 1,100 critical infrastructure assets (you know—bridges, tunnels, and roads) that sustain coastal communities will be at risk of *monthly* flooding by 2050.

Forty percent of the U.S. population lives near a coast, and increasingly, they skew older. Between 1970 and 2022, the number of people aged sixty-five and over living in counties along the country's East, West, Gulf, and Great Lakes coasts rose 159 percent. Meanwhile, the sea level during this time frame has risen—to the tune of five to eight inches, and more along the East and Gulf Coasts—so when hurricanes or atmospheric rivers hit these areas, they are causing more destructive storm surges. Even minor flooding can prevent access to food, medicine, or emergency care; shut off power, heat, or air-conditioning; or drain savings. So the next time you visit Grammy and Pop Pop on the beach, the best thing you can do for them is to make sure they are as ready for disruption as they are for early-bird dinners.

If your region is susceptible to extreme rain, flooding, or mudslides, you probably already know something about what to do when a storm hits. But with weather patterns changing all over the world, these events are happening in areas where people aren't as familiar with the best practices. Also, flash floods and mudslides can occur within minutes of heavy rainfall, so you are potentially dealing with multiple issues during these types of storms. Here are some additional ways to prepare for these events before, during, and after they happen. (Also refer to the prep list on pages 161–163.)

Before a Storm

- **Know the differences between a flood "watch" and a "warning."** According to the National Weather Service, a flood watch means conditions are favorable for flooding, but flooding is not currently happening. A flood warning means flooding is either happening or is about to happen, and immediate action is necessary.

- **Assess your level of risk.** Search for your address in FEMA's flood map to see how high the risk for flooding is in your area. However, do not be lulled into a false sense of security simply because you live in an area with low or moderate risk. Even in these lower-risk areas, *your home is still five times more likely to experience a flood than a fire during the next thirty years.*
- **Know your evacuation zone,** which is determined by elevation levels and your home's distance to water. You can find your zone and your evacuation route through local government websites. Consult your local emergency management office if you rely on public transportation. Do this ahead of time. You don't want to try to locate this information after you've lost power and/or internet service.
- **Work with a professional to take further actions to safeguard your home:** Elevate or anchor critical appliances like your furnace and water heater; build barriers like a levee or floodwall; waterproof your basement; install a flood alarm; maintain a battery-operated sump pump; and/or install flap or check valves to temporarily block drainpipes.
- **Know what your homeowner's insurance policy covers.** Almost 30 percent of the U.S. population lives in coastal zones, and yet nationwide only one in twenty-five homeowners has flood insurance (because, yes, it's very expensive). In some states, you may have access to government-sponsored flood insurance, like the National Flood Insurance Program (which still existed at the time of writing). Waiting until the last minute to get flood insurance doesn't work: It typically takes about thirty days to enter into effect, although there are some exceptions to this waiting period. If you are renting, familiarize

yourself with tenant rights in your state—renters can often face evictions after a disaster.

- **Keep gutters and downspouts clear,** and trim weak or dead tree branches from your yard as part of your routine home maintenance.
- **Learn to recognize the signs of natural disasters that could occur locally.** For example, a landslide may be preceded by loud sounds of trees or boulders cracking against each other as they flow downhill. Seeing suddenly muddy water in a stream that was previously flowing clear may be a sign of flash flooding.
- **When a storm is imminent, use sandbags** to divert water away from the foundation of your home.
- **Bring in outdoor furniture and secure heavy objects** like grills and propane tanks.
- **Listen to NOAA Weather Radio or local news and weather stations** for important news and storm updates, as well as instructions about possible evacuations. If your zone is advised to evacuate, grab your family and your go bags and leave (see chapter 6).

How to Prepare for Landslides

Landslides, also known as mudslides or debris flows, are caused by excessive rain and flooding and are most likely to occur in areas with steep slopes, especially if the vegetation is gone from logging or wildfires (see page 222). Environments with loose soil, like hillside and mountains or sandy or gravelly areas, are more prone to landslides because soil particles can easily detach and flow. Debris, including rocks and vegetation, can also be carried along in the mudslide. What to do?

- If possible, clear a path to deflect possible debris flows.

Trying to dam or stop a flow is never a good idea. Work with your neighbors and avoid deflecting the debris in ways that will make it worse for them.

- Board up windows and doors before an imminent storm. This won't stop a powerful landslide but will strengthen the structure and keep some debris out if the slide is small.
- The root systems of plants help hold soil in place and can provide a buffer to water or debris flowing downhill. Make sure the plants near your house can survive the heavy rains or wildfires that might precede landslides.
- Inspect slopes for increases in cracks, holes, and other changes.
- Consult with a soil engineer or an engineering geologist to minimize the potential impacts of landslides.

During a Storm

If you are inside your home:

- Fill containers with water for drinking and fill the bathtub with water for washing in case there's damage to public water systems.
- Elevate any items on the floor, including furniture, to prevent damage in case of flooding.
- Get to higher ground inside your home; that could mean the roof or the highest room (but avoid attics where you could get trapped). If water is rising and there is higher ground nearby, just a few feet could make a difference; go there.
- If water threatens to break your home loose from its foundation and sweep it downstream, get out and get to higher ground if possible. It would be better to be out in the storm than in a building swept away by floodwaters. You will not

survive a house being crushed around you as it hits trees, a bridge, or other buildings.

If you are outside your home or on the road:

- Do not walk through fast-moving water. Anything above your ankles can knock you down and sweep you away. Fast water to your knees is even harder to negotiate. Also, you don't know what is in that water or where it has been. Floodwaters are usually contaminated with sewage and other nastiness, and exposure could make you sick.
- Have you heard the phrase "Turn Around Don't Drown"? It's popular—and a campaign of the National Weather Service—for good reason. Do not drive into a flooded area. Even in daylight it is hard to tell how deep the water is, how fast it's moving, or what kind of debris it may contain. And even if you know the road, you don't know what condition it may be in under the water—you could be driving into a hole where the road used to be.
- Stay away from downed power lines; if they have fallen into the water, they could electrocute you.
- Like people, critters—including snakes, fire ants, rodents, raccoons, and bats—look for safe ground during a storm. Try to avoid them.

What to Do If Your Car Gets Trapped in Floodwater

- Take a beat to collect yourself and try to stay calm. This will help everything else go smoother and faster. Call 911 as soon as you are able, but understand there may be a delayed response; you will likely need help getting to safety once you're out of your car.

- Undo seatbelts quickly. Cut them if you must. Having an emergency tool kit (see page 105) where you can reach it is a good idea, just in case.
- Open windows as soon as possible (and before water has reached halfway up). They won't keep the water out for long, and you need them open to make your escape. Even electric windows (which almost all cars now have) will work for a minute when submerged.
- If you can't open the windows, try to break the glass, but be aware that some windows in newer cars may be laminated and thus functionally impossible to break. "Tempered" glass can be broken with a glass-breaker. If you have laminated side windows and cannot lower them, you will have to open the door, which will make the car fill up with water faster. This will be nearly impossible until the water pressure equalizes as your car fills up while it sinks. This is dangerous, obviously, as you might have to wait until your car is nearly full of water to open the doors and escape.
- Help kids and the elderly out of the car first. If it's not safe to cross the floodwaters, crawl on top of the car and wait for help.

After a Storm

- **If you have first aid training (see page 22), use it.** If not, simple things like covering injured people with blankets to keep them warm and putting pressure on bleeding wounds can help. Be sure to check children carefully for injuries, as well as people who might not be able to communicate effectively because of language issues, emotional shock, or neurodivergence.
- **Communicate with your friends and family** and have them

spread the word that you're okay. Sometimes you can mark yourself "safe" from a particular disaster on social media. Understand that there may be circumstances in which you might *not* be able to communicate, and if so, try not to panic. It won't change anything. Do your part to help and try to be patient and calm, even if you know people are worried about you or if you are worried about someone else.

- **Listen to first responders when they show up,** and do what they ask if you're able (Note: Sometimes the best way to help is to stay out of the way).
- **Call your insurance provider** as soon as possible to report damage and find out about the process of filing a claim.
- **If you are renting, call your landlord.** Renters can often face evictions after a disaster, so familiarize yourself with tenant rights in your state.
- **Wait until you get the "all clear" from local officials before returning to your home or the affected area,** and don't enter a damaged building (even if it's your house) until the authorities tell you it's safe. If local officials have deemed it safe to go into your home, look for structural damage and/or foundation cracks. Sniff for gas. Use extreme caution if you notice sagging ceilings or floors and/or damaged stairs.
- **Check for loose power lines** around your home, and if you see one, don't go any farther. Leave the property and report it to your local utility.
- **If the building shifts or makes strange noises, get out immediately** and consult authorities or first responders so the building can be checked to see if it poses a hazard.
- **When the weather clears, open windows** to improve ventilation and help your home air out.
- **Avoid floodwater.** Moving water is dangerous and will almost certainly be infected with sewage and other awful stuff that you don't want to be wading around in. Don't stand in floodwater if

you can help it, and most definitely don't stand in it when turning your electricity on or off; leave the house and contact an electrician, who will shut off the power at the utility's meter.

- **Start cleaning up.** After the water has receded, little bits of residual standing water can be removed using a wet vac. If you don't have electricity, use a generator to power a wet vac, but be sure to place the generator at least twenty feet away from your house as carbon monoxide may build up (which is bad) and can kill you (which is worse) if you use a gas-powered engine indoors.
- **Before restarting your HVAC and electrical systems,** consult with a professional to make sure there aren't damaged wires or mold growing in them. Even without the presence of standing water, the motors in some of your appliances, such as refrigerators or washing machines, may have been damaged. Consult with a specialist before turning them back on.
- **Immediately discard anything that may pose a health risk from mold or contamination,** including food, clothes, rugs, and other belongings. For insurance purposes, you will need to take pictures of some items first, including serial numbers on major appliances. Discard damaged items appropriately. Unfortunately, there is almost nothing you can do to save water-damaged upholstered furniture, electronics, and appliances. When disposing of damaged items, separate home goods from organic matter such as tree limbs and spoiled food, so they can be thrown away according to your city's municipal waste disposal guidelines.
- **Make whatever temporary repairs you can before insurance repairs can kick in.** For example, you may need to patch holes or brace walls.
- **Seal off any gaps caused by storm damage** until permanent repairs can be made. Use plywood boards or plastic tarps to seal broken windows or other small siding or roof gaps.

- **Watch out for insect-borne viruses.** Disease-carrying mosquitoes and midges (any small flies, also known as no-see-ums) love warm weather and standing water. To protect yourself after a flood, limit outdoor activity during peak periods, inspect existing window and door screens for holes, and install window and door screens where necessary.
- **Take pictures** (both closeups and wide shots) of any damage to the interior and exterior of the home as you will need them for filing insurance claims (and hopefully you are insured).
- **Be wary of anyone who shows up at your door after a disaster claiming to represent FEMA or another agency.** FEMA will never ask you for money. The safest way to apply for aid is through FEMA's Disaster Assistance Improvement Program's website at disasterassistance.gov, assuming that FEMA is still in operation.
- **Be wary of contractors and/or construction workers who show up immediately following a disaster offering to help you rebuild.** Many cities require permits for rebuilding work, and it is common for scammers to pose as contractors.
- **Don't drink the tap water** until you receive notification from city officials that it is safe, as it may have become polluted during the storm or subsequent flooding.

Dealing with Mold

If there has been standing water in your home for twenty-four hours or more, assume mold is growing. Exposure to mold can lead to asthma attacks, eye and skin irritation, and allergic reactions, as well as severe infections for those with weakened immune systems, and its remediation should therefore be left to a pro. But if you're the do-it-yourself type, make sure you have a hard hat, goggles, waterproof boots and gloves, and an N95 mask before you begin cleaning (a respirator is also recommended), and follow the steps below.

1. Put on the personal protective equipment described above.
2. Open all doors and windows when you are working and leave as many open as is safe when you leave. Open doors to closets and interior rooms to increase airflow. Open kitchen cabinets and bathroom vanities; remove, clean, and stack drawers to dry. If you have an attic, open it, too, to let air flow.
3. Once electricity is safe to use, turn on fans and dehumidifiers to remove moisture (Note: Do not use fans if mold has already started to grow, because fans may spread the mold spores).
4. Remove standing water and wet materials. Use a wet vac to remove water from floors, carpets, and hard surfaces within twenty-four to forty-eight hours if possible. Throw away any items that cannot be cleaned and dried within this time frame to prevent further development and spread of mold.
5. Clean, disinfect, and thoroughly dry everything salvageable that the floodwater has encountered (cabinetry, wood and metal furniture, countertops and dishes). Use products specifically designed to clean each item.
6. Remove all visible mold with water and detergent and let the area dry. Note: Painting or caulking over mold will not prevent it from growing.

14. Hurricanes and Tornadoes

Tropical cyclones are large, powerful, long-lasting rotating storms that form over warm ocean waters, and hurricanes are a geographical subset of these that form specifically in the Atlantic or the northeastern Pacific Ocean. Tornadoes, sometimes called twisters, are also powerful rotating storms, but they are smaller and shorter-lived, form over land, and often come paired with severe thunderstorms.

Hurricanes

Two hundred and thirty-four people died because of 2024's Hurricane Helene. And a 2024 study in *Nature* by Rachel Young and Solomon Hsiang found that the mortality burden caused by tropical cyclones that hit the United States between 1930 and 2015 was far greater than the average of twenty-four immediate deaths reported per storm. In fact, they estimated that the average tropical cyclone indirectly caused between seven thousand and eleven thousand excess deaths *each,* as the displacement of households and the destruction of social networks ate away at public health. Cost-wise, a preliminary estimate by AccuWeather put the direct damage and ripple economic impacts of Hurricane Helene alone at between $225 and $250 billion. Meanwhile, in the North Atlantic, hurricane activity has increased, and there's a trend toward more intense storms, to the point that there's been talk of bumping up the Saffir-Simpson Hurricane Wind Scale from a maximum of category 5 to category 6. Record-breaking warming ocean temperatures are expected to fuel more major hurricanes, which are more likely to undergo rapid intensification and inflict more rainfall than usual. While climate change is producing more and bigger hurricanes, cuts to NOAA make forecasting more difficult.

If your region is susceptible to hurricanes, you probably already know something about what to do when the storm hits. But with weather patterns changing all over the world, hurricanes are affecting areas, including far inland, where people aren't as familiar with the best practices. Here are some additional ways to prepare for a hurricane before, during, and after it happens. (Also refer to the prep list on pages 161–163.)

Before a Hurricane

- **Learn the differences between a "watch" and a "warning."** A hurricane watch means that hurricane conditions (sustained winds of seventy-four mph or higher) are possible within the specified area, generally within forty-eight hours. A hurricane warning means hurricane conditions are expected in the specified area, generally within thirty-six hours.
- **Enable emergency alerts on your phone and know your evacuation zone,** which is determined by elevation levels and your home's distance to water. You can find your zone and your evacuation route through local government websites. Consult your local emergency management office if you rely on public

transportation. Do this ahead of time. You don't want to try to locate this information after you've lost power and/or internet service.

- **Know what your homeowner's insurance policy covers;** almost 30 percent of the U.S. population lives in coastal zones, yet nationwide only one in ten homeowners has flood insurance. In some states, you may have access to government-sponsored flood insurance, like FEMA's National Flood Insurance Program (which still existed at the time of writing). If you are renting, be aware that renters can often face evictions after a disaster, so familiarize yourself with tenant rights in your state.
- **Keep a packed, water-resistant go bag** (or line a non-water-resistant bag with a plastic garbage bag) for every member of your family (see page 89 on how to pack your go bags) and keep them easily accessible so you can grab them and go if necessary.
- **Charge your electronic devices,** and fill up your vehicles with gas and/or make sure the battery is fully charged.
- **Keep the batteries in your carbon monoxide detectors up to date.**
- **Know where the shutoff valves are** for your utilities, including power, water, and gas.
- **Make sure you have adequate storm shutters** or plywood to protect your windows and doors.
- **Bring in outdoor furniture, and secure heavy objects** like grills and propane tanks.
- **Keep gutters and downspouts clear** and trim weak or dead tree branches from your yard as part of your regular home maintenance.
- **If you live in a low-lying coastal home, consider raising it up on stilts.** This is a major effort, but it could ultimately save you

much more money than you invested. Stilts won't protect your house from the wind, but most damage and loss of life from these types of storms are caused by flooding.

During a Hurricane

The power of nature is a wonder to behold and if you are the adventurous type (and/or you don't have the means to go elsewhere), you may choose to ride the storm out at home. If you do stay, you'd better fully accept (no take-backs) that should you end up needing help when it gets bad no one may be available to help you. You may also be putting rescuers at risk and using resources that might have been used elsewhere. Beware of the storm surge, which happens when those hurricane-force winds push water inland for miles and cause an abnormal rise in seawater levels, sometimes in a matter of minutes. Drowning from a storm surge is one of the leading causes of death during a hurricane. During Hurricane Katrina, a twenty-eight-foot storm surge obliterated entire towns on the Mississippi Gulf Coast, killing 238 people.

Be sure you have enough food and water to last at least a full week, and a generator should you lose power. If you live in an evacuation zone or an area prone to flooding (or *not* prone to flooding; see 2024's Hurricane Helene and what happened in Asheville, North Carolina, for reference), consider leaving *before* the storm (when there may be less traffic) or evacuate when instructed.

If you are inside your home:

- Close all windows and doors and turn off the air-conditioning and/or heat.
- If instructed by authorities, turn off water, gas, and electricity.
- Fill containers with water for drinking and bathtubs for washing in case there's damage to public water systems.
- Elevate any items on the floor, including furniture, to prevent water damage in case of flooding.

- Take cover. The safest place to be in your house or apartment building—at least if there's no flooding—is a windowless room closest to the ground in the most interior area. Go there. Exterior walls will likely offer little protection from debris flying at more than one hundred miles per hour. The more walls between you and the outside the better. Close the doors and get under something sturdy, like a worktable, or in an empty bathtub, and protect yourself from flying debris with a heavy blanket or mattress. Avoid buildings with roofs that span great distances, like a school gymnasium or a big box store.
- If your home begins to flood, move to the roof or the highest room (but avoid closed attics where you could get trapped).
- Monitor local news outlets and/or the National Hurricane Center website for updates (www.nhc.noaa.gov); we know from past hurricanes that storms can escalate quickly.

If you are outside or on the road:

- First off, you *should not be driving in a hurricane.* But if for some reason you missed the weather report and were caught unawares, seek shelter in a building or parking garage that's safe from flooding and high winds. Do not get under a highway overpass; these narrow spaces can increase wind speeds dramatically, putting you at much greater risk of injury or death from flying debris.
- If you can't leave your vehicle, close your windows and sunroof and turn on your headlights and hazard lights. Get down on the floor, as low as possible, in case debris comes through the windows.
- If your car is caught in floodwater (see page 194)—which can be deeper than it looks and very fast-moving—try to seek higher ground.

After a Hurricane

Of course, the most important thing with any disaster is that your friends, family, and community make it through without loss of life. But after that come financial concerns. Did you know that according to the National Flood Insurance Program, just one inch of water can cause up to $25,000 worth of damage to an average home? And that denying legitimate claims has become a part of the insurance industry's business model?

- **Wait until you get the "all clear" from local officials before returning to your home or the affected area,** and don't enter a damaged building (even if it's your house) until the authorities tell you it's safe. If you're in your car, remain there for at least thirty minutes after the last clap of thunder.
- **If you have first aid training (see page 22), use it.** If not, simple things like covering injured people with blankets to keep them warm and putting pressure on bleeding wounds can help. Be sure to check children carefully for injuries, as well as people who might not be able to communicate effectively because of language issues, emotional shock, or neurodivergence.
- **Communicate with your friends and family** and have them spread the word that you're okay. Sometimes you can mark yourself "safe" from a particular disaster on social media. Understand that there may be circumstances in which you might *not* be able to communicate, and if so, try not to panic. It won't change anything. Do your part to help and try to be patient and calm, even if you know people are worried about you or if you are worried about someone else.
- **Listen to first responders when they show up,** and do what they ask if you're able (Note: Sometimes the best way to help is to stay out of the way).

- **Contact your insurance provider** as soon as possible to report damage and find out about the process of filing a claim. If you are renting, call your landlord. Renters can often face evictions after a disaster, so familiarize yourself with tenant rights in your state.
- **If local officials have deemed it safe to go into your home,** look for structural damage and/or foundation cracks. Sniff for gas. Use extreme caution if you notice sagging ceilings or floors and/or damaged stairs.
- **Check for loose power lines** around your home, and if you see one, don't go any farther. Leave the property and then report it to your local utility.
- **If the building shifts or makes strange noises,** get out immediately and consult authorities or first responders so it can be checked to see if it poses a hazard to anybody.
- **When the weather clears,** open windows to improve ventilation and help your home air out.
- **If there has been standing water in your home** for twenty-four hours or more, assume mold is growing (see page 198).
- **Avoid floodwater.** Moving water is dangerous and will almost certainly be infected with sewage, bacteria, and other icky stuff that you don't want to be wading around in. Wear protective gear, including gloves, boots, masks, and goggles, if you have to enter flooded areas. Don't stand in floodwater if you can help it, and most definitely don't stand in it when turning your electricity on or off; leave the house and contact an electrician, who will shut off the power at the utility's meter.
- **Start cleaning up.** After the water has receded, small amounts of residual standing water can be removed using a wet vac. If you don't have electricity, use a generator to power a wet vac, but be sure to place the generator at least twenty feet away

from your house as carbon monoxide may build up (which is bad) and can kill you (which is worse) if you use a gas-powered engine indoors.

- **Disinfect and thoroughly dry *everything*** with which the floodwater has come into contact.
- **Before restarting your HVAC and electrical systems,** consult with a professional to make sure there aren't any damaged wires or mold growing in them. Even without the presence of standing water, the motors in some of your appliances, such as refrigerators or washing machines, may have been damaged. Consult with a specialist before turning them back on.
- **Immediately discard anything that may pose a health risk from mold or contamination,** including food, clothes, rugs, and other belongings. For insurance purposes, you will need to take pictures of some items first, including serial numbers on major appliances. Discard damaged items appropriately. Unfortunately, there is almost nothing you can do to save water-damaged upholstered furniture, electronics, and appliances. When disposing of damaged items, separate home goods from organic matter such as tree limbs and spoiled food, so they can be disposed of according to your city's municipal waste disposal guidelines.
- **Make whatever temporary repairs you can before insurance repairs can kick in.** For example, you may need patch holes or brace walls.
- **Seal off any gaps** caused by storm damage until permanent repairs can be made. Use plywood boards or plastic tarps to seal broken windows or other small siding or roof gaps.
- **Watch out for insect-borne viruses.** Disease-carrying mosquitoes and midges (any small flies, also known as no-see-ums) love warm weather and standing water. To protect yourself

from them after a flood, limit outdoor activity during peak periods, inspect existing window and door screens for holes, and install window and door screens where necessary.

- **Take pictures** (both closeups and wide shots) of any damage to the interior and exterior of the home as you will need them for filing insurance claims. (Hopefully you are insured.)
- **Be wary of anyone who shows up at your door after a disaster claiming to represent FEMA or another agency.** FEMA will never ask you for money. The safest way to apply for aid is through FEMA's Disaster Assistance Improvement Program's website at disasterassistance.gov, assuming that FEMA is still in operation.
- **Be wary of contractors and/or construction workers who show up immediately following a disaster offering to help you rebuild.** Many cities require permits for rebuilding work, and it is common for scammers to pose as contractors.
- **Don't drink the tap water** until you receive notification from city officials that it is safe, as it may have become polluted during the storm or subsequent flooding.

Tornadoes

According to the National Weather Service, there were 1,796 tornadoes in 2024, which ranks second behind 2004, which saw 1,817. In the first seven months of 2025, NOAA received more than 1,350 tornado reports, more than sixty people in the United States were killed by the storms, and insurers estimated damages topped $10 billion.

Different from hurricanes, which are categorized on the basis of their wind speed, tornadoes are classified by how much damage they cause. The storms remain very difficult to predict. Making it harder is that the areas where we expect them to form have changed. In recent years, tornado outbreaks have increased, and the traditional area where they occur, known as "Tornado Alley," has noticeably shifted hundreds of miles toward the Southeast, Midwest, and Northeast United States. Powerful and multiple tornadoes are now common in areas where they weren't seen in the past.

If your region is susceptible to tornadoes, you probably already know something about what to do when one is spotted. But as with our stronger rainstorms and hurricanes, the changing climate has altered the nature of tornadoes, making them an issue for people who never thought about them before. Here's how to prepare for a tornado before one happens, if it strikes where you are or nearby, and after it ends. (Also refer to the prep list on pages 161–163.)

Before a Tornado

- **Know the difference between a "watch" and a "warning."** A tornado watch means the conditions are right for a tornado and you should be alert. A tornado warning means a tornado has been spotted nearby, so you should take cover immediately.
- **Identify where in your home to shelter during a tornado.** The safest place to be in your house or apartment building is a windowless room closest to the ground in the most interior area. Exterior walls will likely offer little protection from debris flying at more than one hundred miles per hour. The more walls between you and the outside the better. Close the doors and get under something sturdy, like a worktable, or in an empty bathtub, and protect yourself from flying debris with a heavy blanket or mattress.
- **Keep the batteries in your carbon monoxide detectors up to date.**
- **Know where the shutoff valves are** for your utilities, including power, water, and gas.
- **Make sure you have adequate storm shutters** or plywood to protect your windows and doors.

- **Trim weak or dead tree branches** from your yard as part of your regular home maintenance.

During a Tornado

If you are at home:

- If a tornado is imminent, bring in outdoor furniture, and secure heavy objects like grills and propane tanks.
- Close all windows and doors and turn off the air-conditioning and/or heat.
- If instructed by authorities, turn off water, gas, and electricity.
- Fill empty containers with water for drinking and fill bathtubs with water for washing in case there's damage to public water systems.
- Take cover and monitor local news outlets for updates.
- Be aware that multiple tornadoes can occur in a single storm, and you may need to be alert even after the initial danger seems to be over.

If you are outside or on the road:

- Take cover in the nearest sturdy structure (avoid buildings with roofs that span great distances, like a school gymnasium or a big box store).
- You *should not be driving in* a tornado unless you're a professional storm chaser (yes, we saw both *Twister* movies, and while it looks like fun it is also extremely dangerous). But if for some reason you missed the weather report and were caught unaware, get out of your car and seek shelter in a building or lie flat in the lowest place you can find, such as a ditch or ravine. Do not get under a highway overpass—these narrow spaces can increase wind speeds dramatically, putting you at much greater risk of injury or death from flying debris.
- If you can't leave your vehicle, close the windows, turn on

your hazard lights and headlights, and get down on the floor as low as possible in case debris comes through the windows.

After a Tornado

- **Wait until you get the "all clear" from local officials before returning to your home or the affected area,** and don't enter a damaged building (even if it's your house) until the authorities tell you it's safe. If you are home and there is structural damage, you might want to get out until the safety of the structure can be assessed.
- **If you have first aid training (see page 22), use it.** If not, simple things like covering injured people with blankets to keep them warm and putting pressure on bleeding wounds can help. Be sure to check children carefully for injuries, as well as people who might not be able to communicate effectively because of language issues, emotional shock, or neurodivergence.
- **Communicate with your friends and family** and have them spread the word that you're okay. Sometimes you can mark yourself "safe" from a particular disaster on social media. Understand that there may be circumstances where you might *not* be able to communicate, and if so, try not to panic. It won't change anything. Do your part to help, and try to be patient and calm, even if you know people are worried about you or if you are worried about someone else.
- **Be careful of power lines or gas lines that might have been damaged** and so might pose a threat. Downed power lines are particularly common and dangerous; check for loose power lines around your home, and if you see one, don't go any farther and leave the property. Contact the appropriate authorities to report these issues and note that your community might have a special number for these situations.

- **Listen to first responders when they show up,** and do what they ask if you're able (Note: Sometimes the best way to help is to stay out of the way).
- **Contact your insurance provider** as soon as possible to report damage and find out about the process of filing a claim. If you are renting, call your landlord. Renters can often face evictions after a disaster, so familiarize yourself with tenant rights in your state.
- **If local officials have deemed it safe to go into your home,** look for structural damage and/or foundation cracks. Sniff for gas. Use extreme caution if you notice sagging ceilings or floors, and/or damaged stairs.
- **If the building shifts or makes strange noises,** get out immediately and consult authorities or first responders so it can be checked to see if it poses a hazard to anybody.
- **Make whatever temporary repairs you can before insurance repairs can kick in.** For example, you may need patch holes or brace walls.
- **Seal off any gaps** caused by damage until permanent repairs can be made. Use plywood boards or plastic tarps to seal broken windows or other small siding or roof gaps.
- **Take pictures** (both closeups and wide shots) of any damage to the interior and exterior of the home as you will need them for filing insurance claims. (Hopefully you are insured.)
- **Be wary of anyone who shows up at your door after a disaster claiming to represent FEMA or another agency.** FEMA will never ask you for money. The safest way to apply for aid is through FEMA's Disaster Assistance Improvement Program's website at disasterassistance.gov, assuming that FEMA is still in operation.
- **Be wary of contractors and/or construction workers who show up immediately following a disaster offering to help**

you rebuild. Many cities require permits for rebuilding work, and it is common for scammers to pose as contractors.

- **Don't drink the tap water** until you receive notification from city officials that it is safe, as it may have become polluted during the storm or subsequent flooding.

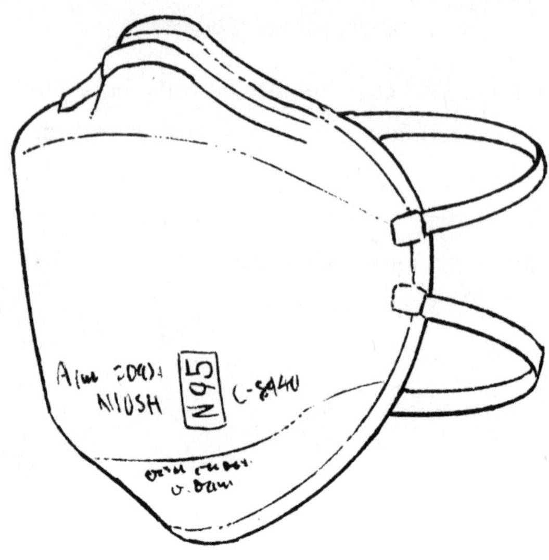

15. Pandemics

As most of us learned in 2020, a pandemic is the outbreak of a disease that spans countries, political parties, celebrities, age groups, and ethnicities, consequently affecting large numbers of people. Caused most often by a virus, it spreads easily from place to place and person to person because, let's face it, in the immortal words of Robert B. and Richard M. Sherman, "It's a small world after all," and these days almost everyone is on their way to somewhere else, creating a more mobile population.

Although the COVID-19 public health emergency officially ended in May 2023, new variants of the virus keep popping up, and there have been multiple warnings from the World Health Organization on mPox (also known as monkeypox, a zoonotic viral disease that spreads through close contact), an alarming spread of previously rare mosquito-borne illnesses (hello, Eastern equine encephalitis), and the is-it-happening-or-is-it-not H5N1 bird flu (with cases of birds and mammals infected with the virus continuing to explode). The appearance of a new transmissible pandemic strain is not an "if" but a "when." And while it's virtually impossible to predict when or where the next new pandemic will emerge, one thing is certain: The (still) current pandemic won't be *the last pandemic*. And if political efforts to defund or eliminate the U.S. government's agencies and programs for pandemic prevention and early warning systems are successful, we may not know when the next pandemic starts until we're dying from it.

How a Warming Planet Increases the Risks of More Pandemics

- Infection-spreading creatures such as mosquitoes and ticks thrive on a warmer planet.
- The introduction of non-native plants and animals and chemicals such as herbicides and fungicides exacerbate losses in biodiversity, leaving surviving populations more vulnerable to illness.
- A hotter world of ravaged ecosystems will be more hospitable to many parasites.
- As diseases become more rampant in animals, the likelihood of "spillover" events that would expose humans to new pathogens increases—for example, the spillover events that likely caused COVID-19 and are causing the ongoing spread of H5N1 bird flu.

We've all been through this before, but as a reminder, here are some additional ways to prepare for a pandemic before, during, and after it happens.

Before a Pandemic

- **Get vaccinated.** Vaccines stimulate your immune system to produce antibodies and—as we've seen from smallpox to typhus—*prevent* diseases. While this is a proven fact, these days otherwise intelligent people dispute the effectiveness of vaccines, leading most recently to a resurgence of measles, one of the most infectious viruses there is. Following the 2025 death of a child in West Texas from the measles, in an interview with CNN Health, Catherine Troisi, an epidemiologist at UTHealth Houston, noted, "I very rarely say I'm 100% sure of something, but I am 100% sure we will see an increase in cases. . . . Texas as a state is undervaccinated, so there are susceptible people." Troisi added, "Measles is the most infectious virus we know. However, it's a harbinger of low vaccination rates, and it is quite likely we will start seeing outbreaks of other diseases that are vaccine preventable as well as these vaccine rates decrease."
- **Stock up on supplies.** When COVID-19 pretty much shut down the world in early 2020, most people realized they didn't have N95 masks lying around, leading to all kinds of "how to make a mask out of your bra or his jockstrap" tutorials. Don't make that mistake again. Lay in a supply over time (you're *preparing,* not hoarding) so you're not caught short.
    - While you're at it, why not stock up on the basics: toilet paper, hand sanitizer, and food, and pretty much all the other essentials you didn't have (but wished you did) the last go-round. Having a supply at home is safer than having to venture out and gives you time to observe, learn, and plan what to do next.
- **Make sure you have the latest COVID home testing kits,** which can detect recently mutated strains of the virus. Molecular tests detect the virus's genetic matter with accuracy rates above 90 percent.

During a Pandemic

Depending on how your experience played out last time, it would be totally understandable if you chose to curl up in the fetal position and have a good cry. After that . . .

- **Seek reliable information.** The guidance of the Centers for Disease Control and Prevention (CDC) may be useful, if that federal agency is not being defunded or politically pressured. Other potential sources to consult are the Center for Infectious Disease Research and Policy (CIDRAP), the World Health Organization (WHO), the European Public Health Association (www.eupha.org), the American Public Health Association (www.apha.org), the American Medical Association (www.ama-assn.org), the American Academy of Pediatrics (www.aap.org), the Mayo Clinic, the Cleveland Clinic, and the Kaiser Family Foundation (KFF). You could also check with your healthcare provider, not your crazy conspiracy-theory-touting relatives. (See page 126.)
    - Think back to what you learned in health class and/or check a reputable resource to learn about how diseases spread. Keep in mind that some viruses can be spread from a nonliving object to a person and by people who are infected but don't have symptoms. Use proven scientific information to inform how you protect yourself and others.
- **Wash your hands often** with soap and water for at least twenty seconds (or sing the happy birthday song through twice) and don't forget to pile on the moisturizer . . . you don't want to come out of this with your hands looking like tortoise shells. Feel free to dance while you sing (it's exercise, which keeps the dopamine flowing), and try not to touch your eyes, nose, or mouth (head, shoulders, knees, and toes, however, are permitted).

- **Keep at least six feet between you and other people** who are not part of your household (to determine six feet, try to imagine a prone Michael B. Jordan, Steph Curry, or Adam Driver).
- **Cover your mouth and nose with a mask when in public.** We know; you don't like wearing one. No one likes wearing one. While any mask is better than none, N95 or KN95 respirators remain the most effective and, when properly fitted, filter out at least 95 percent of airborne particles, including those carrying the virus.
- **Hum when in crowded, enclosed spaces** and soon after, as it stimulates blood flow to mucosa and thus supports immune defense against infection.
- **Cover coughs and sneezes with a tissue;** if you don't have a tissue, sneeze or cough into the inside of your elbow.
- **Clean and disinfect high-touch objects and surfaces.** Research shows that viruses—from those that cause COVID to those that cause the flu (which is also no fun)—typically live longer on stainless steel, plastic, and other nonporous surfaces than on fabric, tissue, and other porous surfaces. And while cold germs on hard surfaces lose effectiveness after the first twenty-four hours, the flu virus can live for up to forty-eight hours and the coronavirus can live from a few hours to a few days. Bacteria such as *E. coli* and *Salmonella* can live for up to four hours on hard surfaces, while *Clostridium difficile* (*C. diff*), which can cause colitis and severe diarrhea, can live for up to five months (and for that long should at least be paying rent).
- **Lay in a stash of extra Clorox and your favorite brand of hand sanitizer.** As much as it sucks to have to clear space in your closet or your man cave to make room for supplies, it's even more sucky to have to put on that jockstrap mask and a HAZMAT suit and venture out to your local retailer to buy

extra hand sanitizer, which—if history repeats itself—they'll most likely be out of anyway.

- **Stay at home as much as possible** to prevent the spread of disease. You've done this before. You know the drill. And stay home when you're sick (except to get medical care).
- **Keep yourself busy.** By now you've probably had some practice (at least a year's worth) in the art of entertaining yourself at home. Pull out the hardly ever used bread maker and a few of those jigsaw puzzles. Learn a new card or board game, take up knitting, or learn to play the guitar. Teach yourself a new language. Try meditation.
- **Keep moving.** Look, there's no easy way to say this, but that 2020 shutdown did not do any favors to our waistlines. We're making no judgments, but staying completely sedentary on the couch while eating Pirate's Booty and scrolling through social media for another year is just not healthy. For most adults, the Department of Health and Human Services recommends getting at least ninety minutes of moderate aerobic activity or seventy-five minutes of vigorous aerobic activity a week, or a combination of each. Since you'll possibly be on some level of lockdown and/or may not want to leave the house, think at-home aerobics (or just dancing), yoga, and/or weight training.
    - Kids aged six and older should get at least an hour of moderate or vigorous aerobic activity a day, combined with vigorous activities such as running or biking at least three days a week (the latter of which may not be possible and/or advisable depending on the size of your home). But for your own sanity, a physically tired kid is what you're after, so be creative if you must, and feel free to improvise.
- **Prepare for the possibility of schools, workplaces, and**

community centers being closed. Investigate and prepare for virtual coordination for school, work (telework), and social activities.

- **If you think you've been exposed** to whatever illness is the pathogenic cause of the pandemic:
    - Immediately quarantine. Don't pass go or stop for a bagel on your way home.
    - Contact your doctor and then follow quarantine instructions.
    - Monitor your symptoms. If you are experiencing a medical emergency, call 911 and shelter in place with a mask, if possible, until help arrives.
- **Share only accurate, science-based information** about the disease with friends, family, and people on social media. Sharing bad information may have serious health outcomes.
- **Be aware of the tendency to stigmatize people for making different choices or to create scapegoats** based on where the disease started and who it first infected. It's often very hard—even for those tasked with doing so—to say who might have infected others, but way easier for our imagination (often with help from the media and government) to find somebody to blame. Some groups will have higher rates of illness because of the jobs they hold, or the makeup of their households, or just bad luck even though they're careful. Try not to blame individuals or a group for illnesses that are often incredibly complex. Remember that stigma hurts everyone and often causes discrimination against people, places, and/or nations.
- **Take care of yourself.** It's normal to feel anxious or stressed during a pandemic and lockdown. It helps to engage virtually with your family, friends, and community through regular video and phone calls. Exercise. Talk to someone if you are feeling especially upset. And take comfort in the fact that you are, to the best of your ability, prepared.

After a Pandemic

It's hard to pinpoint the "after" when it comes to pandemics, especially when the media and government send out mostly "nothing to see here" messages. Sure, we're now free to go out and about mostly mask-free, but many people are still getting sick enough to be hospitalized and dying. That said:

- **If you feel sick** you should use a reliable test to confirm what your illness is caused by.
- **If you test positive** you should stay home if possible. If not, wear a mask to prevent the spread of germs.
- **Grow up.** Peer pressure is very real, which (1) may deter you from wearing a mask or (2) may prompt your family and friends to ask why you're still wearing "that damn stupid representation of government overreach." But you're no longer thirteen years old, and you remember what it was like the last time you got sick, so . . .
- **Keep masking.** If you're in a situation where there's little ventilation and a big crowd, or if your job involves coming face-to-face with a lot of people, you should wear a mask.
- **Don't assume that the pandemic is over when some of the restrictions are lifted.** As we've seen during COVID, decisions are based on economics, fear, frustration, and weariness as much as public health. Continue to keep informed even when it looks like the worst is over.
- **Continue to get appropriate vaccines.**

16. Wildfires and Dangerous Air Quality

Wildfires are spreading a whopping 400 percent faster in California today than they were twenty years ago. Quick-moving blazes like the Palisades and Eaton fires near Los Angeles are becoming common as climate-driven swings between drought and deluge intensify. But it's not only in California. A third of the U.S. population now lives in wildfire risk zones. And while climate change is certainly making things worse, wildfires are nothing new.

The haze and catastrophically bad air quality that enveloped New York City in June of 2023 was reminiscent of New England's Dark Day in May of 1780, when smoke darkened the sun all over the Northeastern United States. Three million acres were burned in northern New Brunswick, Canada, in the Miramichi Fire in 1825. In October 1871, there was the Great Chicago Fire and also—on the very same day!—fires in Michigan and Wisconsin. The largest wildfire yet recorded was in 2003 in Siberia, when fifty-five million acres burned.

We learned a lot from some of those fires about fireproofing buildings, fire suppression techniques, and urban planning, but it seems we never quite aced the test. Chicago was rebuilt rapidly in 1871 with similar wooden structures, only to see another big fire erupt three years later. People would often rebuild using what they knew, even if what they knew was what had led to the previous disaster. During the 2025 fires in Los Angeles, historic neighborhoods were almost completely destroyed, partly because of their locations close to natural areas, but also because of outdated construction techniques.

Once a fire starts—and more than 80 percent of U.S. wildfires are caused by people (turns out Smokey Bear was right!)—warmer temperatures and drier conditions help them spread more quickly and make them harder to put out. According to the Red Cross, a wildfire can move at a rate of up to fourteen miles an hour, with embers taking the lead. Faster-moving wildfires are becoming more common and are responsible for nearly 80 percent of homes and other structures destroyed in the United States over the past two decades, according to a first-of-its-kind study by Jennifer Balch et al. in *Science* in 2024.

As we have seen in just the past couple of years, once started, wildfires can spread quickly and burn towns *to the ground.* You do not want to mess with a wildfire.

Smoke Gets in Your Eyes

It's not just the fire that can kill you. Wildfire smoke is composed of a mixture of carbon monoxide, hazardous air pollutants, and water vapor. And while those ingredients don't quite evoke the scent of a classic *parfum,* it's the 90 percent of tiny particles called PM2.5 that constitute the principal public health threat. Turns out that breathing in those little suckers (think thirty times smaller than the diameter of a strand of hair) can cause and/or amplify problems for the approximately thirty-four million people in the United States who are living with lung disease, while putting millions more at risk of developing chronic illness including emphysema, chronic bronchitis, asthma, lymphoma, lung cancer, heart attacks, and stroke.

According to research by Minghao Qiu et al., published in the September 2025 issue of *Nature,* if the planet continues to warm at its current rate, exposure to wildfire smoke will kill an estimated seventy thousand Americans each year by 2050. Making matters worse, while N95 masks are good for filtering out the fine particles associated with fire smoke, they filter little to nothing of the chemical-laced infernos produced by burning plastic and other petrochemicals. Only a gas mask can filter them out.

But it's not only wildfire smoke that presents a danger. A 2025 article published in the journal *PLOS One* estimates that every day, particularly in indoor environments, people are breathing in as many as sixty-eight thousand tiny plastic particles, which can penetrate deep into the pulmonary system.

Those most at risk from wildfire smoke:

- Pregnant women often have increased respiratory rates, so they're inhaling more smoke. A 2024 study by Sally Picciotto et al. found that exposure to PM2.5 from wildfire smoke was associated with higher odds of premature birth. Babies born early are more likely to have immature lungs and developmental delays and are also more likely to die in their first year.
- Children tend to be more physically active and breathe more air relative to their weight. And the main pollutant in smoke is particulate pollution, which is often bound to heavy metals and toxic chemicals that are really bad for kids' underdeveloped lungs and other organs.

- Adults with asthma and COPD.
- People over sixty-five, especially those who have lung and/or cardiovascular risks.
- Those who work outdoors, including farmworkers, construction crews, bike messengers, and landscapers.
- Pets, including birds.

Air Quality

The Air Quality Index (AQI) is broken up into six color-coded categories, each corresponding to a range of index values. Per AirNow.gov, the categories are as follows:

- **Good (green) 0–50:** Air quality is satisfactory, and air pollution poses little or no risk.
- **Moderate (yellow) 51–100:** Air quality is acceptable. However, there may be a risk for some people, particularly those who are unusually sensitive to air pollution.
- **Unhealthy for sensitive groups (orange) 101–150:** Members of sensitive groups may experience health effects. The general public is less likely to be affected.
- **Unhealthy (red) 151–200:** Some members of the general public may experience health effects; members of sensitive groups may experience more serious health effects.
- **Very unhealthy (purple) 201–300:** The health risks are increased for everyone.
- **Hazardous (maroon) 301 and higher:** Health warning of emergency conditions. Everyone is more likely to be affected.

If the AQI is above 100, avoid outdoor exercise. If it's above 150, wear a tight-fitting N95 mask when you're outside. Run your air conditioner with a high-efficiency filter installed—the EPA recommends MERV 13 or above—or use a portable HEPA air purifier.

Pay attention to air quality alerts because these days, even if you're outside, it's more likely you'll be looking at some type of screen than the actual, you know, sky. If smoky conditions exist, stay inside (if you are in a safe place), and if you have one (you should), run an air filtration device, or move to a location where the air is clearer.

Get an app for your mobile phone to help you plan for localized, real-time data on the AQI and potential health impacts from pollutants like PM2.5 and ozone. The app AirNow is free and provides current and forecasted local air quality data from the U.S. government's Environmental Protection Agency (EPA). Other popular apps (not associated with the EPA) include IQAir, AirVisual, BreezoMeter, and Air Matters, which in addition to air quality includes pollen data. There are also home air quality monitors that can be purchased online or at home improvement stores for $100 or less.

If your region is susceptible to wildfire, you probably already know something about what to do when a fire is nearby. But with weather patterns changing all over the world, wildfires are moving into areas where people aren't as familiar with the best practices. Here are some ways to prepare for wildfires and the poor air quality that often accompanies them before, during, and after. (Also refer to the prep list on pages 161–163.)

Before a Wildfire

- **Learn the difference between a "watch," an "advisory," and a "red flag warning."** A wildfire watch means conditions could lead to wildfires. An advisory means hazardous conditions are actively occurring or imminent. A red flag warning means critical fire weather conditions are happening or will happen soon.

- **Know your risk.** First Street Technology, Inc., estimates climate risks at the property level and makes its risk scores available to the public for free—via popular real estate search sites, including Redfin. About 95 percent of the homes destroyed in Altadena, California, in 2025 had a fire-risk level of at least 7 on a 10-point scale as assigned by First Street.
- **Download Watch Duty,** one of the most popular fire-tracking apps in the United States, which distills and reports emergency communications for those who may be in harm's way.
- **Know what your homeowner's insurance policy covers.** Most standard insurance policies *do* cover damage from fires, but several major insurers have paused or outright canceled coverage in many states (including California), citing the high risk of fire, state caps on premiums, and increased construction costs. If you are renting, familiarize yourself with tenant rights in your state—renters can often face evictions after a disaster.
- **Harden your home.** Experts say there is no such thing as a fireproof home, but you can make yours fire *resistant.* Note that at the time of this book's writing, California is the first state to require sellers in high-risk areas to disclose what they've done to protect houses. There are three ways your home can be exposed to a wildfire: (1) direct flames from a wildfire or burning neighboring home; (2) radiant heat from nearby burning plants or structures; and (3) flying embers, which can destroy homes up to a mile away and are responsible for the destruction of most homes.
    - Taking the necessary measures to prepare your home can help increase its likelihood of survival when wildfire strikes, and for some residents in fire-prone areas of California, making these changes is the difference between keeping and losing homeowner's insurance.

- Use fire-resistant materials to build, renovate, or make repairs.
- Install a fire-resistant roof with concrete or clay tile, fiberglass asphalt composition shingles, or metal. If you are retrofitting an existing roof to try to fend off fire damage, a professional roofer will need to determine whether your roof can handle the weight of concrete or other tiles.
- Regardless of roof type, check for spaces (like between the roof and the eaves) where rodents or birds might have squirreled away debris—which can easily ignite. This material can compromise your roof's fire rating.
- Install tempered glass windows.
- Replace your home's siding with fire-resistant materials such as stucco or a cement-based product like fiber cement, which won't ignite or burn. The space between the ground and your house is an area likely to collect embers during a fire. If your existing home has combustible siding like cedar or vinyl, you'll need at least a six-inch portion from the ground up built with a product that won't burn, such as concrete.
- For those on a limited budget, replace wood shingles on your roof with asphalt or clay tiles, install dual-pane, tempered windows, and coat doors and siding with flame-retardant.
- Shield air vents from burning debris by installing ember-proof vents or covering conventional vents with metal screens. Use a golf tee to ensure that the mesh is tight enough: If the pointed tip of the tee can easily enter the screen, embers can too.
- Use high-efficiency filters in your central air-conditioning system to capture fine particles from smoke.
- Make sure patios, decks, and roadways are free of leaves,

debris, or flammable materials for at least thirty feet from your home.

  - Create at least five feet of fire-resistant hardscape (think gravel or decorative stones) around the house to make a firebreak.
  - You don't need a lot of money to make your landscape fire resistant. Use rock, mulch, flower beds, and gardens as ground cover for bare spaces and as effective firebreaks. There are no "fireproof" plants, but there *are* fire-retardant plant species that resist ignition (fire-resistant plants such as rockrose, ice plant, and aloe vera are often drought tolerant too). Select high-moisture plants that grow close to the ground and have a low sap or resin content, and fire-resistant shrubs such as hedging roses, bush honeysuckles, currant, cotoneaster, sumac, and shrub apples. Plant hardwood maple, poplar, and cherry trees that are less flammable than pine, fir, and other conifers. Bonus! A fire-resistant landscape can increase your property value and conserve water while beautifying your home. Check your local nursery, landscape contractor, or county's co-operative extension service for advice on fire-resistant plants suited for your area.
  - Be sure you have an outdoor water source with a hose that can reach any area of your property.

- **Put away deck furniture, patio decor, and the like** that could catch and spread fire.
- **Keep multiple fire extinguishers on hand** and train your family on how to use them (check expiration dates regularly).
- **Follow instructions from local authorities** who will provide the latest recommendations based on the threat to your community and appropriate safety measures.
- **Keep your tennis shoes close.** During wildfire season, skip the

heels and keep a sturdy pair of shoes near your bed or exit door in case of a sudden evacuation.

- **Be ready to go.** If a wildfire starts near your home and the evacuation zones are getting closer and closer, grab your pre-packed bags and go. The earlier you leave in an emergency situation, the easier it will be to get out of the area.

During a Wildfire

Because many wildfires begin with a spark from a power line, a growing number of utility companies are simply turning off the power to avoid billion-dollar lawsuits. You read that right: According to an analysis of data compiled by researchers at Stanford University, electric companies providing service to roughly twenty-four million homes and businesses across the fire-prone U.S. West now have plans to preemptively cut electricity during dangerous fire conditions. So even if you aren't forced to leave your home, chances are you'll be left sitting in the dark without even cable to keep you company—unless you have a backup generator (see page 35).

Since it is hard to predict whether you should stay or go without looking at the details of a situation, and since you might have to do both at some point, prepare for both scenarios.

If you are trapped in your home during a wildfire:

- Call 911, but be aware that emergency response could be delayed or impossible.
- Turn on lights (if your electricity is working) to help rescuers find you, and unlock your doors so they can easily get inside if needed.
- Close all doors and windows.
- Designate a room that can be closed off from outside air, and set up a portable air cleaner to keep indoor pollution levels low when smoky conditions exist.

- If you have a central air-conditioning system that has fresh air intake, set the system to "recirculate" mode and close the outdoor intake damper.
- Have an N95 respirator, if possible, to keep smoke particles out of the air you breathe. (Note: Respirators are not meant to fit children.)
- Make sure you and your family members know where your gas, electric, and water main shutoff controls are located and how to safely shut them down if necessary (and keep a wrench or pliers nearby to do so).
- Be careful with flammable or combustible household products that can cause fires or explosions, such as aerosols, cooking oils, rubbing alcohol, and hand sanitizer.

An encroaching wildfire will not give you the choice of staying or going. Once a fire begins, it can spread at a rate of up to *14.29 miles per hour.* Fire burns more rapidly when moving uphill by preheating unburned fuels and making them more combustible. Wind also moves more quickly up slopes, increasing the speed at which a fire can spread.

If you have to evacuate quickly:

- Keep your go bags, which you already have packed with essentials for you, your family, and your pets (see page 89), near exits in case you have to grab and go.
- If you plan to take a car and have time to load it, pack the other emergency items you have gathered for this very situation.
- Cover up to protect against heat and flying embers. No matter the weather, wear long pants, a long-sleeve shirt, heavy shoes/boots, a cap, a dry bandanna for face cover, and goggles or glasses. Natural fibers like cotton or linen are preferable as heat will cause most synthetics to *literally* melt on your body. Compared to some other fabrics, wool is relatively fire resistant, as is silk.

- Follow the evacuation plan you created in chapter 6 (see page 85) and take the safest route away from the fire to your safe meeting spot.

After a Wildfire

It's not all clear to return once the flames are put out. Flash flooding and debris flows, structural damage, road instability, and damaged trees are just some of the dangers that exist after a wildfire.

- **Wait until you get the "all clear" from fire officials before returning to your home or the affected area,** and don't enter a damaged building (even if it's your house) until the authorities tell you it's safe.
- **If you have first aid training (see page 22), use it.** If not, simple things like covering injured people with blankets to keep them warm and putting pressure on bleeding wounds can help. Be sure to check children carefully for injuries, as well as people who might not be able to communicate effectively because of language issues, emotional shock, or neurodivergence.
- **Communicate with your friends and family** and have them spread the word that you're okay. Sometimes you can mark yourself "safe" from a particular disaster on social media. Understand that there may be circumstances in which you might *not* be able to communicate, and if so, try not to panic. It won't change anything. Do your part to help, and try to be patient and calm, even if you know people are worried about you or if you are worried about someone else.
- **Be careful around trees, power lines, and other tall structures that may have lost stability during the fire.** Downed power lines are particularly common and dangerous; contact the appropriate authorities to report these issues and note that your community might have a special number for these situations.
- **Stay away from storm channels and natural drainages** such as

rivers, creeks, and engineered channels because these can convey deadly flows of water and debris if it rains. Remember, the rain could be happening far upstream, so be careful even if it's not raining at your location.

- **Check the ground for hot spots.** Avoid hot ash, charred trees, smoldering debris and stumps, and live embers, as these can burn you or spark another fire.
- **Monitor emergency updates, weather forecasts, reports of flash flooding, and news reports.**
- **Listen to first responders when they show up,** and do what they ask if you're able (Note: Sometimes the best way to help is to stay out of the way).
- **Contact your insurance provider** as soon as possible to report damage and find out about the process of filing a claim. If you are renting, call your landlord. Renters can often face evictions after a disaster, so familiarize yourself with tenant rights in your state.
- **If local officials have deemed it safe to go into your home, look for smoke, burning sparks, or embers (including in the attic and on the roof).** Keep a "fire watch."
- **If you haven't already, turn off power until you've completed your inspection.** Note: Use a battery-powered flashlight and turn it on before entering as the battery may produce a spark that could ignite leaking gas if present.
- **Wear protective clothing when cleaning, and use appropriate masks or respirators to limit your exposure.** Wet debris to minimize breathing dust particles. Children and those with asthma and/or other lung conditions should not help with cleanup efforts.
- **When checking the interior for fire damage,** make sure all appliances are turned off and the meter is not damaged before turning on the main circuit breaker.
- **If the breakers are on and power is still not present,** contact

your utility company. If you have a propane tank or system, contact a propane supplier, turn off valves, and leave them closed until the supplier inspects your system. If you have a heating oil tank system, contact a heating oil supplier for an inspection before you use it. If you have a solar electrical system, it should be inspected by a licensed technician to verify that the solar panels and electrical wiring are safe for continued operation.

- **Do not drink or use water from the faucet until emergency officials say it is okay;** water supplies can be damaged and become polluted during wildfires or because of postfire flooding. If your well has been damaged by fire, contact a local licensed and bonded well constructor or pump installer to determine the extent of the damage and what must be done to either repair or decommission the well.
- **Discard any food that has been exposed to heat, smoke, floodwaters, or soot.**
- **Take pictures** (both closeups and wide shots) of any damage to the interior and exterior of the home as you will need them for filing insurance claims. (Hopefully you are insured.)
- **Be wary of anyone who shows up at your door after a disaster claiming to represent FEMA or another agency.** FEMA will never ask you for money. The safest way to apply for aid is through FEMA's Disaster Assistance Improvement Program's website at disasterassistance.gov, assuming that FEMA is still in operation.
- **Be wary of contractors and/or construction workers who show up immediately following a disaster offering to help you rebuild.** Many cities require permits for rebuilding work, and it is common for scammers to pose as contractors.

17. Civil or Political Unrest

Let's start by clarifying what we mean by civil and political unrest, which can range from the systematic oppression of a particular group to civil war. Protests in the street are not usually oppressive or violent, even when they are labeled a "riot," but the *response* to protests can be oppressive (see: Chicago in 1968, Minneapolis in 2026). Until recently, attending or organizing a peaceful protest in the United States was considered a basic human right. Acts like strikes, roadblocks, or throwing tomato juice at a painting protected by bulletproof glass may cause inconvenience, but they don't usually reach the level where you would be concerned with your immediate safety. What we mean when we talk about civil and political unrest are actions that lead to and/or end in bloodshed and loss of life. We mean situations like the 2025 uprising in Nepal or the ongoing civil war in Sudan. We don't mean largely peaceful protests like the demonstrations following the death of George Floyd in

2020 or the No Kings events from 2025. We're talking about oppressive responses by armed authorities to otherwise peaceful protests, like we've seen from ICE in the United States. These can cause loss of freedom, bodily harm, or death.

We can use history as a guide, but while the intention of the oppressors may be the same—to divide people by creating fear and anger—the examples will be a little different (turns out humans are pretty easy to fool). The first step is identifying that political oppression is happening and assessing the degree. This might sound easy, but history shows that oppression sneaks up on people when they're busy looking elsewhere. There might not be a clear red line that is crossed, but there might be numerous pink ones that suggest things are going very wrong.

What follows are some things to consider as you assess the particulars of the situation in which you find yourself. As you'll see, unlike previous chapters, which encourage calm and positivity, this one focuses on not underestimating a situation and on acting as soon as you recognize the potential problem. Rather than waiting to be 90 percent sure that something is about to happen before you bring your lawn chairs inside, as you would in a natural disaster, you might want to respond sooner here, like when you are only 50 percent sure. Because the stakes are high, your options might become limited very quickly, and you really want to protect those lawn chairs.

Before Civil or Political Unrest

One common denominator with these types of situations is the speed with which they escalate, and how they catch those caught in the crosshairs by surprise. Maybe you aren't seeing clearly because you don't want to believe that things can really be this bad. Or maybe you're so busy trying to cover your groceries, make your mortgage payments, and meet your healthcare deductibles that you're not really paying attention to the events unfolding around you. We want to believe that oppression must stop at some point, because this is America and this type of thing just doesn't happen here, right? Evidently not so much anymore. It happened before (see Native American genocide, the enslavement of Black people, and Japanese American internment) and will happen again.

Sure, there's oppression and injustice everywhere. Here we are considering situations in which oppression is severe, threatens to get worse, and puts lives and liberty at risk. This can transpire in a hundred different ways, and one situation might look very different from the next. In some cases, oppression can arise quietly, with minimal disruption to the lives of those who are not directly affected. In other situations, violence is widespread, and tensions explode into a full-blown armed conflict.

A 2023 investigation by Reuters identified more than two hundred cases of political violence between January 6, 2021, and August 2024, noting that "America is grappling with the biggest and most sustained increase in political violence since the 1970s," which, as a reminder, was a period that included the rise (again) of white supremacy, antiabortion organizations, and militia groups. Oppression and violence brought on by civil or political unrest are what we consider catastrophes here, and it is during these particularly unpleasant events that you should always make like a drum and beat it.

Here are a few questions to ask yourself (and answer) about the current state of affairs. Bonus points if you spot what's already happening:

- Have certain groups been identified by the government as "criminals," "killers," or "animals" and blamed for societal problems? The first step to demonizing a group is to dehumanize them.
- Do these groups have to identify themselves in some way with a government ID or some type of official paperwork? If members of the group typically look different from the (white) majority, those differences could make them targeted. If there is no visual clue to the identity of a person, they might have to identify themselves in other ways (like a yellow star, for instance).
- Has the movement of certain groups been limited?

- Have rights been rescinded, officially, for certain groups? These could be rights to vote, to own property, or to own a firearm. It is not uncommon for minorities to have rights denied unofficially (through redlining, Jim Crow, or hiring practices), but when the denial of rights is officially codified, that is a major escalation.
- Are people being detained or disappeared merely for being (or suspected of being) part of a group? This could include criminalizing previously noncriminal acts, like overstaying a visa (which up until recently was a *civil violation* in the United States, not a criminal action).
- Is violence against this group going unpunished? Is it tacitly or explicitly encouraged by the government, or is incitement to violence going unpunished?

Oracle cofounder and billionaire Larry Ellison has been quoted saying that he wants to build a system that keeps the entire U.S. population on its "best behavior," which hews a little too close to George Orwell's dystopian nightmare for comfort. So, one of the first tasks here is to realize what is *actually happening* and how quickly. One of Trump's first actions as president was to rescind the passports of transgender persons. Whether that affects you directly or not, it's something of which you should take note; our opportunity to vamoose might be restricted sooner than we think.

Here is where your strategy should be different than in other scenarios in which staying in place may be a safer option than bugging out. That is not the case with severe political oppression or violence. History is filled with stories of people whose relatives left Germany in 1933 or, more recently, left Mariupol, Ukraine, before February 24, 2022. Their lives and the lives of their descendants were changed by those decisions. Identity-based persecution may start in one way and shift its focus over time. You may not be in the group initially targeted—these days it's everyone from immigrants, transgender folks, gays, and people of color to the media, scientists, and even librarians (yes, you read that right)—but how will that group change or grow?

You have probably heard parts of the poem by Martin Niemöller that starts, "First they came for the socialists, but I did not speak out because I was not a socialist." It ends with "them" coming for him, but nobody is left to help. Violence and oppression start with political enemies and scapegoats but rarely end there. When they start, you may think you will be okay since others are the ones being targeted, but time and time again people have learned that is not necessarily true.

Oppression spreads to all but the oppressing group, no matter how it begins. Listen to how people in power talk, watch how often they give a Nazi salute (which seems to be making a comeback), and *believe what they say,* even before it becomes action. Often, we see that the intention was broadcast long before it actually happened. As soon as you see a threat, make plans to leave. If the threat has already arrived, and you can possibly get out, leave. If it blows over, you might be embarrassed for overreacting, but then again, you'll be alive, so there's that. If you're right and it doesn't blow over? You need to be somewhere else. So before it gets bad, consider the following.

- **If you think you might want or need to leave your town,** your state, or the country, go see an emigration lawyer. They will know about options, how to start the process of moving somewhere else, and what resources are out there to help you. Also, they probably have a better understanding of what is happening in your community, since this is their job and they deal with it every day.
- **Reach out to family or friends in other places.** Can you come to where they are, at least for a while? Having allies who are familiar with a place that is foreign to you will be invaluable. If you have any such potential connections, go ahead and start cultivating them.

    - Were your parents or grandparents born in another country? If so, you may be eligible for a passport in that country.

- **Think about your assets.** Can you move money or stocks to someplace that is not under the thumb of the oppressors? If you have a business, can that be moved? Do you need to consider selling your home, car, or boat in preparation for leaving? Might your property be confiscated? Do you have a trusted person who is not in an oppressed group who might buy them from you (or have them transferred to their name) and sell or give them back later? Lives are more important than things, obviously, but a little homework ahead of time might put you in much better shape in the future.
- **Think about the risks, and who will be affected.** Are you the parent of small children? That might mean you make a different decision than a seventy-five-year-old with no children. Are you a well-known and respected person in your community? A leader or public figure? Your choice could influence others, and that might factor into your decision. Also, consider the consequences of staying versus leaving. Losing a job or even being deported is different from losing your life or freedom, so the potential consequences should be always part of the equation.
- **Get all the information you can.** Don't rely on anecdotes or single instances, but look at the big picture and patterns. Talk to people who are facing the same decision. Listen to trusted leaders. Find a variety of sources of information, including some from other countries, to help you assess the situation.

We would love to be able to provide a clear-cut handy-dandy checklist that could make the decision easier, but as we know from history it's never as simple as that.

During Civil or Political Unrest

First, let's talk about one reason why people do not leave when they should, and that is not wanting to look like they're overreacting. Embarrassment is a powerful force, and we see it across the board when people face life-or-death situations. People who have survived being lost or stranded in the wilderness often report their greatest fear wasn't death, the dark, or wild animals but being mortified that they got lost in the first place. Calling for help when they would have (eventually) found their own way out could only make their embarrassment worse. But think of it this way: If you leave and you've miscalculated the seriousness of the situation, it's probably better than staying and being wrong. If you stay despite all signs telling you to leave, your loss may be greater (and this time we're talking about a lot more than lawn chairs).

If you choose to stay, for whatever reason (elderly parents, extended family), or can't leave, here are some different scenarios and how you might need to adapt.

- If you are a member of an oppressed group (or adjacent enough that you might be next) and you can't leave, you might need to lie low, try to blend in, or even hide. Limit your travel outside of your residence or neighborhood. Have things delivered if possible. Have other people run errands for you if they can.
- When driving, make sure your license plates are current, ensure that all your lights work, and drive conservatively to remain anonymous. Some cars are more noticeable or memorable, for their style or sound, and that may come into play as well.
- And remember, while it's important to resist, protest, and make your voice heard, there may come a time to let others—with less to lose—fight publicly for you. Likewise, if you are not in one of the groups being oppressed, it may be time to make your voice heard in opposition to that oppression.

If you are not afraid of the potentially dire consequences of opposing an oppressive government, or if you are unlikely to suffer by virtue of being in a group that is not being targeted, by all means, stay and fight. Otherwise, when oppression by violence appears as a tool of the powerful, it's time to pack your bags, grab your family, and go. As noted above, things can change quickly, and you may be trapped before you realize you have no means of escape.

We've all seen examples of such things happening in the movies, but how does it play out in real life? If my political party lost the election, should I flee? Of course not. Isolated or relatively few instances of violent oppression? Cause for concern, but that's not what we mean. Ultimately you will have to be the judge, so let's talk about how to assess the danger.

If you decide to leave:

- Learn as much as you can about the conflict, how large an area it might affect, and who might be targeted.
- Make a list of nearby safe areas and try to establish trusted contacts.
- Contact friends, families, or appropriate organizations in those nearby or accessible safe areas (emergency management agencies, Red Cross or Crescent, UNICEF) and ask if you could join them in case of an emergency.
- If you need to leave, map out several different routes and means of transportation to get there. These might include means of transportation that you might not have considered in normal times:
    - Walking. Most reasonably fit people can walk fifteen to twenty miles a day on roads or trails. If you don't have access to a trail, this distance will be much less—maybe five to ten miles, depending on the terrain and vegetation.
    - Biking. Fifty or so miles a day is not too difficult if you're in shape (and for better mental and physical health, you should be!).

  - Driving. Several hundred miles on good roads should be doable, but keep in mind that others may have the same idea. Being stuck in traffic is never ideal. On heavily traveled roads you may not be able to travel as far, but you will also be less conspicuous.

- Know what documents you'll need to travel (driver's license, passport, visas, vaccination info). Keep those handy and make both digital and hard copies. Put the digital copies on a flash drive or two, email the digital copies to yourself, and store them in the cloud if you are able. Make copies (digital, at least) of birth certificates, marriage licenses, financial information, diplomas, training certificates, wills, and medical information. Store this info on flash drives, email it to yourself, put it in the cloud, and make hard copies if possible.
- If you think you might need to hide information, put it on a micro SD card that can be hidden in places like a hem, shoe, or backpack strap.
- Make plans (A, B, *and* C), and decide where to go and how to get there.
- Pack a bag with supplies you might need, and keep it nearby. Depending on your daily activity and the urgency of the situation, you may want to keep it with you.
- If you have space, include camping-type equipment like sleeping bags and pads, and a tent.
- Think about how to be inconspicuous. Maybe you want to blend in by dressing like everyone else. Maybe you want to put on a hi-viz vest and carry a clipboard so you look like you're working. You might have heard the story of a man walking across and out of Nazi Germany by walking with a cow. He was assumed to be a local going a short distance and was able to pass unhindered. We don't know if that story is apocryphal or true, but it illustrates the idea.

The Worst-Case Scenario: Armed Conflict

What if things have turned violent and the bullets and bombs are flying? Leave if you can, of course. If you're trapped in an active war zone, here are some things to know to help you make decisions.

- Expect power and water to be lost, and use your stockpile of food, water, and medicine.
- Try to stay put as much as you can. In most cases, you will be safer in a building, out of sight, than walking or driving around.
- Cities are especially dangerous because even legitimate military targets could be in proximity to civilians.
- In modern warfare, most people are killed or injured by artillery or bombs. When these things explode, they kill from the blast and/or shrapnel. A typical small mortar shell, the kind fired out of a short tube, will kill or seriously injure people within about a hundred feet / thirty meters of the impact.
- Consider reinforcing the walls of your home with sandbags, bricks, or even books.
- Designate a basement or other interior room to which you can retreat.
- A competent person with a rifle can easily hit something the size of a smartphone from one hundred yards or more (roughly the length of a football field) with less than a second to aim. So keep your head down!
- No matter where you are, if you hear incoming artillery, lie flat on the ground with your head away from where you anticipate the impact.
- When inside, stay away from windows. You might be visible and therefore a target. Keep in mind that the wall

won't protect you from blasts, and you could be injured by flying glass.

- Bullets penetrate a lot more than you might imagine. Even from a pistol, they can go through a person, several sheets of drywall, plywood, a cast-iron skillet, and a car door. Brick or stone walls, a dirt berm, or sandbags will stop a lot, but big bullets from powerful guns like those mounted on vehicles will be hard to stop.
- Any time guns or explosives are involved, blood loss is a big risk. Bleeding out is a real possibility, even with wounds that would otherwise not be fatal or even cause permanent damage. The answer? A tourniquet. If possible, carry one and learn how to use it (before the shooting starts). CATs (combat application tourniquets), like the ones soldiers carry, can be purchased online, in outdoor stores, and in hunting equipment stores.
- Modern militaries and even some local police forces can track cellular and/or satellite phones, turn off cell service and internet, and use drones and satellites to observe particular areas. They can access public and sometimes private surveillance cameras, like the one on your doorbell, and they have night vision and thermal vision, making it incredibly difficult to do anything unobserved, even if you are dressed in black in the dark.
- You are not the hero of an action movie, whose courage and determination will somehow protect you. Unless you have a shield like Captain America or bracelets made from Amazonium like Wonder Woman, when bullets and bombs are flying, you need to take cover.
- If you are in the vicinity of an active shooter, follow the "run, hide, fight" advice that is endorsed by the FBI and the Department of Homeland Security. First, try to evacuate the area—maybe not by actually running but by

removing yourself from the situation. If that doesn't work, find a place out of sight and with some protection between you and the shooter, like a door you can lock. You don't want to trap yourself, so an area with another exit is best. Silence your phone, breathe deeply and slowly, and remain silent. As a last resort, fight back. Be aggressive. Throw things, try to create an opening to escape. You must commit to this if it becomes necessary. You can't fight back halfway, as you will be fighting for your life.

After Civil or Political Unrest

When the threat or conflict is over, what do you do? This isn't as clear-cut as some of the other scenarios, as so much depends on what happened and how it was resolved. Can you just return home and go back to your previous life? Probably not. What happened to the perpetrators? Was there a reckoning, or are the same people still in power? What is the place like now, in terms of infrastructure, economy, and political system? Is there still a threat? Is your home still there? Can you file an insurance claim? Almost certainly not. Is your job intact? There are so many variables that we can't make any statement that is likely to be helpful except to say that you should expect everything to be different and you might have to start over. Hopefully, if it comes to that, some of your advance preparation helped put you in the best position possible to persevere.

18. Economic Crisis

Disasters of all sorts can trigger an economic crisis, and this is nothing new. Looking back historically, we see that a breakdown in trade, production, or access to resources often accompanies the end of an empire. Sometimes the crisis begins with economic issues, and sometimes other problems come first. Historians cite excessive taxation, out-of-control military spending, and a decline in the agricultural surplus as major factors in the collapse of the Roman Empire. The Ottoman Empire faltered after trade routes changed.

The changes in the past that have led to economic problems still sound as familiar as last year's song of the summer. Inflation, tariffs, overspending, and too much (or too little) taxation are as much on our minds today as they were for the ancient Romans. Add to that job loss across industries affected by AI (from teachers to accountants), the stock market falling and rising and falling again because of overvalued securities, and the housing insurance market slo-mo crashing because of extreme climate events—and conditions seem more than well aligned for a crisis.

In general, uncertainty and instability are bad for economies. Here are some of the specific factors that can lead to an economic crisis:

- **Artificial intelligence.** A 2023 McKinsey report by Kweilin Ellingrud et al. projects that by 2030, 30 percent of current U.S. jobs could be automated, with 60 percent significantly altered by AI tools. Goldman Sachs predicts that *up to 50 percent of jobs could be fully automated by 2045,* driven by generative AI and robotics. And we're not just talking about blue-collar jobs. AI's impact is already visible in white-collar sectors like finance, coding, and legal services.
- **Runaway inflation.** The U.S. Federal Reserve likes to keep inflation around 2 percent, and the U.S. average is around 3 percent. At its height in 2022, inflation was around 9 percent. Compare this to Hungary in 1946, when inflation was around 41 quadrillion percent (that's forty-one followed by fifteen zeros), with prices doubling every fifteen hours. But inflation over 50 percent in a month is considered hyperinflation (that's over 12,000 percent per year) and can lead to problems very quickly.
- **The collapse of the housing insurance market.** A September 2025 article in *Yale Environment 360* quotes Dave Jones, the former insurance commissioner of California and current director of the Climate Risk Initiative at the Center for Law, Energy and the Environment at the University of California, as saying, "The insurance crisis in the U.S. is the canary in the coal mine, and the canary is dead. We are marching toward an uninsurable future in this country and across the globe; marching into the abyss." According to a 2024 report from personal finance site Bankrate, approximately one in four U.S. homeowners is financially unprepared for the costs of ex-

treme weather damage. Further, 7 percent of those polled said they do not have homeowner's insurance, a number that rises to 15 percent for those earning less than $50,000 a year. And of those who do have insurance, 15 percent responded that they would not be able to pay their deductible without going into debt if their home was damaged. As Bloomberg recently noted, "Insurance coverage is not keeping up with growing losses, leading to more underinsured or uninsured households and businesses." This is all bad news as homeowners in areas most susceptible to natural disasters are slowly waking up to an underinsurance nightmare.

- **Currency devaluation.** This deliberate act of changing the value of a currency related to other currencies can lower the cost of exported goods, making the import/export balance more favorable. Devaluation can also represent a loss of faith in the currency. Sometimes it can be a benefit. Other times, it can be the nail in the coffin of a struggling economy.
- **A prevalent "buy now, pay later" mentality** and subsequent default on loans to pay for college, housing, or just more stuff.
- **Unrestricted crypto.** As of August 2025, the White House will allow retirement savers to contribute to their 401(k)s in crypto. According to investment professionals quoted by Reuters, these investments "are inherently riskier, lack the same disclosures, and carry higher fees than traditional retirement plans."
- **Breakdown of established trade connections.** As a country, we have our favorite trading partners, and changing those is not easy. Trade is complex and involves many steps that we can't reproduce just anywhere on a moment's notice. Disrupting something like trade, such as by imposing tariffs, and then lifting and imposing them again, can have wide-ranging and often unanticipated consequences.

- **A loss of productivity.** This could be due to many factors, including drought, crop failure, the mass deportation of the people who are doing the work (hello, ICE), natural disaster, warfare, or population decline.
- **Bad behavior combined with a lack of regulation.** Think buying on margin in October 1929, or the subprime mortgage crisis of September 2008. When big financial institutions fail, they can cause a lot of collateral damage.
- **Loss of confidence.** Much of our economic system depends on people believing the economy works. When they don't, it doesn't.

Of course, all of these systems can interact in complex ways. Climate change can affect agriculture, which can trigger inflation, which can cause people to lose confidence and change their spending habits. All of this can put pressure on financial institutions. And once economic change starts rolling, it can be hard to stop without skillful intervention. A government without expertise, experience, or good intentions may be unable to stop an economic disaster once it begins.

Depending on where you live, the specifics might be different, but here are some signs that a financial crisis is imminent.

- **Issues that may indicate supply chain problems:** empty shelves, changes in available goods, brands you never saw before, limits on quantities you may purchase (gas, groceries, medications)
- **Price instability,** including rapid inflation or deflation (usually inflation)
- **A loss of trust in banks** as people begin withdrawing money and looking for other ways to store currency or exchanging money for goods that may hold value should financial institutions go under
- **Banks limiting access to your money** via shorter hours, branch closings, ATM malfunctions, or withdrawal limits

- **An increase in foreign currency use**
- **An increase in bartering** for goods and services
- **The emergence of black markets** for currency, basic necessities, and luxury goods
- **Increased security,** such as military, ICE, or the National Guard on the streets or guards in stores—all signs that the authorities are worried
- **People starting to leave the area,** especially wealthier, powerful people who may have inside information about the situation
- **Large corporations' suspension of operations** in your area
- **Enactment of restrictions on travel and freedom of movement,** in part to keep people from leaving and also to prevent people from bringing in foreign currency or goods

In general, be sensitive to changes that indicate behind-the-scenes changes, attempts to limit access or information, and nervousness or fear on the part of the authorities or others with insider knowledge of the economy.

We all live and work in local, national, and global economies. Most of us can't insulate ourselves completely from these systems, meaning we will all most likely suffer in an economic crisis. Don't wait until it's too late. When you see one coming, here are some steps to take to protect yourself and your assets.

Before an Economic Crisis

- **Budget and save.** This is getting harder to do, especially for younger people who are struggling to find work or trying to pay off college and first houses (if they can afford them). Nevertheless, emergency savings can protect you financially in times of crisis, such as job loss or unexpected medical expenses.

- **Diversify your banking.** There has been some talk about dismantling the Federal Deposit Insurance Corporation (FDIC), which provides up to $250,000 of insurance at FDIC-insured banks (which, currently, most banks are). Just in case, make sure you don't keep over $250K in the same bank. In fact, you might keep your money in a couple of different banks in case one of them goes under. And it's also wise, should you be unable to access your money, to keep some cash on hand (as much as makes sense for you) and to tuck it away where you can easily access it.
- **Make sure you have adequate health and home insurance** to protect against potential losses.
- **Diversify your investments** among cash, real estate, stocks, and bonds.
- **Be careful about turning your currency into a commodity that you think might hold its value better**—sometimes it doesn't. Bitcoin is not magically valuable, and if people don't want it, it's not worth much. The same goes for diamonds, jewelry, ammunition, or alcohol. You may not be able to predict what will retain its value, so study the situation and listen to trusted experts before you convert your retirement account to Rolexes, gold, or whiskey.
- **Identify things you own for which there will be no market in the upcoming crisis but that are still valuable today.** These could be luxury goods, items that are rare or collectible, or cryptocurrencies. Do you own investment real estate that you've intended to sell at some point? Now might be the time.
- **Look for other options (aside from the bank and stock market) to keep your cash and other assets.** Can you invest in foreign currency? If so, pick a stable currency like the Swiss franc or the euro.

- **Get liquid.** Do you have assets tied up in the stock market, such as retirement accounts? Now might be the time to cash out or change up your portfolio. Some consumer staples (like food, beverages, household supplies), healthcare, and utilities fell less than other stocks in recent downturns, like the one in 2008.
- **Consider withdrawing your cash**—which means finding a safe and secure place to keep it. If access was limited, or there was a run on the banks, could you get to your money? If things look bad, take it out. You can always put it back if it turns out you have overreacted.
- **Since high inflation may be a concern, consider buying something that could be of use and retain value.** Examples include tools, medicine, food, and real estate, especially farmland or forested land with resources. Historically, precious metals have held value, but that may not always be the case. You can't actually do much with most precious metals besides trade them, and that relies on everyone agreeing that they are (still) valuable.
- **Stock up on essentials** like food and water for your family and pets. Buy cleaning supplies and anything else you'll need to keep your household running in case of shortages. Stock extra pain medications like ibuprofen or aspirin, diarrhea medicine (loperamide), and an antihistamine like diphenhydramine (Benadryl). If possible, get backups of prescription meds and antibiotics (more on stockpiling prescriptions on page 94), along with first aid supplies. Once you've bought something, inflation in its price can't affect you.
- **Stay informed.** Find multiple sources of information that you can trust and keep abreast of what's happening. Don't fall for rumors or panic, but understand that things can change quickly.

Protect Yourself from Scams

Many will try to take advantage of a bad situation by, for example, price gouging, war profiteering, or running some type of deception on desperate people. Stay alert to the possibilities and follow these tips.

- Use strong, unique passwords. Avoid using the same ones across multiple platforms, and ensure they are hard to guess (use a mix of letters, numbers, and symbols). A password manager can help you generate and store complex passwords so you don't have to remember each one.
- Enable two-factor authentication for logins when you can. This extra step adds a layer of security by requiring you to verify your identity with a second factor (like a text or email) before you can access your online account.
- Make regular software updates. Updates often contain fixes to protect against security vulnerabilities. Set your apps and devices to automatically update.
- Monitor your financial accounts regularly. Check your bank and credit card statements for unauthorized charges. You can also get a free credit report every year from either Experian, Equifax, or TransUnion. Read through it to be sure the information is accurate and complete.
- Build and maintain a community to help if things get bad. Having a group of friends and neighbors who can provide mutual aid can be priceless.

During an Economic Crisis

- **Avoid public Wi-Fi networks for sensitive communications and transactions.** They are often insecure, making it easier for hackers to access your information. Use a VPN, or Virtual Private Network, for added protection when browsing on public networks.
- **Beware of phishing, spoofing, and other types of financial scams.** Question unsolicited emails, texts, or calls asking for personal information or payment, especially if there is an urgency to the request. Don't click on links unless you are certain of the source. Always verify the legitimacy of the request before responding. Note: AI can create almost perfect voice replication, and who can say no to Aunt Helen when she calls asking for money? Have a safe word or question to verify ID before you send money, or call Aunt Helen directly to make sure it's her.
- **Get together with your neighbors.** As a group, you have more options. You can trade among yourselves, share information, and establish a trusted group of people.
- **Prepare for the possibility of losing your job and income.** We often tie our identity and mental well-being to our professional or work life. Understand that this may change. You may not be a lawyer, ad executive, or real estate agent any longer. Be willing to do what it takes and understand that you might have to cobble together a number of side hustles to make ends meet.
- **Take stock of the skills you have that might become valuable,** such as the ability to fix or make things from available materials. Can you do plumbing, car repair, sewing, or woodworking? Can you fix electronics or computers? Can you speak other languages? If travel is difficult, somebody with knowledge and experience could become a guide. Brush up on the

skills you have and make sure you have the tools required to do them.

- **Limit expenses and don't waste anything.** That means saving things like boxes, old clothes, and empty food containers that could be used for something else. Spend money on staples and necessities and avoid large expenses if possible. Do not take on more debt if you can avoid it.
- **Be fair and trustworthy in your dealings with others.** All of your skills and goods won't be worth anything if nobody wants to deal with you. Try to make interactions mutually beneficial, and don't squeeze a desperate person for everything you can get. In the end, you get more by being fair.

After an Economic Crisis

- **Understand that things may never return to the way they were before.** Don't kid yourself; be realistic and face the fact that there is likely to be a new reality. It could be better than the old one, at least for those who benefited least from the previous status quo, but it will be different.
- **Take stock of what you have.** Your financial situation could have changed, perhaps radically, and you need to know where you stand. What assets are still worth something? What about currency? Credit? You may be in much different shape than at the beginning of the crisis.
- **Consider where you have your assets and assess whether you should move them now that the crisis has passed.** Maybe you took out a bunch of cash or invested in gold. While that might have made sense at one moment in time, if things are returning to some version of normal, now would be the time to assess how to manage your assets going forward.
- **Prepare for the next crisis.** Hopefully we all learned some-

thing, and that knowledge could help you prepare for future economic crises. What worked well and what didn't? What things held value? What ended up being the most successful strategy for managing assets during a tumultuous time? Use the past to inform your future actions.

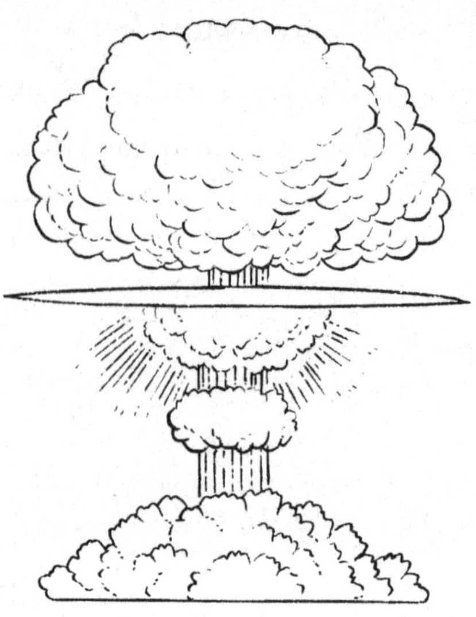

19. Nuclear Attack or Accident

On March 11, 2011, a magnitude 9.0 earthquake followed by a massive tsunami on Japan's Pacific coast caused the Fukushima Daiichi nuclear plant and six reactors to lose power. The tsunami flooded the backup diesel generators, leading to the complete loss of all capacity and ultimately devastating the agricultural and fishing industries near the plant. It was consequently rated the second-worst nuclear accident in history after the Chernobyl disaster in 1986.

Closer to home, the Three Mile Island nuclear plant near Harrisburg, PA, where the Unit 2 reactor partially melted down in 1979, is scheduled to reopen in 2027, rebranded as the Crane Clean Energy Center—to help power Microsoft's data centers. To the South, two large nuclear reactors are currently under construction in Georgia, while CNBC reported (in July 2025) that Westinghouse Electric plans to build ten large nuclear reactors in the United States, with construction slated to begin by 2030. There are already concerns about the enormous costs and where the radioactive waste will be deposited, not to mention that more nuclear facilities equals a higher probability of an accident.

In a full-blown nuclear *exchange*, more than half of humanity would die (and that's according to the more optimistic studies). While lethal fallout can disappear within minutes to a day, the effects can last indefinitely. And what the radiation, fires, smoke, dust, and fallout will do to the planet is something most people can neither escape nor survive. Even if you did manage to make it out alive, you might be facing nuclear winter conditions where producing agriculture would become difficult to impossible. The reality is that few people today have ever seen the power of atomic destruction up close or experienced the human-scale reality of what happens when cities vanish in seconds. A full-blown nuclear war might result in something that would resemble an apocalyptic movie. (Finally, some realistic cinematic representation!)

Of course, it is possible that a nuclear exchange or accident could be limited (if leaders realize the hopelessness of retaliation) and survivable. Imagine a nuclear weapon like the one dropped on Hiroshima. That bomb had a yield of sixteen kilotons—the equivalent of sixteen thousand tons of regular explosives—which is small for today's weapons. Now the average nuclear weapon is around two hundred kilotons, or something like fifteen times the power of the bomb dropped on Hiroshima (Note: When it comes to nukes, bigger is never better).

If the target was something like a missile silo, the bomb would explode on or very near to the ground. If the target was troops or a city, it would probably explode in the air above. The weather, the size of the bomb, and where it exploded would change some of the details, but an average-yield nuclear weapon dropped over a city and exploding a thousand feet or more above the ground would detonate with great heat, light, and pressure. The initial explosion would create more of the former (heat and light) and less of the latter (pressure), making the air and everything around it rapidly superheat and expand. Temperatures would be millions of degrees Celsius, or several times the temperature of the surface of the sun, causing the atmosphere to swell and creating a massive pressure wave of superheated, compressed material that would move outward at something like four miles a second.

Close to impact, everything would be vaporized. Game over. The heat and light from the fireball would ignite objects and burn people up to a mile or more away from ground zero. In the right conditions, large-scale fires could start, like the firestorm that incinerated everything within four miles of Hiroshima. Beyond that, you would have damage from heat, the blast, and radiation. Shot. Chaser. For a bomb of this size, most scientists say there would be an area of severe damage extending out a half mile or so, where no structures would remain standing and almost everyone would be killed in the initial blast. A zone of light damage from one mile to four miles beyond that would result in broken windows and some structural damage.

If you didn't cover it in high school science class, enormous amounts of radiation are released by a nuclear explosion, and those close to detonation would receive a lethal dose. For a Hiroshima-sized bomb, lethal radiation would kill anybody within three-quarters of a mile. Farther away, most of the concern would be with fallout—material suspended in the air from the blast that would now be radioactive. FEMA has noted that it takes about fifteen minutes for fallout to descend back to ground level outside the immediate blast zones, which is enough time for you to be able to prevent significant radiation exposure.

Those not in the severe damage zone would be more likely to survive. If you were in a zone with substantial damage to buildings, it is possible that first responders wouldn't or couldn't rescue you because of the impassability of roads (there would be rubble everywhere in an urban setting) and the radiation danger. If you were not injured by flying debris or burns, your biggest problem would be radiation from the fallout.

Before a Nuclear Attack or Accident

There are no good options here aside from collectively hoping that humanity gets its act together before things get too out of control. Use your vote, if you have one, to elect people who will avoid this at all costs. If you want to join a protest, do that, too.

If you think an attack is imminent, you could consider taking potassium iodide tablets. This is a salt that can protect your thyroid, a small gland located in the front of your neck that produces hormones and controls many aspects of your body's metabolism; the thyroid is the part of your body most susceptible to damage from radiation. Thyroid cells use iodine to function.

By taking potassium iodide prior to coming into contact with radiation from nuclear fallout, you essentially saturate the thyroid with good iodine. Once radiation is in there, the potassium iodide won't get radiation out or reverse the damage, but it will keep any more from getting in. Potassium iodide can be bought without a prescription in many pharmacies and online, so it may be a good time to stock up now.

And while, ideally, you should take potassium iodide only on the advice of a doctor or emergency management personnel (because taking too much of it or when it's not needed can cause problems), if the situation is such that doctors aren't available, you may have to take a chance. Potassium iodide pills typically come in 65 mg and 130 mg doses. When called for, the typical dose for an adult or teenager over 150 pounds is 130 mg a day. A teenager under 150 pounds or a child from three to twelve years old would take 65 mg a day. Children from a month old to three years old would take 32 mg, and infants under a month old would take 16 mg. If you are instructed to take potassium iodide, do so until you are instructed to stop. Once you are no longer exposed to radiation, you should stop taking it. Note: Potassium iodide does not protect any part of your body except your thyroid. Some people may have allergic reactions to it, especially those over forty years of age.

During a Nuclear Attack or Accident

- Get indoors and stay there and hope you are far from ground zero.
- Look away from the blast. The bright light can damage your eyesight or blind you.
- Immediately seek shelter in the lowest part of a sturdy building. The basement would be best. This is partly to protect you from the blast, but more to protect you from radioactive fallout, detailed below.
- One of the main dangers, beyond the initial blast, is radioactive fallout, radioactive debris, and remains of the fissionable material in the bomb. Most of this decays pretty rapidly, so staying indoors for twenty-four to forty-eight hours will greatly decrease the risk of exposure.
- The intense heat of the blast can cause widespread fires, or even firestorms that could consume everything in a given area. Some fires will not be manageable by an individual, but others might be, so be ready to grab fire extinguishers and/or water, and if you have a choice, look for a shelter with little combustible material.

After a Nuclear Attack or Accident

- If you have been exposed to any dust or debris, change your clothes or remove the outer layer, being careful not to stir up any dust or ash that might, in fact, be radioactive fallout. Simply removing the outer layer (coat, shirt) can reduce your radiation exposure up to 90 percent. Put the contaminated clothes outside of the area you are using for shelter.
- If you have no change of clothing, brush off the dust (outside of your shelter, if possible, being careful not to breathe it in) and then wash your hands. Use a mask and gloves if you have them.

- Shower with soap and water, if possible. Wash your hair with soap or shampoo, but do not use conditioner, which can cause radioactive material to stick to your hair. If you can't shower, wash your head, face, and hands. If you have no water, wipe them off with something. Do the same with children and pets.
- Stay indoors for at least twenty-four hours. The longer the better, as the radioactive fallout will decay rapidly and be much less dangerous as time goes on. In most cases, radiation danger decreases dramatically every hour. Some radioactive fallout can have isotopes that do not decay for years, but most will be gone in a day or two.
- Listen to the radio for instructions and updates. If you are lucky, there will be a functioning emergency response. You can learn what happened, what areas are dangerous, and what you should do next. If you can't immediately get information from outside, do not get anxious and leave; you are better off waiting it out if you aren't otherwise injured.

Should I Fear an Electromagnetic Pulse (EMP)?

A favorite threat of doomsday preppers, an EMP is the electromagnetic field produced by the pulse of energy emitted by a nuclear weapon or by a device designed to produce an EMP that can disrupt or destroy electronics and computer chips. Since just about everything has a computer chip in it nowadays, an EMP has the potential to disable many of the electronics we rely on, such as computers, cellular phones, radios, and automobiles. The range of an EMP depends on the size of the nuclear weapon and whether it was detonated on the ground or in the air, but its range could be several hundred miles. A small weapon detonated on the ground might not affect an area larger than the zone of severe damage. A large bomb detonated in the air could affect electronics hundreds of miles away. Depending on the strength of the EMP, the impact on electronics could range from a momentary disruption to permanent damage or destruction.

There is not much you can do to stave off the damage from an EMP aside from turning off and unplugging electronics (if you know the blast is imminent), or placing them in a Faraday cage (an enclosure used to block some electromagnetic fields by a continuous covering of conductive material), or shielding them with aluminum, copper, or steel. Wrapping your electronics in several layers of aluminum foil, with no gaps anywhere, can offer some protection.

A nuclear exchange would be one of humanity's worst possible scenarios. Not only do political realities make it likely that a limited exchange would escalate, but there is very little that the average person can do to get ready beforehand or to deal with the destruction that follows (read *Nuclear War: A Scenario* by Annie Jacobsen for a glimpse of the global disaster that could result from any nuclear exchange).

Much of the threat comes from the reactionary and retaliatory strategies that nuclear powers have built into their military and political systems, so something that could be only a small exchange, devastating for the immediate area but not a global catastrophe, would likely trigger an escalation that becomes a global disaster. Once again, we see that the initial disaster is only part of the problem—the reactions to that disaster become an even more devastating issue. So what can we do? Well, we can't wait until the bombs are launched. At that point, we have very limited options. What we *can* do is to understand the seriousness and risk of this scenario and ensure that we put people in power who are able to handle it (better luck next time). Blowhards and saber-rattlers may seem harmless, but even tiny fingers can push big buttons, and with nuclear weapons, the results are deadly.

CONCLUSION

Keeping the Faith When Things Get Bad

In all our searching, the only thing we've found that makes the emptiness bearable is each other.

—CARL SAGAN

What do you do when you have faced the worst and survived? Historically, people recover and keep on going. We see this again and again, from the mutual aid groups that formed during the COVID-19 pandemic to the way Appalachian residents looked after one another and rebuilt after devastating floods in the early 2020s. Even the national response after 9/11 was remarkable and unifying—at least initially. We also learn from these catastrophes. We can't change the results of the magnitude 9.0 earthquake and tsunami that struck Indonesia in 2004 and claimed the lives of more than 220,000 people (one of the largest disasters in terms of loss of life in modern history). But as a result, we have significantly improved tsunami detection and warning systems.

When we survive something, relief and joy can also feel . . . well, wrong. It is at odds with the understanding that something bad has happened and that not everyone was as lucky. Survivor's guilt is common and is built on that disconnect. Should you look for the silver lining? Does finding that silver lining somehow diminish the suffering that others endured?

Starting over has a lot of challenges. As you know now from reading this book, some of your needs are very clear-cut—food, water, and shelter. Some are a little less so—you need to feel like part of a community, you need hope for the future, and you need to deal with the emotional and psychological toll that surviving a disaster can inflict. Any significant disaster or trauma will have an impact. And while some people hide those impacts, everybody experiences them.

Survivors of trauma may have intense, volatile emotions that vary from moment to moment or frequent arguments with family and friends as they adjust. Sometimes people withdraw from social situations to avoid conflicts. And reactions to triggers of the initial disaster (a storm or the smell of smoke) can create strong feelings of dread or fear.

> After the severe floods in Appalachian Kentucky in 2022, I was part of a team reporting on the disaster for public radio stations in the area. I interviewed teachers who recounted that many students broke into tears when it started to rain. And a woman whose house had been flooded called to ask me if I was still going to make the two-hour trip to interview her since it was raining. For her, the rain made it too hazardous, with too much potential for disaster, to think about an interview. Rain, even modest amounts, brought out strong emotions in people who had gone through the fear and uncertainty of the day of torrential rain that caused the flooding.
>
> —Chris

Finally, survivor's guilt can develop when you make it through something that others did not. A version of that can happen even if nobody lost a life—surviving with less loss than others can trigger this feeling too. Survivor's guilt is often considered a form of post-traumatic stress disorder and can have real effects on one's ability to move on. Some of the symptoms include hopelessness, lack of motivation, and physical symptoms such as loss of appetite, headaches, or even chest pain. Dwelling on the past makes it worse, and a phenomenon called hindsight bias leads people to believe that they could have done more to influence past events than they actually could have, making them feel responsible for something even if they could not have done much to prevent it.

Getting to the other side of these common responses to trauma doesn't happen right away. We need time to adjust to what happened and start to live with our new normal. We need time to mourn and to adapt to a new emotional state or perhaps a new life entirely. Knowing this can even help us get through it. As Winston Churchill purportedly once said, "If you're going through hell, keep going."

Talking to people about what happened can help too. Find a professional or share your experience with a close friend or family member. Communicating what you've gone through and how you are thinking about it may help you to work through it. Establish new routines that you look forward to. Do things you like, no matter how trivial they seem (reading trashy novels or playing videogames). Routines give us a sense of control, no matter how illusory, that can help us regain our balance. It's also helpful to incorporate healthy habits. Eat right, sleep enough, meditate, spend time outdoors, and get some exercise. Feeling physically better can help your mental outlook as well.

And no, it is not naive to look for a silver lining. It is essential. This does not minimize what happened or disrespect those who suffered. It does not mean that you are thankful for the disaster or trying to convince yourself that it's all for the best. It's not. It would have been better if the worst had not happened, but it did. Finding the good things that are left or that ultimately emerge is something to strive for and celebrate. Rediscover, if possible, your connection to family, friends, and nature. Justin McAffee, a writer, filmmaker, and outdoor educator, noted in his Substack newsletter *Collapse Curriculum* that "wealth is not the accumulation of things, but the depth of our relationships to each other, to the land, to the skills and traditions that sustain us. The myth of scarcity wants us to believe that without money, without consumption, we are empty. But the truth is that a life rooted in reciprocity and belonging is not poor at all. It is the kind of wealth that no market can price and no gate can keep." Perhaps the silver lining is learning about and leaving behind what you don't need—money, power, more stuff—and finding what truly makes you happy. Look for the good, the pleasurable, and the beautiful. It's there, however hidden. We promise.

Be intentional about how you think about the future. Our thoughts and imagination set parameters for what is possible. Dutch sociologist Fred Polak, author of *The Image of the Future,* believed that we need to imagine the future we want to make real. This is more than merely keeping a positive attitude—it's envisioning a future that you will help create.

It is possible, to some degree, to plug along with no hope, but you won't get far. You'll lose motivation, and it's hard to summon the grit to get through something if there is no hope that a better future awaits. You may feel like Sisyphus—pushing the rock up the hill for eternity—and you might know that things will never be the same. But by giving yourself time, talking to people, being part of a community, looking for the good in what is left, and finding joy wherever it exists, you create the conditions for hope to arise from the ashes. You may bend, but with hope, you won't break. And your example may be the thing it takes to spark hope in others. That can make all the difference.

Your Community Is Essential

Way back in 2016, before COVID-19 showed up, one in six people in the United States were on an antidepressant or antianxiety medication, and most had been taking it for at least a year or more. Even more alarming, the World Health Organization (WHO) reports that dying by suicide was the third leading cause of death among fifteen- to twenty-nine-year-olds globally in 2021. Many of us weren't feeling too happy or hopeful *before* the feces hit the fan, and there are certainly other issues at play even when we're not experiencing a pandemic, from work pressures and money problems to political upheaval and relationship challenges. If you don't have hope during the best of times, you're certainly going to suffer during the worst, which is why we want to make a case for having an optimistic attitude; it may give you the best possible chance to survive and thrive through a disaster. Having a loving and supportive community of family, friends, and neighbors around also doesn't hurt. (Remember that creating and maintaining community is a feature of surviving.)

If you don't have a long list of close friends that you see often, you're not alone. Today, even the people who used to show up for everything are more likely to be on social media than at their local block parties. And if you think that's because we're living in a divisive time, keep in mind that the beloved children's program *Mister Rogers' Neighborhood,* a show that highlighted kindness and how to be a good neighbor, debuted in 1968, the year that saw support for the Vietnam War begin to fade, the assassinations of Martin Luther King Jr. and Robert F. Kennedy, and a growing "generation gap"—not especially neighborly moments in our history. More than fifty years after the first episode aired, a 2018 Pew Research Center survey explored several aspects of community life in the United States, including neighborly relations, and it didn't look good.

- Most Americans said they knew only *some* of their neighbors; far fewer, around a quarter, said they knew *most* of them. Americans ages sixty-five and older were more likely than those ages eighteen to twenty-nine to say they knew *most* of their neighbors (34 percent vs. 20 percent). In contrast, about a quarter of adults under thirty didn't know *any* of their neighbors, compared with less than 5 percent among those sixty-five and older.

- Having children at home is not related to stronger ties with neighbors: Parents were just as likely as nonparents to say they knew most of their neighbors.
- Even in a digital age, neighborly interactions are still more likely to happen in person than via text or email, but social events among neighbors are relatively rare.
- Many people are ultimately fine with not knowing their neighbors; 56 percent said they had no interest in getting to know those who lived next door any better than they already did.
- The survey did find that people living in rural areas were only slightly more likely to have friends in their neighborhood than city dwellers, and they still amounted to less than a fourth of respondents.

Why does this matter? To quote Benjamin Franklin, "We must all hang together, or assuredly we shall hang separately." Even if you are well prepared for a disaster, your next-door neighbor might have something you need, be it a skill or an antacid. And odds are they would be more likely to help you if they knew your name. And vice versa. Even if you're holed up in a fully stocked bunker in New Zealand, chances are good that you'll have to learn to get along with your neighbors at some point. Remember, in disasters from floods to hurricanes to an honest-to-God apocalypse, we'll have to work together to rebuild systems and organizations—*big* systems, from water to agriculture, and big organizations, from neighborhood groups to governments. No matter how many guns and how much money or power we have, we'll need help—potentially lots of it—to do that. As Dr. Luke Kemp, from the Centre for the Study of Existential Risk at the University of Cambridge and author of the book *Goliaths,* says, "I'm pessimistic about the future. But I'm optimistic about people."

The Steps to Rebuilding

Once the main event has passed and the dust has settled, there's the matter of moving forward. Here are our recommendations for the best ways to do that.

Step One: Know Who to Listen to for Advice

To move forward in the most effective way possible you need to be able to quickly identify trustworthy people and news sources. You also need to be able to recognize (and avoid) those who are spreading disinformation for political or monetary gain. Bad information, conspiracy theories, and political rhetoric can put you and your community in danger, prevent you from doing what's necessary to prevent the next disaster, and cause you to spend energy on the wrong thing. This is one of the most important parts of your preparation, so make a list and check it twice, as who you can trust may change (also see page 126).

Step Two: Be Willing to Share

After a major catastrophe, the need is usually great, and help doesn't always arrive quickly. Sometimes it doesn't arrive *at all.* In most emergencies that affect entire communities, like hurricanes or wildfires, people come together on the basis of need and proximity, not personal or familial relationships. There are historical instances where people were excluded because of class, race, creed, or other things that make us unique, but we've also seen the opposite, where people overcame their prejudices and fears in service of a larger cause. If you can, prepare extra for your neighbors, even if they did scoff at your early warnings and your urging them to do the same preparation as you.

Even people who do prepare sometimes lose everything, and you might be the one who ends up on the other side of a disaster with nothing. Picture the lone house standing among the ruins of a flood or wildfire while surrounding houses have been destroyed. If we all prepared more than we needed, it would go a long way toward protecting and helping our communities. It's an old-fashioned notion, but we are indeed all in this together. Lead by example.

Step Three: Share Your Skills, Strengths, and Weaknesses

Be upfront about your skills, strengths, and weaknesses, especially as these pertain to things you could do for your group. It may be that the work you did before things went to hell—in finance or law—has less immediate value than someone else's wilderness survival skills or medical training. Suck it up and help where you can. And don't feel lesser-than if your skills are more of the "soft" or arty kind. Musicians, chefs, storytellers, and caretakers also have their place. Think about how many times a song or a meal or the kindness of a friend got you through a tough time. Those things will also matter.

Step Four: Know When (and How) to Step Up

Whether it's in our home life or in business, a lot of us are used to being in charge. It won't take much time to realize, especially after a disaster, that many of life's bigger surprises are outside of our control. That may make some people angry. If so, give them space. It may make *you* angry. If so, try to be patient. Step up if you're able and if that's what the situation requires. But also be open to following directions from someone who may know better how to proceed.

If you are in charge, be honest and don't sugarcoat problems. Work for the good of the group. Take responsibility for your mistakes and share credit for success. Have integrity, and people will see it. These things matter, and these qualities should be present whether you're leading or following, as the success of the community reflects on you, regardless of your role.

Mind Your Manners

Remember manners? We're not talking about writing thank-you emails or opening doors for someone, but about showing respect to and receiving common courtesy from your fellow humans. In a recent survey more than one-third of polled respondents rated the manners of Americans as poor, significantly higher than similar polls from twenty years prior.

Why does it matter? It is our belief that a little of what used to be called "common" courtesy goes a long way, especially when the stakes are so high. "In its simplest sense," noted the authors of *Mind Your Manners,* a book published in 1964, "etiquette is a part of mankind's system for getting along together." Decades later they're not wrong.

Play nice and remember to:

- Always say "please" and "thank you"—remember, you are talking with real people, not to Siri or Alexa.
- Respect the privacy and property of others.
- Majority rules; learn to respect the opinions, ideas, and interests of others.
- Do unto others as you would have them do unto you (i.e., take the Golden Rule to heart).
- Apologize if you do something (or someone) wrong.
- Be courteous.
- Be loyal.
- Keep your promises.

It may be tough, but in the end, hope—along with our fellow humans—may be all we have.

Step Five: Expect to Be Uncomfortable and Aggravated (with Pretty Much Everyone)

As in a marriage, in the aftermath of a disaster there will be times when everything is going well and people are happy or have at least adjusted to what may be a new reality. But the honeymoon always ends, mostly because the adjustment and stress are intense and people are, well, people. To put it simply, living with others is hard. Hell, even on a good day just living with yourself and your family can be difficult.

Know that those with whom you suddenly find yourself in proximity may not always share your opinions and may handle things in ways you never would. Ideas about personal space, how loudly you can talk, and what kind of music should be played (or at what time) may differ. These may seem like relatively minor issues, but when they are magnified by all the other pressures you (and everyone else) may be enduring, it will be easy to get to a breaking point. People are different, and these differences can be fascinating and wonderful, but they can also be stressful and uncomfortable. We need to be prepared for that, along with realizing that *we* may be the one making others stress out.

So, designate a person the majority respects to help sort out disagreements. Learn to take time-outs before a situation gets too heated. And learn to live and let live and compromise because, historically, that's not been one of humanity's strong points.

"

When I was learning Spanish while conducting archaeological research in Central America, I remember how happy and relieved I was when I encountered somebody who spoke English. In those early days, I didn't speak Spanish very well, and English was so easy and familiar.

When I went back to the larger towns, I knew where Peace Corps volunteers could be found, and I would try to find them just to spend some time speaking a language that I didn't have to think about using. Same with the food. I like beans and rice, but I ate it three meals a day for a year, and that was difficult for me. Of course, it was completely normal for everybody I lived with. After a year or so, I was completely comfortable speaking Spanish all the time (it is still the language of our household) and I actually miss beans and rice. The moral of the story? We can get used to almost anything, but it may take some time.

—Chris

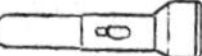

When students are graduating from high school or college, we call it a commencement ceremony. To commence is to begin. Surviving a disaster is not like graduating from school, but it *is* a new beginning. And any new beginning is hard. This one might be the hardest.

We hope this book helps you weather the storm, whatever sort of storm that turns out to be. We know the toughest times might be still to come, and that's where your attitude can play the biggest part yet. You will need information, a plan, and hope, but also you need to be tough and prepared for the hard, unpleasant work ahead. So endeavor to persevere, focusing if you can on the good things that remain. Just keep living; whatever shorthand we use for it, that's the task for now. Easier said than done, but we have faith. We hope you have some too.

As we've said at various times throughout this book, life is an adventure. Seriously, you do have the power to choose how you look at the world. Some moments and some things will suck—no doubt. But they will suck less if instead of whining you find the fortitude to keep putting one foot in front of the other. You can be the hero of your own story. The first step is being prepared.

SOURCES AND FURTHER READING

Introduction: The Prepping Lifestyle

Begley, Chris. 2021. *The Next Apocalypse: The Art and Science of Survival.* Basic Books.

Bendell, Jem. 2020. *Deep Adaptation: A Map for Navigating Climate Tragedy.* IFLAS Occasional Paper 2. 2nd rev. ed. Initiative for Leadership and Sustainability. https://www.lifeworth.com/deepadaptation.pdf.

Flavelle, Christopher. 2018. "New Climate Debate: How to Adapt to the End of the World." Bloomberg, September 26. https://www.bloomberg.com/news/articles/2018-09-26/new-climate-debate-how-to-adapt-to-the-end-of-the-world.

McDonald, Moriah. 2024. "A New Study Revealed Big Underestimates of Greenland Ice Loss—and the Power of New Technologies to Track the Changes." *Inside Climate News,* February 15. https://insideclimatenews.org/news/15022024/new-study-revealed-big-underestimates-of-greenland-ice-loss.

Solnit, Rebecca. 2009. *A Paradise Built in Hell: The Extraordinary Communities That Arise in Disaster.* Viking.

Wallace-Wells, David. 2017. "The Doomed Earth Catalog." *New York Magazine,* July 10.

Chapter 1: What the Past Can Teach Us About the Future

Begley, Chris. 2021. *The Next Apocalypse: The Art and Science of Survival.* Basic Books.

Blaikie, Piers, Terry Cannon, Ian Davis, and Ben Wisner. 2004. *At Risk: Natural Hazards, People's Vulnerability and Disasters.* 2nd ed. Routledge.

Kemp, Luke. 2025. *Goliath's Curse: The History and Future of Societal Collapse.* Knopf.

Klein, Ezra. 2021. "It Seems Odd That We Would Just Let the World Burn." *New York Times,* July 15.

National Research Council. 1991. *A Safer Future: Reducing the Impacts of Natural Disasters.* National Academies Press.

Rajan, S. Ravi. 2019. *Risk, Disaster, and Vulnerability.* University of California Press.

Slovic, Paul, ed. 2000. *The Perception of Risk.* Earthscan Publications.

Chapter 2: How to Make a Plan *Before* Things Go Tits Up

Comfort, Louise K. 2007. *Crisis Management in Hindsight: Cognition, Communication, Coordination.* Routledge.

Elvegård, Rune, Natalia Andreassen, and James Badu. 2024. "Building Collaboration and Trust in Emergency Preparedness: A Model for Planning Collaboration Exercises." *Safety in Extreme Environments* 6:319–31.

Fazeli, Sara, Milad Haghani, Mohammad Mojtahedi, and Taha H. Rashidi. 2024. "The Role of Individual Preparedness and Behavioural Training in Natural Hazards: A Scoping Review." *Safety Science* 175:106232.

Kapucu, Naim. 2008. "Collaborative Emergency Management: Better Community Organizing, Better Public Preparedness and Response." *Disasters* 32 (2): 239–62.

McAffee, Justin. *Collapse Curriculum.* Substack. https://collapsecurriculum.substack.com/.

Nelson, Alexis Nikole. Instagram. @blackforager.

Rivera, Jason D. 2020. "The Likelihood of Having a Household Emergency Plan: Understanding Factors in the US Context." *Natural Hazards* 104 (2): 1331–43.

Shmueli, Deborah F., Connie P. Ozawa, and Sanda Kaufman. 2020. "Collaborative Planning Principles for Disaster Preparedness." *International Journal of Disaster Risk Reduction* 52:101981. PubMed Central ID 9614352.

Wheal, Jamie. *Homegrown Humans Newsletter.* Substack. https://jamiewheal.substack.com/.

Chapter 3: Protection from the Elements

Bloomberg. 2025. "Free Air Conditioner Programs Help Amid Life-Threatening Heat." August 2. https://www.bloomberg.com/news/articles/2025-08-02/free-air-conditioner-programs-help-amid-life-threatening-heat.

Centers for Disease Control and Prevention (CDC). 2020. "Cold Stress." https://www.cdc.gov/niosh/topics/coldstress/default.html.

Centers for Disease Control and Prevention (CDC). 2023. "Extreme Heat: Protecting Yourself." https://www.cdc.gov/disasters/extremeheat/protect.html.

Colorado Mountain Club (CMC) Denver. 2016. *Moderate-Weather Survival Shelter Construction Techniques.* CMC. https://cmcdenver.org/wp-content/uploads/2010/01/Learn-More-%E2%80%93-Moderate-Weather-Survival-Shelter-Construction-2016-051.pdf.

Davis, Ian. 2015. *Shelter After Disaster.* 2nd ed. Practical Action Publishing.

Department of the Army. 1992. *FM 21-76: Survival Manual.* U.S. Government Printing Office. https://dn790002.ca.archive.org/0/items/Fm21-76SurvivalManual/FM21-76_SurvivalManual.pdf.

IQAir. 2025. "2024 IQAir World Air Quality Report Finds Only 17% of Global Cities Meet WHO Air Pollution Guideline." PR Newswire, March 11. https://www.prnewswire.com/news-releases/2024-iqair-world-air-quality-report-finds-only-17-of-global-cities-meet-who-air-pollution-guideline-302397828.html#:~:text=Seattle%2C%20Washington%20was%20the%20cleanest,to%20address%20these%20data%20gaps.

Sphere Association. 2018. *The Sphere Handbook: Humanitarian Charter and Minimum Standards in Humanitarian Response.* Sphere Association.

Chapter 4: Water

Centers for Disease Control and Prevention (CDC). 2025. *Make Water Safe During an Emergency.* https://www.cdc.gov/water-emergency/media/pdfs/make-water-safe-during-emergency-p.pdf.

Environmental Protection Agency (EPA). 2011. *Planning for an Emergency Drinking Water Supply.* EPA 600/R-11/054. U.S. EPA. https://www.epa.gov/sites/default/files/2015-03/documents/planning_for_an_emergency_drinking_water_supply.pdf.

Gleick, Peter H., ed. 2021. *The World's Water, 2020–2021.* Island Press.

Postel, Sandra. 1992. *Last Oasis: Facing Water Scarcity.* W. W. Norton.

U.S. Department of Defense / U.S. Navy. n.d. *Emergency Water Purification.* CNIC / Barking Sands. Accessed October 2025. https://cnrh.cnic.navy.mil/Portals/79/PMRF_Barking_Sands/Documents/Emergency%20Water%20Purification.pdf.

U.S. Geological Survey. 2019. "Water Q&A: How Much Water Do I Use at Home Each Day?" June 20. https://www.usgs.gov/water-science-school/science/water-qa-how-much-water-do-i-use-home-each-day.

World Health Organization (WHO). 2005. *Emergency Treatment of Drinking-Water at the Point of Use: A WHO Guidance Document.* Technical Notes for Emergencies TN 05. WHO. https://cdn.who.int/media/docs/default-source/wash-documents/who-tn-05-emergency-treatment-of-drinking-water-at-the-point-of-use.pdf.

World Health Organization (WHO). 2017. *Guidelines for Drinking-Water Quality.* 4th ed. WHO.

Chapter 5: Food

Alaimo, Katherine, Alyssa W. Beavers, Eva Coringrato, et al. 2023. "Community Gardening Increases Vegetable Intake and Seasonal Food Security." *Current Developments in Nutrition* 7 (5): 100077. PubMed Central ID 10196338.

Altieri, Miguel A. 2018. *Agroecology: The Science of Sustainable Agriculture.* 2nd ed. CRC Press.

Food and Agriculture Organization (FAO). 2023. *The State of Food Security and Nutrition in the World, 2023.* FAO.

Galhena, D. H., R. Freed, and K. M. Maredia. 2013. "Home Gardens: A Promising Approach to Enhance Household Food Security and Nutrition Outcomes." *Agriculture and Food Security* 2 (1): 8.

Garcia, Mariana T., Silvana M. Ribeiro, Ana Claudia Camargo Gonçalves Germani, and Cláudia M. Bógus. 2023. "The Impact of Urban Gardens on Adequate and Healthy Food: A Systematic Review." *Public Health Nutrition* 21 (2): 416–25. PubMed Central ID 10260856.

Kotschi, Jimmy, and Barbara Müller. 2014. *The Role of Agroecology in Food Security and Resilience.* International Union for Conservation of Nature.

Liu, Y., V. Chanse, and F. Chicca. 2025. "Enhancing Post-disaster Food Security Through Urban Agriculture." *Land* 14 (4): 799.

Payen, F. T., Daniel L. Evans, Natalia Falagán, et al. 2022. "How Much Food Can We Grow in Urban Areas? Food Production and Crop Yields of Urban Agriculture: A Meta-analysis." *Earth's Future* 10 (8): e2022EF002748. PubMed Central ID 9540868.

Sioen, G. B., M. Sekiyama, T. Terada, and M. Yokohari. 2017. "Post-disaster Food and Nutrition from Urban Agriculture: A Self-Sufficiency Analysis of Nerima Ward, Tokyo." *International Journal of Environmental Research and Public Health* 14 (7): 748. PubMed Central ID 5551186.

Slater, T., and S. J. Birchall. 2022. "Growing Resilient: The Potential of Urban Agriculture for Increasing Food Security and Improving Earthquake Recovery." *Cities* 131:103930.

Chapter 6: In Case of Evacuation

American Red Cross. n.d. "Survival Kit and Supplies." American Red Cross. Accessed October 2025. https://www.redcross.org/get-help/how-to-prepare-for-emergencies/survival-kit-supplies.html.

Bethea, Charles. 2024. "The Americans Prepping for a Second Civil War." *New Yorker*, November 4.

Federal Emergency Management Agency (FEMA). 2019. *Planning Considerations: Evacuation and Shelter-in-Place.* U.S. Department of Homeland Security. https://www.fema.gov/sites/default/files/2020-07/planning-considerations-evacuation-and-shelter-in-place.pdf.

Federal Emergency Management Agency (FEMA). n.d. *Appendix B: Disaster Supplies Checklists.* U.S. Department of Homeland Security. Accessed October 2025. https://www.fema.gov/pdf/areyouready/appendix_b.pdf.

Federal Emergency Management Agency (FEMA). n.d. "What Should I Bring with Me When I Evacuate My Home Before or During a Disaster?" U.S. Department of Homeland Security. Accessed October 2025. https://www.fema.gov/node/what-should-i-bring-me-when-i-evacuate-my-home-or-during-disaster.

Fekete, Alexander, and Elisabeth Fekete. 2016. "Evacuation Modeling in Flood Risk Assessment." *Natural Hazards* 84 (S1): 118–36.

Lindell, Michael K. 2013. "Evacuation Planning, Analysis, and Management." In *Handbook of Emergency Response: A Human Factors and Systems Engineering Approach*, edited by A. B. Bariru and L. Racz. CRC Press.

Perry, Ronald W., and Michael K. Lindell. 2007. *Emergency Planning.* Wiley.

Ready.gov. n.d. "Build a Kit." U.S. Department of Homeland Security. Accessed October 2025. https://www.ready.gov/kit.

Spector, Nicole. 2016. "60 Percent of People Can't Change a Flat Tire—but Most Can Google It." NBC News, September 27. https://www.nbcnews.com/business/consumer/draft-60-percent-people-can-t-change-flat-tire-most-n655501.

Tierney, Kathleen. 2007. "From the Margins to the Mainstream: Disaster Research at the Crossroads." *Annual Review of Sociology* 33:503–25.

Chapter 7: Tools for the Home and Methods of Communication

Aberle, Steve. 2017. "Ham Radio in Emergency Operations." Domestic Preparedness, June 21. https://www.domesticpreparedness.com/articles/ham-radio-in-emergency-operations.

American Radio Relay League (ARRL). n.d. *Amateur Radio Emergency Communica-*

tions Guidebook. ARRL. Accessed July 2025. https://www.wb2lua.com/papers/Ecom_Guidebook.pdf.

Beaty, Ethan. 2025. "AI Misinformation Is Threatening Emergency Communications. Here's How to Fix That." *Bulletin of the Atomic Scientists,* September 7. https://thebulletin.org/2025/09/ai-misinformation-is-threatening-emergency-communications-heres-how-to-fix-that/.

Carreras-Coch, A., D. Baños, F. J. García, and J. L. García-García. 2022. "Communication Technologies in Emergency Situations." *Electronics* 11 (7): 1155.

Clarke, Arthur C. 1962. *Profiles of the Future: An Inquiry into the Limits of the Possible.* Harper and Row.

Federal Communications Commission (FCC) and Federal Emergency Management Agency (FEMA). n.d. *Tips for Communicating During an Emergency.* FCC and FEMA. Accessed July 2025. https://www.fcc.gov/sites/default/files/fcc-fema_tips_for_communicating_during_an_emergency.pdf.

Federal Emergency Management Agency (FEMA). 2019. *Communication Plan Guide.* DHS / FEMA. https://www.fema.gov/sites/default/files/2020-10/communication-plan-guide.pdf.

Ham Radio Prep. 2024. "Ham Radio Emergency Communications Guide." https://hamradioprep.com/ham-radio-in-emergencies/.

Haupt, Brittany. 2021. "The Use of Crisis Communication Strategies in Emergency Management." *Journal of Homeland Security and Emergency Management* 18 (2): 125–50.

Nolan, Hamilton. 2025. "Where Does News Come From?" *How Things Work,* September 10. https://www.hamiltonnolan.com/p/where-does-news-come-from.

Chapter 8: Money, Bartering, and Other Valuable Things

Graeber, David. 2011. *Debt: The First 5,000 Years.* Melville House.

Greco, Thomas H., Jr. 2014. *Currency: The Hidden Revolution.* Cornell University Press.

Harari, Yuval Noah. 2015. *Sapiens: A Brief History of Humankind.* HarperCollins.

Humphrey, Caroline. 1985. "Barter and Economic Disintegration." *Man,* 20 (1): 48–72.

Pearson, Ruth. 2003. "Argentina's Barter Network: New Currency for New Times?" *Bulletin of Latin American Research* 22 (2): 214–30.

Taleb, Nassim Nicholas. 2012. *Antifragile: Things That Gain from Disorder.* Random House.

Taskinsoy, John. 2023. "The Reincarnation of Barter Trade and Barter Economy." *SSRN Electronic Journal,* May 23. https://ssrn.com/abstract=4456717.

Uyan, Ömer. 2017. "Barter as an Alternative Trading and Financing Tool and Its Role During Economic Crises." *Journal of Economics, Finance and Accounting (JEFA)* 4 (3): 282–95.

Chapter 9: Protecting Yourself and Your Family

American College of Emergency Physicians. 2017. *First Aid Manual.* DK Publishing.

Apian, Nicole. 2024. *Forgotten Home Apothecary: 250 Powerful Remedies at Your Fingertips.* Global Brother.

O'Neill, Brian, and Jim O'Neill. 2013. *Bushcraft 101: A Field Guide to the Art of Wilderness Survival.* F+W Media.

Pollan, Michael. 2021. *This Is Your Mind on Plants.* Penguin Press.

Werner, David. 2022. *Where There Is No Doctor: A Village Health Care Handbook.* With Carol Thurman and Jane Maxwell. Updated ed. Hesperian Health Guides.

Chapter 10: Drought

Ault, Toby. 2024. "How Climate Models Could Be Underestimating Drought." *Bulletin of the Atomic Scientists,* December 17. https://thebulletin.org/2024/12/how-climate-models-could-be-underestimating-drought/.

Bahta, Y. T. 2020. "Smallholder Livestock Farmers Coping and Adaptation Strategies to Agricultural Drought." *AIMS Agriculture and Food* 5 (4): 964–982.

Bryan, Katherine, S. Ward, L. Roberts, et al. 2020. "The Health and Well-Being Effects of Drought: Assessing Narratives and Impacts." *Climatic Change* 162:2271–89.

Danelski, David. 2023. "AI Programs Consume Large Volumes of Scarce Water." UC Riverside News, April 28. https://news.ucr.edu/articles/2023/04/28/ai-programs-consume-large-volumes-scarce-water.

Ebi, Kristie L., and T. A. Semenza. 2008. "Community-Based Adaptation to the Health Impacts of Climate Change." *American Journal of Preventive Medicine* 35 (5): 501–7.

Gebrechorkos, Solomon H., Justin Sheffield, Sergio M. Vicente-Serrano, et al. 2025. "Warming Accelerates Global Drought Severity." *Nature* 642 (June): 628–35.

Hawkins, P., Wendy Geza, Tafadzwanashe Mabhaudhi, et al. 2022. "Dietary and Agricultural Adaptations to Drought Among Smallholder Farming Households." *Weather and Climate Extremes* 35:100413. PubMed Central ID 8889023.

Mardy, T., M. N. Uddin, M. A. Sarker, D. Roy, and E. S. Dunn. 2018. "Assessing Coping Strategies in Response to Drought." *Climate* 6 (2): 23.

McConnell, Eric. 2025. "Unquenchable Thirst: Texas Data Centers Consume 50 Billion Gallons of Water as State Grapples with Historic Drought." Yahoo Finance, August 20. https://finance.yahoo.com/news/unquenchable-thirst-texas-data-centers-010128313.html.

NASA. 2024. "NASA Satellites Reveal Abrupt Drop in Global Freshwater Levels." GRACE Tellus website, November 20. https://grace.jpl.nasa.gov/news/218/nasa satellites-reveal-abrupt-drop-in-global-freshwater-levels/.

Prideaux, Margi. 2025. "The Hydra Is Here." *Radically Local,* Substack, September 18. https://margiprideaux.substack.com/p/the-hydra-is-here?utm_source=%2Fbrowse%2Fclimate&utm_medium=reader2.

ProPublica. 2025. "8 Things to Know About New Research on Earth's Rapid Drying and the Loss of Its Groundwater." July 28. https://www.propublica.org/article/groundwater-fresh-water-depletion-research-science-advances-takeaways.

Salvador, Coral, Raquel Nieto, Cristina Linares, Julio Díaz, and Luis Gimeno. 2020. "Effects of Droughts on Health: Diagnosis, Repercussion, and Strategies for Mitigation." *Science of the Total Environment* 703:134912.

Stanke, Carla, Marko Kerac, Christel Prudhomme, Jolyon Medlock, and Virginia Murray. 2013. "Health Effects of Drought: A Systematic Review of the Evidence." *PLOS Currents: Disasters,* June 5.

Venkataramanan, V., Shalean M. Collins, Kathleen A. Clark, et al. 2020. "Coping Strategies for Individual and Household-Level Water Insecurity: A Systematic Review." *WIREs Water* 7 (5): e1477.

World Meteorological Organization (WMO) and Integrated Drought Management Programme (IDMP). 2016. *Handbook of Drought Indicators and Indices.* WMO.

Chapter 11: Earthquakes and Tsunamis

Bryant, Edward. 2008. *Tsunami: The Underrated Hazard.* 2nd ed. Berlin: Springer.

California Seismic Safety Commission. n.d. "What to Do After an Earthquake." Accessed October 2025. https://ssc.ca.gov/disasters/after_earthquake/.

Demir, Ömer, and Nuran Aydemir. 2025. "Examining Individual Earthquake Preparedness Behaviors in Istanbul, Türkiye: A Stage-Based Study Applying the Precaution Adoption Process Model." *International Journal of Disaster Risk Science* 16:346–60.

Koca, T. T., and Duran Topak. 2024. "Rehabilitation Approach After Earthquake Disaster: A Brief Report from Turkey." *Journal of Rehabilitation Medicine—Clinical Communications* 7:34748. PubMed Central ID 11064675.

Koike, R., Nao Sonoda, Hideaki Furuki, and Akiko Morimoto. 2024. "Individual Preparedness for Large-Scale Earthquakes Among International Students in Japan: A Cross-sectional Questionnaire Survey." *JMA Journal* 7 (4): 496–505. PubMed Central ID 11543362.

Ready.gov. n.d. "Earthquakes." Accessed October 2025. https://www.ready.gov/earthquakes.

Schulz, Kathryn. 2015. "How to Stay Safe When the Big One Comes." *New Yorker,* July 28.

Shearer, Peter M. 2009. *Introduction to Seismology, Earthquakes, and Earth Structure.* 2nd ed. Cambridge University Press.

U.S. Geological Survey (USGS). 2023. "Drop, Cover, and Hold On." Earthquake Hazards Program. https://www.usgs.gov/media/images/drop-cover-and-hold.

U.S. Geological Survey (USGS). n.d. "What to Do After an Earthquake." https://www.usgs.gov/faqs/what-do-i-do-after-earthquake.

Chapter 12: Extreme Heat

Beckmann, S. K., A. H. Berger, L. Reusswig, and P. D. Gohlke. 2021. "Heat Adaptation Measures in Private Households." *Humanities and Social Sciences Communications* 8:217.

Centers for Disease Control and Prevention (CDC). n.d. "Heat-Related Illnesses." Accessed October 2025. https://www.cdc.gov/niosh/heat-stress/about/illnesses.html.

Centers for Disease Control and Prevention (CDC). n.d. "Protect Yourself from the Dangers of Extreme Heat." Accessed October 2025. https://www.cdc.gov/climate-health/php/resources/protect-yourself-from-the-dangers-of-extreme-heat.html.

Frank, Thomas. 2024. "They Died with the AC Off: Why the Government Pays for Heating but Not Cooling." *Politico,* September 15. https://www.politico.com/news/2024/09/15/extreme-heat-deaths-government-agencies-00176697.

Khan, Anas A. 2019. "Heat-Related Illnesses: Review of an Ongoing Challenge." *Saudi Medical Journal* 40 (12): 1195–1201. PubMed Central ID 6969637.

Kiarsi, Maryam, Mohammadreza Amiresmaili, Mohammadreza Mahmoodi, et al. 2022. "Heat Wave Adaptation Paradigm and Adaptation Strategies of Community: A Qualitative Phenomenological Study in Iran." *Journal of Education and Health Promotion* 11:408. PubMed Central ID 9942165.

Mora, Camilo, Bénédicte Dousset, Iain R. Caldwell, et al. 2017. "Global Risk of Deadly Heat." *Nature Climate Change* 7:501–506.

Occupational Safety and Health Administration. n.d. "Heat: Prevention: Protecting New Workers." Accessed October 2025. https://www.osha.gov/heat-exposure/protecting-new-workers.

Perkins, Sarah E., L. V. Alexander, and J. R. Nairn. 2012. "Increasing Frequency, Intensity and Duration of Observed Global Heat Waves and Warm Spells." *Geophysical Research Letters* 39:L20714.

Quilcaille, Yann, Lukas Gudmundsson, Dominik L. Schumacher, et al. 2025. "Systematic Attribution of Heatwaves to the Emissions of Carbon Majors." *Nature* 645:392–98.

Ready.gov. n.d. "Extreme Heat." Accessed October 2025. https://www.ready.gov/heat.

Sherwood, Steven C., and Matthew Huber. 2010. "An Adaptability Limit to Climate Change Due to Heat Stress." *Proceedings of the National Academy of Sciences* 107 (21): 9552–55.

Chapter 13: Extreme Rain, Flooding, and Landslides

American Red Cross. n.d. "Landslide Safety and Preparedness Tips." Accessed October 2025. https://www.redcross.org/get-help/how-to-prepare-for-emergencies/types-of-emergencies/landslide.html.

Centers for Disease Control and Prevention (CDC). n.d. "Preparing for Floods: Flood Safety Tips." Accessed October 2025. https://www.cdc.gov/floods/safety/index.html.

Federal Emergency Management Agency (FEMA). 2022. *How to Prepare for a Flood.* U.S. Department of Homeland Security. https://www.fema.gov/sites/default/files/documents/fema_flood-safety_how-to-prepare.pdf.

Federal Emergency Management Agency (FEMA). n.d. "FEMA Flood Map Service Center: Search by Address." Accessed October 2025. https://msc.fema.gov/portal/search.

Glade, Thomas, Malcolm G. Anderson, and Michael J. Crozier, eds. 2005. *Landslide Hazard and Risk.* Wiley.

Highland, Lynn M., and Peter T. Bobrowsky. 2008. *The Landslide Handbook: A Guide to Understanding Landslides.* U.S. Geological Survey. https://pubs.usgs.gov/circ/1325/pdf/C1325_508.pdf.

McEwen, Lindsey Jo. 2024. *Flood Risk and Community Resilience: An Interdisciplinary Approach.* Routledge.

National Weather Service. 2018. *Flood Safety for You and Your Family* (One-Pager). National Oceanic and Atmospheric Administration. https://www.weather.gov/media/owlie/FloodSafety-OnePager-11-29-2018.pdf.

Nunez, Ashley Seifert. 2024. "New Analysis Finds Rising Seas Threaten US Infrastructure Critical for Millions of People, Hundreds of Communities." Union of Concerned Scientists, June 25. https://www.ucs.org/about/news/new-analysis-finds-rising-seas-threaten-us-infrastructure-critical-millions-people.

Parker, Dennis J., and Sally Priest. 2012. "The Fallibility of Flood Warning Chains: Can Europe's Flood Warnings Be Effective?" *Meteorological Applications* 19 (3): 340–51.

Ready.gov. n.d. "Flooding." Accessed October 2025. https://www.ready.gov/floods.

Rice, Doyle, and Dinah Voyles Pulver. 2024. "Hurricanes Can Kill from 1,000 Miles

Away—and Other Terrifying Dangers." *USA Today,* May 20. https://www.yahoo.com/news/hurricanes-kill-1-000-miles-090554218.html.

Welch, Craig. 2024. "Washed Away." AARP, May 28. https://www.aarp.org/home-living/washed-away.

Wing, Oliver E. J., William Lehman, Paul D. Bates, et al. 2022. "Inequitable Patterns of US Flood Risk in the Anthropocene." *Nature Climate Change* 12:156–62.

Chapter 14: Hurricanes and Tornadoes

Bluestein, Howard B. 2013. *Severe Convective Storms and Tornadoes: Observations and Theory.* Springer.

Elsner, James B., and Thomas Hultquist, eds. 2006. *Hurricanes of the North Atlantic: Climate and Society.* Oxford University Press.

Emanuel, Kerry. 2005. *Divine Wind: The History and Science of Hurricanes.* Oxford University Press.

Federal Emergency Management Agency (FEMA). 2021. *Shelter-in-Place for Tornado.* https://www.fema.gov/sites/default/files/documents/fema_shelter-in-place_guidance-tornado.pdf.

Federal Emergency Management Agency (FEMA). n.d. "Flood Insurance." Accessed October 2025. https://www.fema.gov/flood-insurance.

Hagerty, Colleen. 2025. "On the Road with NOAA as They Face Uncertainty in Their Agency and the Weather." *Rolling Stone,* July 27. https://www.rollingstone.com/culture/culture-features/noaa-tornado-research-extreme-weather-1235393629/.

Insurance Journal. 2024. "AccuWeather Increases Estimate of Helene's Economic Loss to $225B–$250B." October 4. https://www.insurancejournal.com/news/national/2024/10/04/795674.htm.

National Weather Service. n.d. *Tornado Safety.* Accessed July 2025. https://www.weather.gov/media/owlie/TornadoSafety-OnePager-2-27-19.pdf.

National Weather Service. n.d. "2024 Tornado Activity Reached Near-Historic Levels Across the U.S." Accessed October 2025. https://www.weather.gov/news/250703_tornado_activity.

Ready.gov. n.d. "Hurricanes." Accessed October 2025. https://www.ready.gov/hurricanes.

Schmidlin, Thomas W., Barbara O. Hammer, Yuichi Ono, and Paul S. King. 2009. "Tornado Shelter-Seeking Behavior and Shelter Options Among Mobile Home Residents in the United States." *Natural Hazards* 48 (2): 191–201.

Strader, Stephen M., Victor A. Gensini, Walker S. Ashley, and Amanda N. Wagner. 2024. "Changes in Tornado Risk and Societal Vulnerability Leading to Greater Tornado Impact Potential." *npj Natural Hazards* 1 (20).

Walters, J. E. 2020. "Staying Safe in a Tornado: A Qualitative Inquiry into Public Warning Response." *Weather and Forecasting* 35 (1): 203–18.

Wang, C., P. J. Robinson, and W. M. Brown. 2023. "A Case Study of an EF3 Tornado in Jacksonville, Alabama: Survivor Narratives and Implications for Warning and Shelter Behavior." *Weather, Climate, and Society* 15 (1): 123–40.

Young, Rachel, and Solomon Hsiang. 2024. "Mortality Caused by Tropical Cyclones in the United States." *Nature* 635:121–28.

Chapter 15: Pandemics

Barry, John M. 2004. *The Great Influenza: The Story of the Deadliest Pandemic in History.* Viking/Penguin.

Centers for Disease Control and Prevention (CDC). 2025. "How to Protect Yourself and Others | COVID-19." https://www.cdc.gov/covid/prevention/index.html.

Füszl, A., Julia Ebner, Miriam Van den Nest, Lukas Bouvier-Azula, Magda Diab-El Schahawi, and Elisabeth Presterl. 2023. "COVID-19 Patient and Personal Safety—Lessons Learnt for Pandemic Preparedness." *Antimicrobial Resistance and Infection Control* 12:27. PubMed Central ID 10066952.

Güner, R., İmran Hasanoğlu, and Firdevs Aktaş. 2020. "COVID-19: Prevention and Control Measures in Community." *Turkish Journal of Medical Science* 50 (3): 571–77. PubMed Central ID 195988.

Morens, David M., Gregory K. Folkers, and Anthony S. Fauci. 2009. "What Is a Pandemic? The Flu of 1918–1919." *Journal of Infectious Diseases* 200 (7): 1018–21.

Mukherjee, Neha. 2025. "Child in West Texas Is First US Measles Death in a Decade." CNN Health, February 27. https://www.cnn.com/2025/02/26/health/texas-measles-death.

Occupational Safety and Health Administration (OSHA). n.d. "Protecting Workers: Guidance on Mitigating and Preventing COVID-19 in the Workplace." Accessed October 2025. https://www.osha.gov/coronavirus/safework.

Ready.gov. n.d. "Pandemics." Accessed October 2025. https://www.ready.gov/pandemic.

Taubenberger, Jeffery K., and David M. Morens. 2006. "1918 Influenza: The Mother of All Pandemics." *Emerging Infectious Diseases* 12 (1): 15–22.

Whyte, Liz Essley. 2025. "RFK Jr. to Oust Advisory Panel on Cancer Screenings, HIV Prevention Drugs." *Wall Street Journal,* July 25. https://www.wsj.com/health/healthcare/rfk-health-screening-panel-members-c308cbb0.

Chapter 16: Wildfires and Dangerous Air Quality

American Red Cross. n.d. "Wildfire Safety." Accessed October 2025. https://www.redcross.org/get-help/how-to-prepare-for-emergencies/types-of-emergencies/wildfire.html.

Balch, J. K., V. Iglesias, A. L. Mahood, et al. 2024. "The Fastest-Growing and Most Destructive Fires in the US (2001 to 2020)." *Science* 386 (6720): 425–31.

Bowman, David M. J. S., Grant J. Williamson, John T. Abatzoglou, Crystal A. Kolden, Mark A. Cochrane and Alistair M. S. Smith. 2017. "Human Exposure and Sensitivity to Globally Extreme Wildfire Events." *Nature Ecology and Evolution* 1 (3): 0058.

Centers for Disease Control and Prevention (CDC). n.d. "Safety Guidelines: Wildfires and Wildfire Smoke." Accessed October 2025. https://www.cdc.gov/wildfires/safety/how-to-safely-stay-safe-during-a-wildfire.html.

Hamilton, Matthew. 2018. "Behavioral Adaptation to Climate Change in Wildfire-Prone Ecosystems." *Wiley Interdisciplinary Reviews: Climate Change* 9 (4): e553.

Juneja Lakhina, Shefali, Susan D. Kocher, B. Lebeda, et al. 2021. *Wildfire Preparedness and Evacuation Planning in a Pandemic: Case Studies from California and Colorado.* Technical Report, June. CONVERGE, Natural Hazards Center. https://www.researchgate.net/publication/352749605_WILDFIRE_PREPAREDNESS_AND

_EVACUATION_PLANNING_IN_A_PANDEMIC_Case_studies_from_California_and_Colorado.

Picciotto, Sally, ShihMing Huang, Frederick Lurmann, et al. 2024. "Pregnancy Exposure to PM2.5 from Wildland Fire Smoke and Preterm Birth in California." *Environment International* 186 (April): 108583.

Pyne, Stephen J., Patricia L. Andrews, and Richard D. Laven. 2013. *Introduction to Wildland Fire.* 2nd ed., rev. Waveland Press.

Qiu, Minghao, Jessica Li, Carlos F. Gould, et al. 2025. "Wildfire Smoke Exposure and Mortality Burden in the US Under Climate Change." *Nature,* September 18. https://doi.org/10.1038/s41586-025-09611-w.

Reid, Colleen E., Michael Brauer, Fay H. Johnston, Michael Jerrett, John R. Balmes, and Catherine T. Elliott. 2016. "Critical Review of Health Impacts of Wildfire Smoke Exposure." *Environmental Health Perspectives* 124 (9): 1334–43.

Yakovenko, Nadiia, Lucía Pérez-Serrano, Théo Segur, et al. 2025. "Human Exposure to PM10 Microplastics in Indoor Air." *PLOS One,* July 30.

Chapter 17: Civil or Political Unrest

Barrs, C. A. 2010. *How Civilians Survive: Strategies for Self-Protection in Conflict Zones.* November. Oxfam Australia. https://www.oxfam.org.au/wp-content/uploads/2011/08/Casey-Barrs-supporting-documentation-How-Civilians-Survive.pdf.

Chenoweth, Erica, and Maria J. Stephan. 2011. *Why Civil Resistance Works: The Strategic Logic of Nonviolent Conflict.* Columbia University Press.

Goodwin, Jeff. 2001. *No Other Way Out: States and Revolutionary Movements, 1945–1991.* Cambridge University Press.

Hetzner, Christiaan. 2024. "Larry Ellison Predicts Rise of the Modern Surveillance State Where 'Citizens Will Be on Their Best Behavior.'" *Fortune,* September 17. https://fortune.com/2024/09/17/oracle-larry-ellison-surveillance-state-police-ai/.

Kalyvas, Stathis N. 2006. *The Logic of Violence in Civil War.* Cambridge University Press.

Milliff, Aidan. 2024. "Making Sense, Making Choices: How Civilians Choose Survival Strategies During Violence." *American Political Science Review* 118 (3): 1379–97.

Parker, Ned, and Peter Eisler. 2023. "Political Violence in Polarized U.S. at Its Worst Since 1970s." Reuters, August 9. https://www.reuters.com/investigates/special-report/usa-politics-violence/.

Sanaullah. 2020. "Effectiveness of Civilians' Survival Strategies: Insights from Mixed Methods." *Journal of Conflict and Security* 32 (3).

Schon, Justin. 2020. "A Theory of Civilian Survival Strategies." In *Surviving the War in Syria: Survival Strategies in a Time of Conflict,* Cambridge University Press, 19–46.

Shesterinina, Alexandra. 2022. "Civil War as a Social Process: Actors and Dynamics from Pre- to Post-war." *European Journal of International Relations* 28 (3): 538–62. Pub Med Central ID 35971376.

Tilly, Charles. 2003. *The Politics of Collective Violence.* Cambridge University Press.

Chapter 18: Economic Crisis

Ellingrud, Kweilin, Saurabh Sanghvi, Gurneet Singh Dandona, et al. 2023. *Generative AI and the Future of Work in America.* McKinsey Global Institute. July 26. https://www.mckinsey.com/mgi/our-research/generative-ai-and-the-future-of-work-in-america.

Gaul, Gilbert M. 2025. "How Climate Risks Are Putting Home Insurance Out of Reach." *Yale Environment 360,* September 15. https://e360.yale.edu/features/climate-change-home-insurance.

Kelly, Jack. 2025. "These Jobs Will Fall First as AI Takes Over the Workplace." *Forbes,* April 25. https://www.forbes.com/sites/jackkelly/2025/04/25/the-jobs-that-will-fall-first-as-ai-takes-over-the-workplace/.

Kindleberger, Charles P., and Robert Z. Aliber. 2011. *Manias, Panics, and Crashes: A History of Financial Crises.* 6th ed. Palgrave Macmillan.

Lusardi, Annamaria, Andrea Hasler, and Paul J. Yakoboski. 2021. "Building Up Financial Literacy and Financial Resilience." *Mind and Society* 20:181–87.

Martin, Shannon. 2024. "Survey: 1 in 4 Homeowners Feel Financially Unprepared for Costs of Extreme Weather Events." Bankrate, September 9. https://www.bankrate.com/insurance/homeowners-insurance/severe-weather-financial-impact-survey/.

McLeod, Jane, and Michael Shanahan. 2015. "Effects of the Great Recession: Health and Well-Being." *Annual Review of Sociology* 41:1–17.

Minsky, Hyman P. 2008. *Stabilizing an Unstable Economy.* McGraw-Hill.

Reinhart, Carmen M., and Kenneth S. Rogoff. 2009. *This Time Is Different: Eight Centuries of Financial Folly.* Princeton University Press.

Sinor, Mark, Morton Silverman, Jane Pirkis, and Keith Hawton. 2024. "The Effect of Economic Downturn, Financial Hardship, Unemployment, and Recession on Population Health." *Lancet Public Health* 9 (5): e389–e400.

Sornette, Didier. 2003. *Why Stock Markets Crash: Critical Events in Complex Financial Systems.* Princeton University Press.

Chapter 19: Nuclear Attack or Accident

Beres, L. R. 1985. "Surviving Nuclear War: U.S. Plans for Crisis Relocation." *International Journal of Mass Emergencies and Disasters* 3 (1): 43–67.

Chester, C. V. 1987. "Civil Defense Shelters: A State-of-the-Art Assessment." *Energy* 12 (6): 573–84.

Fekete, Alexander. 2022. "Safe from Harm? Massive Attack Nuclear Worst-Case Scenarios and Civil Protection." *Sustainability* 13 (2): 47.

Glasstone, Samuel, and Philip J. Dolan. 1977. *The Effects of Nuclear Weapons.* 3rd ed. U.S. Department of Defense / U.S. Department of Energy.

International Atomic Energy Agency (IAEA). 2015. *Preparedness and Response for a Nuclear or Radiological Emergency* (GSR Part 7). IAEA.

International Commission on Radiological Protection (ICRP). n.d. "Advice for the Public on Protection in Case of a Nuclear Detonation." Accessed October 2025. https://www.icrp.org/protection-nuclear-attack.html.

Jacobsen, Annie. 2024. *Nuclear War: A Scenario.* Dutton.

Kearny, Cresson H. 2016. *Nuclear War Survival Skills: Lifesaving Nuclear Facts and Self-Help Instructions.* Rev. ed. Skyhorse. https://ia802306.us.archive.org/19/items/NuclearWarSurvivalSkills_201405/nwss.pdf.

Leaning, J. 2000. "Civil Defense Planning for Nuclear War." In *Planning for a Nuclear Future,* edited by T. L. Paul. Springer.

Sandia National Laboratories. 2009. *Modeling Fallout and Shelter Effectiveness.* Sandia National Laboratories Report SAND2009-XXXX. Sandia.

Conclusion: Keeping the Faith When Things Get Bad

Allen, Betty. 1964. *Mind Your Manners.* Rev. ed. J. B. Lippincott.

Kemp, Luke. 2025. *Goliath's Curse: The History and Future of Societal Collapse.* Knopf.

McAffee, Justin. 2025. "The Myth of Scarcity." *Collapse Curriculum,* Substack, August 9. https://collapsecurriculum.substack.com/p/the-myth-of-scarcity.

Polak, Fred. 1961. *The Image of the Future.* Oceana Publications.

Wildfire, Jessica. 2025. "Something Stronger Than Hope." *OK Doomer* (blog), August 3. https://www.the-sentinel-intelligence.com/p/something-stronger-than-hope.

ACKNOWLEDGMENTS

In the words of Dr. Sheldon Cooper, "I have spent my whole life trying to bring order to the universe by carefully planning every moment of every day." It hasn't been easy. Thanks to my co-author, Chris Begley, for agreeing to help me write this book and providing his expertise; my agent, Leslie Meredith, and my editor, Julie Bennett, for recognizing the need and supporting us in getting it right; my husband and daughters for their endless love and support; and my blended and extended family, who together with my friends make it all worthwhile.

—AMY

Thanks to my co-author, Amy Edelman, for contacting me about writing this book. I think it's needed now more than ever, and tomorrow more than today. Thanks to my family, who might have wondered where I was for these last few months. Thanks to my agent, Leslie Meredith, for making all of it possible, and to our editor, Julie Bennett, for seeing the value in this book and for her help with organization and making it all make sense. And thanks to everybody who reads the book. You are preparing yourself to make the world a better place when we need you the most.

—CHRIS

INDEX

TEN SPEED PRESS
An imprint of the Crown Publishing Group
A division of Penguin Random House LLC
1745 Broadway
New York, NY 10019
tenspeed.com
penguinrandomhouse.com

A Ten Speed Press Trade Paperback Original

Typefaces: Adobe's Minion Pro, EMME Grafica's Zold, Hoefler & Co.'s Gotham and Gotham Rounded, Latinotypes' Apparel, Monotype's Hideout, Redy Studio's Laguna Hills

Library of Congress Cataloging-in-Publication Data
Names: Edelman, Amy Holman author | Begley, Chris author
Title: The emergency playbook : a bunker-free guide to disaster preparation / Amy Edelman and Chris Begley.
Identifiers: LCCN 2025049291 (print) | LCCN 2025049292 (ebook) |
ISBN 9780593837641 trade paperback | ISBN 9780593837658 ebook
Subjects: LCSH: Emergency management
Classification: LCC HV551.2 .E38 2026 (print) | LCC HV551.2 (ebook)
LC record available at https://lccn.loc.gov/2025049291
LC ebook record available at https://lccn.loc.gov/2025049292

ISBN 978-0-593-83764-1
Ebook ISBN 978-0-593-83765-8

Editor: Julie Bennett | Production editor: Taylor Teague
Designer: Andrea Lau | Production: Dan Myers
Copy editor: Elisabeth Magnus | Proofreaders: Tracy Rothschild Lynch and Julie Ehlers | Indexer: Elise Hess
Publicist: Natalie Yera-Campbell | Marketer: Emily Hotaling

Manufactured in the United States of America

1st Printing

Cover design by Francesca Truman
Back cover icons: FontFont's Mister K Dingbats

The authorized representative in the EU for product safety and compliance is Penguin Random House Ireland, Morrison Chambers, 32 Nassau Street, Dublin D02 YH68, Ireland, https://eu-contact.penguin.ie.

ABOUT THE AUTHORS

Amy Edelman is a PR and marketing professional and the author of *The Little Black Dress* and *Manless in Montclair.* She has appeared on *Today* and been featured in *The New York Times, USA Today, Los Angeles Times, New York Daily News, Chicago Tribune,* and others.

Chris Begley, PhD, is an archaeologist, a professor, a wilderness survival instructor, and the author of *The Next Apocalypse.* He was a Fulbright Scholar and a National Science Foundation Graduate Fellow and was named a National Geographic Explorer and one of the "World's 50 Most Adventurous Men" by *Men's Journal.* He has also been featured in *The New Yorker, National Geographic,* and *American Archaeology* magazine, and in documentaries on the BBC, Discovery Channel, and elsewhere.